US Youth Films and Popular Music

This book brings theory from popular music studies to an examination of identity and agency in youth films while building on, and complementing, film studies literature concerned with genre, identity, and representation. McNelis includes case studies of Hollywood and independent US youth films that have had commercial and/or critical success to illustrate how films draw on specific discourses surrounding popular music genres to convey ideas about gender, race, ethnicity, sexuality, and other aspects of identity. He develops the concept of 'musical agency', a term he uses to discuss the relationship between film music and character agency, also examining the music characters listen to and discuss, as well as musical performances by the characters themselves.

Tim McNelis is a youth film and film music scholar with chapters in *International Cinema and the Girl: Local Issues, Transnational Contexts* and *The Time of Our Lives: Dirty Dancing and Popular Culture*. He has also co-authored pieces on songs in Wes Anderson films and visible playback technology in film.

Routledge Advances in Film Studies

For a full list of titles in this series, please visit www.routledge.com.

US Youth Films and Popular Music

Identity, Genre, and Musical Agency

Tim McNelis

Routledge
Taylor & Francis Group

NEW YORK AND LONDON

First published 2017
by Routledge
711 Third Avenue, New York, NY 10017

and by Routledge
2 Park Square, Milton Park, Abingdon, Oxon OX14 4RN

*Routledge is an imprint of the Taylor & Francis Group,
an informa business.*

Library of Congress Cataloging-in-Publication Data
CIP data has been applied for.

ISBN: 978-1-138-94691-0 (hbk)
ISBN: 978-1-315-67053-9 (ebk)

Typeset in Sabon
by codeMantra

MIX
Paper from
responsible sources
FSC® C013056
www.fsc.org

Printed and bound in Great Britain by
TJ International Ltd, Padstow, Cornwall

For Elena, with love and respect

Contents

List of Figures

Acknowledgements

This book has slowly evolved from my PhD thesis, undertaken at the University of Liverpool. I would first and foremost like to thank Anahid Kassabian and Yannis Tzioumakis for thought-provoking discussions, feedback on my writing, generosity, and friendship over the years. I am also grateful to the editorial team at Routledge for their support, and to the anonymous reviewers of this project for their feedback and criticism. Thanks to all of those who contributed to reading group in the School of Music. The ideas discussed in that group, guided by the encyclopaedic knowledge of theory and brilliant critical analysis of Anahid Kassabian, will be with me always. I would also like to acknowledge Ian Garwood and Rob Strachan for useful suggestions on the much earlier version of this material that appeared in my PhD thesis. I am particularly grateful to Elena Boschi for intellectually and politically stimulating conversations, writing advice, love, and support over the years. Thanks also to my family for their love and support. Finally, I would like to thank all of those colleagues who have provided ideas, comments, criticism, and inspiration at conferences, in workplaces, and in editorial roles. Parts of Chapter 7 were previously published in *International Cinema and the Girl* (edited by Fiona Handyside and Kate Taylor-Jones, 2016, Palgrave Macmillan).

Introduction
Youth Films, Identity, and Musical Agency

The year was 1993, and it was the morning of the annual school picnic at Kennywood Park,[1] the local amusement park. I was 15 years old – yearning for freedom but not yet old enough to drive my friends to our destination. As had become tradition over the past few years, we gathered early, for what would be the last time, to watch *Ferris Bueller's Day Off* (John Hughes, 1996). At the time I didn't really reflect on why this film meant so much to us, and why we identified with its protagonist and narrative. All I knew was that it put us in the mood for a day of what seemed like unbridled freedom at the amusement park. The young love and unshakable friendship portrayed in the film were central to our youthful, naïve aspirations for this day and for a future that still felt wide-open and full of possibility. But I now understand that something else was going on when we watched that film. As white, suburban, middle class, American boys, we saw a somewhat wealthier, more charismatic version of ourselves in Ferris (Matthew Broderick). Back then we never questioned his privilege, we just admired how the world was his oyster, and how he could break the rules and never get caught. But we also identified with the emotions expressed by the film's soundtrack. We felt the excitement of 'Beat City' (by The Flowerpot Men) when Ferris, his girlfriend Sloan Peterson (Mia Sara), and his best friend Cameron Frye (Alan Ruck) drove into downtown Chicago in Cameron's father's prized 1961 Ferrari 250 GT California; the day and the city were theirs to discover. We also felt the hormonally-amplified, yet all-too-real pain and confusion expressed by the instrumental cover version of The Smith's 'Please Please Please Let me Get What I Want' (performed by The Dream Academy). As this song played, we identified with Cameron as he identified with the insecurity of the little girl in Georges-Pierre Seurat's *A Sunday Afternoon on the Island of La Grande Jatte*.

What I now understand is that identity and music were central to our love of that film and to our identification with its protagonist – the processes at work are brilliantly theorised in Anahid Kassabian's *Hearing Film* (2001). But why did Ferris and his friends have such agency? What role did the film's score play in the construction of their identities? And why was *Sloan Peterson's Day Off* never made? As Timothy Shary asserts, youth films "are imbued with a unique cultural significance: they question our evolving identities from youth to adulthood while simultaneously shaping and maintaining those identities" (2014, p. 13). However, youth films are still held by many as unworthy of serious scholarly attention. They even sit low within the canon of popular cinema due to the art/commerce binary, which still shapes the research agenda despite being deconstructed in the classroom. All of this notwithstanding, adolescence and the genesis and evolution of 'the teenager' as a concept have been discussed in many texts concerned with youth film and youth culture.[2] And while there have been a handful of book-length studies and edited collections on youth cinema,[3] none of them have focused on music. Although music is discussed briefly in most of these books, it is only the central concern in a couple of chapters and journal articles from the whole body of literature on youth cinema. As Kay Dickinson succinctly states, "without popular music, the representation and self-definition of the category 'teenager' – from its inception up until the present day – would be almost unrecognisable" (2004, p. 99). With the acknowledgment of music's importance to youth identity construction from a number of different academic disciplines, including popular music studies, youth studies, music and moving image studies, and cultural studies, it would seem that the time for a book-length study of music in youth films is long overdue.

In this book I examine the relationships between popular music, identity, and agency in US youth films. Although I draw some conclusions regarding popular music's role in defining youth films, the outlining of a genre is not my central concern. Rather, my intention is to bring together theory from film music studies, popular music studies, film studies, and cultural studies, among others, to create a better understanding of the meanings popular music brings to the construction of character identities and how these musically-imbued identities affect character agency. In addition, I discuss what I am calling 'musical agency', or the agency resulting from the coming together of certain uses of music and certain facets of identity (more on this later). Songs – whether source music, dramatic score, or source score[4] – are central to these issues. But I also consider how teenage characters engage with music in the narrative, including access to instruments and musical performance, social context of music consumption and performance, engagement with recorded music and visible playback technology,[5] and the appearance of visible signifiers of music not directly commented on by characters, such as posters, stickers, album covers, and so on.

Aside from youth films being ideal texts for studying identity construction through popular music, I have chosen to study youth films because they are, quite simply, of immense cultural importance. In addition to being extremely popular in the United States, the international importance of youth films has also been acknowledged by the publication of

Youth Culture in Global Cinema (editors, Timothy Shary and Alexandra Seibel, 2007). In his ground-breaking work on the genesis and evolution of the teen film genre, *Teenagers and Teenpics: The Juvenilization of American Movies in the 1950s*, Thomas Doherty (1988) states the following about the target audience of US films at the time of the book's publication:

> Strictly speaking, American motion pictures today are not a mass medium. As any multiplex marquee attests, theatrical movies cater primarily to one segment of the entertainment audience: teenagers. Without the support of the teenage audience, few theatrical movies break even, fewer still become hits, and none become blockbusters. In America movies reflect teenage, not mass—and definitely not adult—tastes.
>
> (p. 1)

While the complete separation of teenage and adult tastes oversimplifies film viewing practices and the statement that films reflect taste ignores their role in *shaping* taste, Doherty nonetheless suggests that films aimed at teen audiences are an incredibly powerful cultural force. In a chapter on teen films of the 1990s, Wheeler Winston Dixon (2000) makes a similar statement about the film industry at the turn of the millennium: "in the late 1990s, 'teen presence' is essential in the enterprise of selling a motion picture, and so no matter what genre these individual films might belong to, their overriding audience appeal is to contemporary teenage filmgoers" (p. 126). Since technological advances ensure that young people with the financial means to buy phones or tablets can now watch films anywhere and at any time, teens remain an important segment of the market. Despite the above claims, films that focus on teenage experiences, which are by no means universal, tend to include certain tropes and trials related to coming-of-age in its many forms. Thus, not all films marketed to teens are teen films.

Throughout this book I use the term 'youth films' rather than 'teen films' or any of its variants. My decision to do so stems from the discussions of Doherty (1988), Shary (2014), and Catherine Driscoll (2002 and 2011). Doherty uses the term 'teenpics' to discuss a particular genre that grew out of US exploitation films in the 1950s. For Doherty, "the teenpic [...] begins around 1955, a product of the decline of the classical Hollywood cinema and the rise of the privileged American teenager" (p. 14). He studies the development of this genre rather than focusing on its definition and is concerned with films that target teen audiences. Instead of choosing films that fit within this category, I have decided to study films concerned with teen identity, some of which are intended to have more widespread appeal and are not solely marketed to teenagers (although, as discussed above, this is a complicated issue). I use 'teen films' occasionally, however, when referring to films that are typical of the genre.

Like Shary, I use the term 'youth films' to reference "the entire sphere of films made about young adults" (2014, p. 20). I only focus on films with teenage protagonists. While Doherty, Driscoll, and Shary use genre analysis as their main analytical method, they do so in very different ways. For Doherty, studying the history of the genre's development is more important than the more traditional method that involves defining genre characteristics and classifying films. Shary sets out a classification system of youth film subgenres, employing "genre theory to study social representation" of youth (2014, p. 13). Driscoll's approach is "predominantly discursive rather than aesthetic", looking beyond the film text itself to broader constructions of adolescence in society (2011, p. 2). While discussing histories, generic conventions, and limitations of genre definitions, she considers how various social and legal constraints shape the content of teen films, as well as studying the 'adaptability' of teen films, or how their ability to incorporate new cultural trends and forms is a key characteristic. In her book *Girls* (2002), Driscoll separates teen films and youth films based on gender connotations. She argues that youth films focus on rebellious subcultures and are considered boys' films, whereas teen films are considered girls' films and contain "romantic narratives of transformation mediated by overt commodification" (p. 217). Central to this division is the nature of conflict – youth films contain mostly physical conflict, while in teen films conflict is focused on "interiorized disciplines and exclusions" (p. 220). While Driscoll abandons this distinction in *Teen Film: A Critical Introduction* (2011), insisting that many films are concerned with the interdependence of institutionalised adolescence and resistance to it, her earlier distinction is still relevant due to its implications for the study of identity and agency in youth films. As I argue throughout this book, music, identity, and agency are intimately connected in youth films. This binary distinction between resistance and dependence is central to the social functions of different types of popular music and their attachments to different identities.

In *American Film Cycles*, Amanda Ann Klein (2011) considers how the juvenile delinquent teenpic cycle of the 1950s represented and exploited various aspects of contemporary youth culture, including rock 'n' roll music.[6] As Klein explains, "film studios appeal to teenagers precisely by making a spectacle of their so-called deviant behaviors: listening to and dancing to rock 'n' roll music, racing hot rods or stealing cars, engaging in 'confrontational dressing,' and taking or distributing illegal drugs" (p. 103). She goes on to describe how the exploitative films, in an attempt to placate conservative audiences, always contained such 'antisocial' behaviour by punishing the teenage offenders through reformation, jail, death, or exile. Another important point Klein makes is that "this cycle was also integral to the proliferation, diffusion, and active shaping of how subcultures and their teenage participants understood themselves" (p. 103). She argues that the containment of criminal activities and deradicalisation of subcultural behaviour was necessary to appeal to a general audience but also asserts that the films retained some element of subcultural edginess and threat in order to appeal to their target audience. This safely exploitative approach to subcultural representation is typical of how youth films represent musical cultures, be they subcultures or more mainstream practices. Of course, filmic representations of subcultures feed back into the subcultures themselves, altering them in the process. As Klein states, "the media plays an integral role in shaping the future of subcultures by singling out certain elements of the subculture and redefining them for mass consumption" (p. 107). Popular music has continued to play a central role in both the narratives and soundtracks of youth films since their early days as exploitation fare. Rock 'n' roll teenpics of the 1950s established the convention of using songs and diegetic performances to associate the films with contemporary youth culture and therefore better entice their target audience.

Driscoll's (2011) emphasis on the liminality of both teen film characters and the content and form of the genre itself gets to the heart of why identity is so important in these films. She argues that, while coming-of-age and maturity are central concerns of teen film narratives, "teen film is less about growing up than about the expectation, difficulty, and social organisation of growing up" (p. 66). Popular music plays an integral part in the social organisation depicted in youth films, as it does in the real world. In this book, I group films together based on three narrative tropes: teenage girls who play guitars, white characters who use black music to express identity and improve agency, and characters whose ethnic identity is musically constructed in contradictory ways.[7] This strategy of categorisation foregrounds hybrid identity constructions that challenge fixed notions of gender, race, ethnicity, class, and sexuality, as well as elucidating the relationship between these complex identities and agency.

The films I have chosen for this study were released from 1997 to 2007. While this choice may seem more arbitrary than focusing on a single decade, it is actually less so, since it partly corresponds with a cycle of US youth films. Both Shary (2014) and Stephen Tropiano (2006) recognise a resurgence of teen-focused youth films in the mid-1990s. Shary describes the gap in youth film production after the group of teen stars known as the 'Brat Pack' grew into adult roles in the late 1980s, arguing that aside from the mini-cycle of films about urban African-American youth concerned with questions of gang membership and gun violence in the early 1990s, there were relatively few youth films made until a resurgence occurred in the mid-1990s (2014, p. 12). He goes on to explain how this cycle waned in the early 2000s and was later replaced with a cycle coinciding with the rise in teen fantasies. Tropiano suggests that the mid-1990s surge was due to a small number of "mega-media conglomerates" targeting teenagers, who had more spending money due to a healthy economy and who "were the fastest-growing segment of the U.S. population" between 1990 and 2000 (pp. 202–204). More importantly, representations of identity and difference were becoming more complex as the 1990s drew to a close. As Shary explains, "by giving youth more powers of self-identification, recent youth films have placed more responsibility on their protagonists to deal with their ascent through adolescence, an ascent that can take any number of directions en route to maturity" (2014, p. 300). Shary goes on to say that his study "has been an attempt to show how images of youth in American cinema at the turn of the millennium are evolving, and its main argument has been that adolescent depictions are becoming increasingly complex, dynamic, and revealing" (p. 302). My interest in this increasing complexity influenced the decision to focus on films from this period.

Of course, I have also made choices about inclusion and exclusion from within this period. Although interactions between popular music, identity, and agency can be found in most youth films, I have favoured films that foreground character interactions with music in some cases. In addition, I have included a mix of Hollywood and independent films. In his introduction to *Youth Culture in Global Cinema*, Shary argues that in Hollywood films, "youth culture is portrayed as primarily white, middle class, non-religious, suburban, and fun", with more diverse youth experiences being represented in American independent films (editors, Shary and Seibel 2007, p. 1). While independent films do not always contain a critical analysis of identity, it is nevertheless true that the foregrounding of difference is often more considered and less simplistic in these films. The major reason for including Hollywood films in this study is that they have the widest cultural impact of all films made in the US. To focus simply on independent cinema would be to ignore those films that influence the greatest number of young people (and adults) and their conceptions of identity.

Music, Identity, and Agency

In recent years, conceptions of identity have become more fluid, open, and traversable than ever before, yet fixed identities can still be vital to collective social movements. With regard to the "interdeterminacy and ambivalence that shape [...] identity politics," Sharon Willis states, "in popular representations, as in the world, identity politics is likely to go both ways, to become either a site for the progressive use of diversity or an opportunity for the conservative management of difference within existing power structures" (1997, p. 3). Thus representations, generally marked by ambivalence as Willis asserts, are never simply good or bad. Likewise, Pam Cook argues that, "contrary to the claims made by much film theory that 'the cinematic institution' works to endorse and sustain dominant ideology, popular cinema problematises all social categories – of class, race and ethnicity, national identity, gender, sexuality, age and so forth" (1998, p. 234). Gaining an understanding of how music can articulate identities is critical to the study of popular cinema due to its representational ambivalence and wide appeal. Youth films are the perfect object of analysis for this task, due to the social relevance of music in youth films and in the lives of everyday teenagers.

Despite some basis in social background and biological factors, identity is constantly under construction, with every new experience or interaction potentially influencing how one perceives oneself. As Stuart Hall explains, this is a process dependent on external discourses and internal subjectivities:

> I use 'identity' to refer to the meeting point, the point of *suture*, between on the one hand the discourses and practices which attempt to 'interpellate', speak to us or hail us into place as the social subjects of particular discourses, and on the other hand, the processes which produce subjectivities, which construct us as subjects which can be 'spoken'. Identities are thus points of temporary attachment to the subject positions which discursive practices construct for us.
>
> (1996, pp. 5–6)

Elsewhere, Hall similarly describes "the post-modern subject [...] conceptualized as having no fixed, essential or permanent identity". In this case, "identity becomes a 'moveable feast': formed and transformed continuously in relation to the ways we are represented or addressed in the cultural systems which surround us" (1992, p. 277). While these conceptualisations are somewhat restrictive with regard to agency, their emphasis on the liminality and social construction of identity is useful for understanding the role music and other forms of popular culture can play in identity construction. Hall does incorporate agency when considering why identity is experienced as less fragmented than that of the post-modern subject, arguing "if we feel we have a unified identity from birth to death, it is only because we construct a comforting story or 'narrative of the self' about ourselves" (1992, p. 277). This complete identity is made to feel whole by incorporating external attributes, "by the ways we imagine ourselves to be seen by *others*" (1992, p. 287). Similarly, Hall asserts that "identities are constructed through, not outside, difference" (1996, p. 4). Individuals no doubt draw on narratives present in popular cultural texts when constructing this "narrative of the self"; teens are likely to identify with youth film narratives and their depictions of identity formation when imagining their own personal narratives.

Despite criticisms of identity as a concept fundamentally based on exclusion, it is still useful for theorising real world struggles and the power relations that affect agency in filmic representations of youth. In *Sacrificial logics*, Allison Weir (1996) considers such criticisms of identity in feminist theory. She contests the idea that identity is always exclusionary and disempowering, arguing for "a model of self-identity as a capacity for participation in a social world" (p. 8), where "the individual can be understood as a participant in a social world of contested meanings" (p. 13). After discussing the criticism of identity and its evolving theorisation from Simone de Beauvoir through Julia Kristeva, Weir proposes the following conception of identity for future studies:

> We need to make a space for an understanding of self-identity and autonomy which will not clash with our conviction that individuals must be understood as embedded, embodied, localized, constituted, fragmented, and subject to systems of power, oppression, and exploitation. We need, still, to understand ourselves clearly as actors capable of learning, of changing, of making the world, and ourselves, better.
>
> (pp. 184–185)

Thus Weir acknowledges the subject's constitution in ideology and power relations, and its fragmentation, but also argues for the potentially positive effects of self-identity on attainment of agency. The inclusion of oppression and agency within such theories of identity is somewhat contradictory, but it also reflects the complexity of identity politics in vivo. Any theory of identity that is wholly dismissive or celebratory is necessarily incomplete, ignoring the contradictory aspects of living and acting within a society.

What role, then, does popular music play in the construction of these complicated, sometimes transient identities? In a discussion of music and identity, Simon Frith suggests that "the question we should be asking is not what does popular music reveal about the people who play and use it but how does it create them as a people, as a web of identities?" (1996, p. 121). For Frith, music is central to creating a narrative of identity, and any identity is an ideal version of the self. He also claims that listening to music allows one to "participate in imagined forms of democracy and desire" (p. 123). Echoing Hall, Frith goes on to state that "music constructs our sense of identity through the direct experiences it offers of the body, time and sociability, experiences which enable us to place ourselves in imaginative cultural narratives" (p. 124). While it is true that individuals from a variety of different backgrounds can use music to construct their personal identity narratives, this is not simply a straightforward matter of choice. The agency suggested in Frith's discussion is perhaps more restricted than the words imply. But Frith goes on to suggest music has its own particular liberating potential:

> [...] what makes music special – what makes it special for identity – is that it defines a space without boundaries [...] Music is thus the cultural form best able both to cross borders – sounds carry across

fences and walls and oceans, across classes, races and nations – and to define places; in clubs, scenes, and raves, listening on headphones, radio and in the concert hall, we are only where the music takes us.

(p. 125)

The ability of music to cross borders and define places offers unlimited possibilities for identity construction. This begs the question – to what extent do social background and socially-mediated biological traits affect one's capacity for constructing a narrative from musical texts? Not all musics are available to all people, for reasons ranging from gender to class to race to age. Thus, the construction of a narrative of the self through music is dependent on a complex mix of choice, exposure, and agency.

Elsewhere in his argument, Frith does acknowledge the role that culturally-articulated biological traits and social background play in identity construction, as well as arguing that "anti-essentialism is a necessary part of musical experience" (p. 122). But he also contradicts the above quote about border crossing by stating that "[m]usic, whether teenybop for young female fans or jazz or rap for African-Americans or nineteenth century chamber music for German Jews in Israel, stands for, symbolizes *and* offers the immediate experience of collective identity" (p. 121). While Frith does not exactly argue for a universal musical experience based on biological or cultural traits, his examples range from specific cases to more general arguments about audiences, making this claim is somewhat dubious. Conversely, an individual from a different racial/ethnic/gender/age group could experience feelings of collective identity from the same type of music for different reasons.

Underpinning many discussions of identity in popular music studies, and vital to the theorisation of musical articulations of identity in this book, is Pierre Bourdieu's writing on the social dynamics of culture. His concepts of 'habitus', 'field', and 'cultural capital' developed in *Distinction* (2010) and elsewhere provide a useful model for understanding the connections between identity, agency, and expressions of culture. For Bourdieu, taste, or 'disposition', is a product of education, and therefore primarily dependent on class background. 'Habitus' refers to class-based "systems of dispositions" (2010, p. xxix), which more or less determine one's relationship with cultural forms. The effect of habitus on cultural competence and taste, and the resulting influence on agency within a cultural field, is summarised in the following quote:

The denial of lower, coarse, vulgar, venal servile – in a word, natural – enjoyment, which constitutes the sacred sphere of culture, implies an affirmation of the superiority of those who can be satisfied with the sublimated, refined, disinterested, gratuitous, distinguished pleasures forever closed to the profane. That is why art and cultural consumption are predisposed, consciously and deliberately or not, to fulfil a social function of legitimating social differences.

(p. xxx)

This theorisation of class-based taste and the ways that cultural products reinforce social difference can be extended to other aspects of identity when discussing popular music. Furthermore, this legitimation of social differences is intertwined with the legitimation of particular forms of art. The implications of this on agency within any cultural field are clear. Cultural capital, the sort of currency resulting from existing within a certain habitus and gained through the application of cultural competence, provides one with agency and the ability to act as a gatekeeper within a cultural field. Discussing the literary field in 'The Field of Cultural Production or, the Economic World Reversed', Bourdieu argues that "the field of cultural production is the site of struggles in which what is at stake is the power to impose the dominant definition of the writer and therefore to delimit the population of those entitled to take part in the struggle to define the writer" (1993, p. 42). While this statement refers specifically to writers and cultural *production*, there is no reason why the same could not be said for cultural *consumption*. With regard to music, various facets of identity play a role in determining who is entitled to define the composer or performer and who should be considered a legitimate fan of certain genres or styles.

The concept of 'cultural capital' has been extended to cover 'popular cultural capital' by John Fiske (1989 and 1992) and 'subcultural capital' by Sarah Thornton (1996) with regard to fandom and club cultures, respectively. As Fiske points out in 'The Cultural Economy of Fandom', Bourdieu's model suffers from two main weaknesses – his focus on class (while ignoring other aspects of identity) and his failure to develop a theory that accounts for the practices of the "culture of the subordinate" (1992, p. 32). In fact, when Bourdieu does consider popular culture, he argues that such art refuses formal experimentation and privileges function over form (2010, pp. xxvii–xxviii). Fiske argues that textual and social discrimination are central to fandom, and that this discrimination "involves the selection of texts or stars that offer fans opportunities to make meanings of their social identities and social experiences" which "may at times be translated into empowered social behavior" (1992, p. 35). He identifies three types of productivity in which fans engage – 'semiotic productivity' ("making of meanings of social identity and of social experience from the semiotic resources of the cultural commodity"), 'enunciative productivity' (including fan talk and style), and 'textual productivity' (pp. 37–39). Each of these is intimately linked to self-conceptions of identity, and thus agency within fan cultures. The ability to produce depends on how one defines one's identity in relation to music, as well as how one discriminates against music and people understood to fall outside of this self-definition. Fiske also emphasises the relationship between knowledge and power in fan cultures. While few youth film characters are depicted as belonging to the type of fan cultures Fiske describes, they are nevertheless sometimes depicted as fans of particular artists or genres of music. The agency that can develop from acquiring a particular body of musical knowledge and performing a particular identity can transfer into agency within the overall narrative when music is present.

Similarly, in *Club Cultures* Sarah Thornton (1996) describes how knowledge is central to the embodiment of 'subcultural capital' in the form of using current slang and performing the latest dance styles as if second nature. She considers age, rather than class, to be the primary factor determining taste in popular music, with gender being the second most important social difference. Echoing Bourdieu, Thornton states that "subcultural capital would seem to be a currency which correlates with and legitimizes unequal statuses", with the mainstream often being classified as feminine and 'unhip' in dance cultures (p. 104). Furthermore, she emphasises the role of the media in both circulating subcultural capital and destroying it through overexposure, such that "the difference between being *in* or *out* of fashion, high or low in subcultural capital, correlates in complex ways with degrees of media coverage, creation and exposure" (p. 14). As I explore in greater detail, particularly in Part I, the mediation of popular music genres and artists influences how films portray youth culture in relation to certain types of music.

Furthermore, Lawrence Grossberg (1996) argues that "agency involves relations of participation and access, the possibilities of moving into particular sites of activity and power, and of belonging to them in such a way as to be able to enact their powers" (p. 99). This is where identity becomes a useful tool for social organisation to combat power imbalances. While some restraints to participation and access are structural and reside outside of the agent, there are also internalised mechanisms that restrict agency. As Judith Butler states:

> Power does not exist over and against the subject or, perhaps better said, it does not exist only in such an exterior relation. The subject is itself constituted through the embodiment of certain norms that establish in advance and with considerable social force what will or will not be a recognizable subject.
>
> (2000, pp. 33–34)

For those identities not officially recognised as legitimate, any struggle for agency will be all the more difficult.

As previously discussed, music is essential to the construction of identity in representations of teenagers, as well as in their own expressions of identity. In *Music in Everyday Life*, Tia DeNora (2000) asserts that music is a powerful tool for regulating the self, constructing identity, and enabling agency:

> At the level of daily life, music has power. It is implicated in every dimension of social agency [...] Music may influence how people compose their bodies, how they conduct themselves, how they experience the passage of time, how they feel – in terms of energy and emotion – about themselves, about others, and about situations. In this respect, music may imply and, in some cases, elicit associated modes of conduct. To be in control, then, of the soundtrack of social action is to provide a framework for the organization of social agency, a framework for how people perceive (consciously or subconsciously) potential avenues of conduct. This perception is converted into conduct *per se*.
>
> (pp. 16–17)

Thus, music is important for self-regulation and motivation, but control of music in social spaces also provides access to a different sort of power. In a similar manner, social expression of musical identity (and access to the knowledge necessary to construct this identity) is a source of power that can facilitate agency in certain social spaces. DeNora acknowledges the value of social presentation of the self (p. 62) and goes on to discuss the importance of music as a source of aesthetic material for identity construction and body regulation:

> Within social spaces, then, prominent music may allude to modes of aesthetic agency – feeling, being, moving, acting – and so may place near-to-hand certain aesthetic styles that can be used as referents for configuring agency in real time, for the bodily technique of producing oneself as an agent in the full sense of that word [...]
>
> (p. 123)

This conceptualisation of "aesthetic agency" brings the entire body, and not just the mind, into the consideration of agency and expressions of power. For DeNora, this function of music is essential to the articulation of true agency. Music can enable agency via different yet interconnected routes, from its use as a semantically rich toolkit for identity construction to its affective properties. DeNora's study of individuals' everyday use of music sheds light on sources of agency both in personal spaces and in shared social contexts.

   In addition to depicting how some teens use music in the formation of identities, films also use music to represent characters' subjectivity and imply certain aspects of their self-identity. However, the musically-articulated connotations understood by a perceiver, whether intended by filmmakers or not, depend on the perceiver's background. With regard to film music and identification, Kassabian describes the ways "assimilating identifications" (more often created with composed scores) "draw perceivers into socially and historically unfamiliar positions, as do larger processes of assimilation", while "affiliating identifications" (more often created with compiled scores) "depend on histories forged outside the film scene, and they allow for a fair bit of mobility within it" (2001, p. 3). She adds that "assimilating identifications narrow or tighten possibilities, while affiliating identifications open outward" and discusses how personal histories may affect the ways perceivers understand music and identify with characters (pp. 141–142). This suggests that the cultural and personal background of the perceiver is just as important to her or his understanding of film music connotations as the context of the music within the film.

I use the term 'musical agency' to describe character agency intimately connected to, and influenced by, one or both of the following categories of music use: (1) music performed and listened to by characters and (2) music played in association with characters. The former category involves character engagement with source music and includes playing instruments, listening to music, and adopting elements of self-identity such as clothing style and attitude directly related to music. The latter category refers to dramatic score that is heard when the character is present or that alludes to the character. Of course, source score can bridge these two categories. Thus, I am not considering 'narrative agency', understood as the actions of the theoretical narrator (not to be confused with a film character) who, as described by Jerrold Levinson (1996) in 'Film Music and Narrative Agency', "presents the events of the film's world from within it, whereas the implied author of a film [...] presents the world of the film [...] from a position external to it" (p. 253). My second category of music use that affects musical agency does overlap somewhat with the concept of 'musical agency' employed by Daniel Goldmark, Lawrence Kramer, and Richard Leppert (2007) as a unifying concept to group three chapters together in *Beyond the Soundtrack: Representing Music in Cinema*. Goldmark, Kramer, and Leppert use the term to refer to music's power to construct the film world, as well as "the power of music in film to move or "transport" the audience into recognitions, subject-positions, and reflective understanding that could be accessed in no other way" (p. 7). While I am not referring to the agency *of* the music as they do, I am nevertheless concerned with the ways in which music can be responsible for enabling character agency, as well as the perceiver's understanding of and relation to this process.

Authoritarian Musical Agency in *Coach Carter*

Before considering how popular music affects the agency of teen characters, I would like to provide a counter-example to illustrate how composed dramatic score can also be used to appoint musical agency, while popular music can be depicted as corrupt in comparison. In *Coach Carter*

(Thomas Carter, 2005), sporting goods store owner Ken Carter (Samuel L. Jackson) is asked to coach the Richmond High School basketball team, for which he was a star player as a teenager. He eventually tries to turn the misbehaved teens into good students and good players by emphasising mutual respect, hard work, and education. The team goes from a losing record in the previous year to an undefeated season. In the end, they all manage to pass high school and several of them even go to college.

The film opens with a shot of 'Carter's Sporting Goods' just after the start of 'Untouchable' by DMX, a mix of rap and soulful R&B. The words "we untouchable, baby" are heard as Carter locks up his shop, and the song continues over cuts between action shots of the Richmond High basketball team playing the decidedly superior St. Francis High and Carter driving from his shop to the game. The song ends after Carter enters the gym and sees the star player of St. Francis dunk the ball in slow motion. Carter reacts with a look that is both impressed by the dunk and embarrassed for Richmond, his former team. This title sequence sets up Carter as the protagonist of the film and the Richmond High basketball team as the problem that needs to be solved. The rest of the game, which soon ends in a fight started by one of Richmond's players after a taunt from the other team, has no music. The title sequence establishes a theme that carries on throughout the film: popular music, especially rap and R&B, is mostly used to suggest delinquency, degradation, and poor judgement.

One scene where an R&B song narrates urban crime and decay begins just after Coach Carter's son, Damien (Robert Ri'chard), tells him that he wants to leave St. Francis High, an expensive private school, and attend Richmond in order to play on the team that his father now coaches. Anthony Hamilton's 'Comin' From Where I'm From' plays as Coach Carter drives through town contemplating his son's decision. As Carter passes street corners with young African-American men selling/buying drugs and just generally being idle, Hamilton sings about a life wasted hustling, starting with the line "Sittin' here guess I didn't make bail." Carter fears that Damien may suffer the same fate if he goes to Richmond.

Figure 0.1 Coach Carter ensures the party's over.

Rap is used to similar ends on two other occasions. In one scene, rap is used to connote racially coded violence as a former player who was kicked off the team pretends to mug two current players at gunpoint. He and his friend are just playing a joke on the others, and the music foregrounds their childish and potentially dangerous actions. In another scene, rap music accompanies delinquent behaviour after Richmond wins a prestigious out-of-town tournament. Rap is heard as the players sneak out of their hotel and take a taxi to a party. Eventually, Carter notices the boys are missing and goes after them. With a cut to the team arriving at the party, rap music can be heard outside, and it continues inside the house as players flirt, drink, and generally 'misbehave'. Carter soon shows up and collects his players, and as he yells at them on the bus ride home, tragic sounding dramatic score reflects his feelings of disappointment. In this sequence, the players are portrayed as misbehaved children. Thus, the popular music associated with the players in their everyday teenage existence is associated with immature or unacceptable behaviour.

Coach Carter utilises military-informed discipline, which is reflected in the original score during the players' moments of struggle and victory in the name of 'becoming men'. While his military background is never explicitly stated, it is certainly implied in the mise-en-scène. Composed dramatic score with a military march rhythm plays during scenes of triumph on the basketball court, transferring all musical agency to Coach Carter. Thus, the teens are denied agency and get no musical recognition for their accomplishments. Coach Carter has plenty of musical agency in this film because the score during scenes of triumph closely matches his identity as an authoritarian figure. This is not a film about student athletes; it is a film about a saviour basketball coach, and the film's conservative musical strategies and designation of musical agency make this clear.

Youth Films, Identity, and Musical Agency

Film music participates in identity construction through the cultural connotations it brings to a film; popular music genres are central to this process. Music can also evoke ideas related to deeply ingrained stereotypes in various forms of popular media and discourse. Of course, what filmmakers intend to convey and how perceivers interpret films are not always aligned. A perceiver's understanding of character identity depends on her or his knowledge of a particular genre of music or the cultural context of a song. Therefore, identity can never be set; different perceivers will always come to an understanding of a character's identity based on the knowledge available to decode connotations brought to characters by music. I discuss the cultural context of various songs and genres to suggest possible connotations from which perceivers may construct an understanding of character identity. One's understanding of such connotations, one's knowledge of popular culture, can completely change one's comprehension of a film's identity construction and the resulting political meaning. The same musical elements that affect one's understanding of identity also affect one's comprehension of musical agency. Identity and agency are tightly entwined in filmic narratives, and music plays a key role in the construction of both. Musical agency is related to narrative agency, but it also involves characters' access to musical performance, as well as their musical representation through source music, source score, and dramatic score. The characters with the most musical agency are those who use music to their own benefit or benefit from music in the soundtrack.

Analysis of films in this book is divided into three larger sections based on unifying tropes. In Part I: 'She's a Rebel?: Girls, Guitars, and Agency', I consider how guitar playing, identity, and agency interact for female characters in the films *10 Things I Hate About You* (Gil Junger, 1999), *Love Don't Cost a Thing* (Troy Beyer, 2003), *All Over Me* (Alex Sichel, 1997), and *Juno* (Jason Reitman, 2007). In these films, access to instruments and performance spaces, masculine connotations of the electric guitar, and musical self-identity all affect agency in ways that complicate simplistic understandings of gender as a binary construction. In addition, discourses surrounding different genres/movements of popular music, such as riot grrrl, folk, punk rock, and R&B, serve to empower, feminise, sexualise, or infantilise characters in ways that can emphasise, alter, or disguise the ideological work of other narrative elements.

In Part II: 'Listening to the Other: Cultural Borrowing and Critical Reflection', I examine the use of 'black music' by white characters in the films *Ghost World* (Terry Zwigoff, 2001), *Save the Last Dance* (Thomas Carter, 2001), *Bring It On* (Peyton Reed, 2000), *Mean Creek* (Jacob Aaron Estes, 2004), and *Napoleon Dynamite* (Jared Hess, 2004). Characters typically engage in this cultural borrowing because they wish to access characteristics associated with certain discourses of blackness, such as authenticity, depth, masculinity, coolness, sex appeal, and righteousness. In these films, different types of whiteness are highlighted or modified through the borrowing of black music. Here I argue that characters who engage critically with cultural forms of the Other are likely to benefit in terms of agency; such depictions also force the perceiver to reflect on the implications of cultural borrowing and the constructed nature of racial discourses. Uncritical borrowing, however, often leaves characters unfulfilled and reduces music of the Other to a set of essentialised characteristics. Thus, depictions of white characters engaging with black music are not simply positive or negative, but they present a whole range of ethical questions regarding agency and illuminate how racial discourses are constructed and altered.

In Part III: 'Unheard Ethnicities: Musical Construction of Ethnic Identity and Agency', I consider how music enforces ethnicity or constructs identities that are more complex and hybrid in *Real Women Have Curves* (Patricia Cardoso, 2002), *Quinceañera* (*Echo Park, LA* – alternate title,

Richard Glatzer and Wash Westmoreland, 2006), and *Better Luck Tomorrow* (Justin Lin, 2002). In the first two films, hybrid forms of Latina/o identities are created through contrasts between traditional and modern forms of music. In addition, these films draw on music genre connotations that interact with other elements of character identity to produce new and complex meaning and problematise simple conceptions of ethnicity. In *Better Luck Tomorrow*, direct ethnic connotation is absent altogether from the soundtrack. Instead, restricted representations of Asian-American ethnicities are challenged through the alignment of the central male characters with feminist alternative rock, as well as electronic music. Overall, I argue that a careful study of the musical (and not just the visual) construction of ethnicity can provide insight into the true hybridity of these characters' identities and highlight how such characters are allowed or denied access to mainstream US culture.

The common thread that connects all of the chapters in this book is an interest in how music constructs identity and affects agency, whether characters are playing the guitar, engaging with recordings, or being affected by dramatic score beyond their control. Music does more than simply accompany these characters; it serves a vital function in constructing the filmic narrative. Throughout this book, I argue that music, particularly pre-existing songs, constructs identity in a manner that is complex, fluid, and unfixed. Finally, I argue that musical agency is affected by a film's internal contradictions – by which I mean the areas of tension between music, identity, and storyline. Characters tend to have the greatest musical agency in films where musical connotations align with other elements of character identity and the character's treatment in the storyline. Thus, musical agency tends to be less when there are contradictions between characters' musical performance, the music they listen to, music on the soundtrack (source music, source score, or dramatic score) that they do not choose, other elements of their identity, and their narrative behaviour unrelated to music.

Notes

1 Interestingly, Kennywood Park doubles for Adventureland in the film *Adventureland* (Greg Mottola, 2009).
2 See, for example, Thomas Doherty (1988) and Catherine Driscoll (2011). For a genealogy of identity that considers its origins in relation to Cold War youth culture, see Leerom Medovoi (2005).
3 See, for example, Thomas Doherty (1988), John Lewis (1992), Jonathan Bernstein (1997), Frances Gateward and Murray Pomerance (2002), Timothy Shary (2002/2014), Murray Pomerance and Frances Gateward (2005), Roz Kaveney (2006), Stephen Tropiano (2006), Timothy Shary and Alexandra Seibel (2007), and Catherine Driscoll (2011).
4 These are the terms used by Kassabian (2001). 'Source music' roughly equates to the more common 'diegetic music', while 'dramatic score' is used in place of 'non-diegetic music'. Kassabian defines 'source score' as

"music that falls between diegetic and nondiegetic music [...] [It] combines aspects of source music and dramatic scoring in terms of both its relationship to the film's narrative world and its coincidence with the onscreen events" (p. 45).

5 For a discussion of the meaning of playback technology in film, see Tim McNelis and Elena Boschi (2013).

6 For a detailed study of the history and industrial context of the use of popular music in films, see Jeff Smith (1998).

7 These categories are full of problematic terms that I discuss in depth throughout this book.

References

Bernstein, Jonathan (1997) *Pretty in Pink: The Golden Age of Teenage Movies*, New York: St. Martin's Griffin.

Bourdieu, Pierre (1993) 'The Field of Cultural Production, or: The Economic World Reversed' in Randal Johnson (ed.), *The Field of Cultural Production: Essays on Art and Literature*, Cambridge, UK: Polity Press, pp. 29–73.

Bourdieu, Pierre (2010) *Distinction: A Social Critique of the Judgement of Taste*, London: Routledge.

Butler, Judith (2000) 'Agencies of Style for a Liminal Subject' in Paul Gilroy, Lawrence Grossberg and Angela McRobbie (eds), *Without Guarantees: In Honour of Stuart Hall*, London: Verso, pp. 30–37.

Cook, Pam (1998) 'The Women's Picture From *Outrage* to *Blue Steel*' in Steve Neale and Murry Smith (eds), *Contemporary Hollywood Cinema*, London: Routledge, pp. 229–246.

DeNora, Tia (2000) *Music in Everyday Life*, Cambridge, UK: Cambridge University Press.

Dickinson, Kay (2004) 'My Generation': Popular Music, Age, and Influence in Teen Drama of the 1990s' in Glyn Davis and Kay Dickinson (eds), *Teen TV: Genre, Consumption, Identity*, London: British Film Institute, pp. 99–111.

Dixon, Wheeler Winston (2000) '"Fighting and Violence and Everything, That's Always Cool": Teen Films in the 1990s' in Wheeler Winston Dixon (ed.), *Film Genre 2000: New Critical Essays*, Albany, NY: State University of New York Press, pp. 125–141.

Doherty, Thomas (1988) *Teenagers and Teenpics: The Juvenilization of American Movies in the 1950s*, Boston, MA: Unwin Hyman.

Driscoll, Catherine (2002) *Girls: Feminine Adolescence in Popular Culture & Cultural Theory*, New York: Columbia University Press.

Driscoll, Catherine (2011) *Teen Film: A Critical Introduction*, Oxford, UK: Berg Publishers.

Fiske, John (1989) *Understanding Popular Culture*, Boston, MA: Unwin Hyman.

Fiske, John (1992) 'The Cultural Economy of Fandom' in Lisa Lewis (ed.), *The Adoring Audience: Fan Culture and Popular Media*, London: Routledge, pp. 30–49.

Frith, Simon (1996) 'Music and Identity' in Stuart Hall and Paul du Gay (eds), *Questions of Cultural Identity*, London: Sage, pp. 108–127.

Gateward, Frances and Murray Pomerance (eds) (2002) *Sugar, Spice, and Everything Nice: Cinemas of Girlhood*, Detroit, MI: Wayne State University Press.

Goldmark, Daniel, Lawrence Kramer and Richard Leppert (eds) (2007) *Beyond the Soundtrack: Representing Music in Cinema*, Berkeley, CA: University of California Press.

Grossberg, Lawrence (1996) 'Identity and Cultural Studies: Is That All There Is?' in Stuart Hall and Paul du Gay (eds), *Questions of Cultural Identity*, London: Sage, pp. 87–107.

Hall, Stuart (1992) 'The Question of Cultural Identity' in Stuart Hall, David Held, and Tony McGrew (eds), *Modernity and Its Futures*, Cambridge, UK: Polity Press, pp. 274–325.

Hall, Stuart (1996) 'Introduction: Who Needs 'Identity'?' in Stuart Hall, and Paul du Gay (eds), *Questions of Cultural Identity*, London: Sage, pp. 1–17.

Kassabian, Anahid (2001) *Hearing Film: Tracking Identifications in Contemporary Hollywood Film Music*, New York: Routledge.

Kaveney, Roz (2006) *Teen Dreams: Reading Teen Film and Television from 'Heathers' to 'Veronica Mars'*, London: I.B. Tauris.

Klein, Amanda Ann (2011) *American Film Cycles: Reframing Genres, Screening Social Problems, & Defining Subcultures*, Austin, TX: University of Texas Press.

Levinson, Jerrold (1996) 'Film Music and Narrative Agency' in David Bordwell and Noël Carroll (eds), *Post-Theory: Reconstructing Film Studies*, Madison, WI: University of Wisconsin Press, pp. 248–282.

Lewis, John (1992) *The Road to Romance and Ruin: Teen Films and Youth Culture*, New York: Routledge.

McNelis, Tim and Elena Boschi (2013) 'Seen and Heard: Visible Playback Technology in Film' in Marta García Quiñones, Anahid Kassabian, and Elena Boschi (eds), *Ubiquitous Musics: The Everyday Sounds That We Don't Always Notice*, Farnham, UK: Ashgate, pp. 89–106.

Medovoi, Leerom (2005) *Rebels: Youth and the Cold War Origins of Identity*, Durham, NC: Duke University Press.

Pomerance, Murray and Frances Gateward (eds) (2005) *Where the Boys Are: Cinemas of Masculinity and Youth*, Detroit, MI: Wayne State University Press.

Shary, Timothy (2014) *Generation Multiplex: The Image of Youth in Contemporary American Cinema*, Revised Edition, Austin, TX: University of Texas Press.

Shary, Timothy and Alexandra Seibel (eds) (2007) *Youth Culture in Global Cinema*, Austin, TX: University of Texas Press.

Smith, Jeff (1998) *The Sounds of Commerce: Marketing Popular Film Music*, New York: Columbia University Press.

Thornton, Sarah (1996) *Club Cultures: Music, Media and Subcultural Capital*, Middletown, CT: Wesleyan University Press.

Tropiano, Stephen (2006) *Rebels & Chicks: A History of the Hollywood Teen Movie*, New York: Back State Books.

Weir, Allison (1996) *Sacrificial logics: feminist theory and the critique of identity*, New York: Routledge.

Willis, Sharon (1997) *High Contrast: Race and Gender in Contemporary Hollywood Film*, Durham, NC: Duke University Press.

Filmography

10 Things I Hate About You (1999, USA) directed by Gil Junger, music by Richard Gibbs, music supervision by Alfonso E. Chavez, Buena Vista Home Entertainment.

Adventureland (2009, USA) directed by Greg Mottola, music by Yo La Tengo, music supervision by Tracy McKnight, Miramax.

All Over Me (1997, USA) directed by Alex Sichel, music by Miki Navazio, music supervision by Bill Coleman, Alliance.

Better Luck Tomorrow (2002, USA) directed by Justin Lin, music by Michael J. Gonzales and Semiautomatic, music supervision by Ernesto M. Foronda, Paramount.

Bring It On (2000, USA) directed by Peyton Reed, music by Christophe Beck, music supervision by Billy Gottlieb, Universal Home Entertainment.

Coach Carter (2005, USA) directed by Thomas Carter, music by Trevor Rabin, music supervision by Jennifer Hawks, Paramount.

Ferris Bueller's Day Off (1986, USA) directed by John Hughes, music by Arthur Baker, Ira Newborn, and John Robie, music supervision by Taquin Gotch, Paramount Home Video.

Ghost World (2001, USA) directed by Terry Zwigoff, music by David Kitay, music supervision by Melissa Axelrod and Christine Bergren, Icon Home Entertainment.

Juno (2007, USA) directed by Jason Reitman, music by Mateo Messina, music supervision by Peter Afterman, 20th Century Fox.

Love Don't Cost a Thing (2003, USA) directed by Troy Beyer, music by Richard Gibbs, music supervision by Michael McQuarn, Warner Home Video.

Mean Creek (2004, USA) directed by Jacob Aaron Estes, music by tomandandy, music supervision by Robin Urdang, Palisades Tartan.

Napoleon Dynamite (2004, USA) directed by Jared Hess, music by John Swihart, music consultancy by Tracy Lynch-Sanchez, Paramount Pictures.

Quinceañera (*Echo Park, LA* – alternate title, 2006, USA) directed by Richard Glatzer and Wash Westmoreland, music by Victor Bock and Micko Westmoreland, music supervision by Shaun Young, Metrodome Distribution.

Real Women Have Curves (2002, USA) directed by Patricia Cardoso, music by Heitor Pereira, music supervision by Margaret Guerra Rogers, Home Box Office Home Video.

Save the Last Dance (2001, USA) directed by Thomas Carter, music by Mark Isham, music supervision by Michael McQuarn, Paramount Home Video.

Part I

She's a Rebel? Girls, Guitars, and Agency

Introduction

While the relationship between character identity and film score has been studied in other contexts, the relationship characters have with musical recordings has been considered less often, and musical performances by characters in contexts other than the film musical and documentary are almost never discussed. When it comes to musical performance by girls and young women, filmic representations are particularly problematic. The restricted nature or complete absence of musical performance by girls in youth films says a great deal about how society still views the gender coding of musical performance and agency. Rather than analysing these performances in a filmic vacuum, I am considering characters, music genre, and the meaning of the guitar in relation to real world contexts to gain a better understanding of how identity and agency are constructed in relation to musical practices. This approach also helps to identify which discourses surrounding popular music these films draw on to create characters that audiences with a certain cultural competence will be able to understand.

Unlike many other genres of mainstream US cinema, youth films often have girl protagonists, and this means greater agency is available for girls in these films. In addition, girl protagonists in youth films tend to have complicated identities and more ambivalent characterisations. Despite being fairly normal teens their representations are multidimensional when compared with familiar teen stereotypes, and they are often outsiders in some way; the audience is made aware of this through their style, hobbies, interest in scholarly pursuits, and frequently, taste in music. However, initial challenges to hegemonic constructions of femininity are usually suggested to be expressions of individuality later in the films rather than transgressions of traditional gender roles, so that any deviant behaviour by the girl protagonist is contained. Few of these young women have an opportunity to express themselves through music, though there are some notable exceptions. Andie in *Pretty in Pink* (Howard Deutch, 1986) works in a record store, hangs out in a rock club, and has a superior knowledge of 'cool' music compared to Blane, her generally vapid love interest. In *Some Kind of Wonderful* (Howard Deutch, 1987), Watts, the tomboy friend of protagonist Keith, is a fan of music *and* a drummer (although she is never shown performing outside of the confines of her own home). *Ghost World* (Terry Zwigoff, 2001) finds Enid using music recordings of various genres and formats to experiment with and display her identity (see Chapter 4). These are just a few examples of musical expression by girl protagonists in youth films, but even in each of these cases agency is restricted in some way.

Throughout Part I, I examine the freedoms and limitations of girls who play guitars in the films *10 Things I Hate About You* (Gil Junger, 1999), *Love Don't Cost a Thing* (Troy Beyer, 2003), *All Over Me* (Alex Sichel, 1997), and *Juno* (Jason Reitman, 2007). I wish to interrogate the contexts of performance in each film and discuss how sexuality, gender, race, and ethnicity map onto these important expressions of identity. In addition, I discuss how other sources of musical signification – both aural and visual – contribute to character development and expression of identity. Finally, I consider how all of these elements affect the agency of the protagonist in each film.

Music listened to and performed by characters plays an important role in characterisation by employing certain signifiers that have been circulated in various forms of media. These media constructs, often associated with specific musical genres or movements, are expected to be recognised and understood by audiences without the provision of supplementary contextual information. Two of the films I discuss in this section draw on the music of a single cultural movement with very different results, while the other two use multiple genres to signify different character traits at different points in the film, depending on the dramatic needs of the narrative. What unifies all four of these films is that they include a girl who plays the guitar, and that specific popular music genres and artists are used to bring subcultural cachet to each of the characters. In *10 Things I Hate About You* and *All Over Me*, riot grrrl music, which is more of a feminist political project than a genre in the strict sense, is employed both explicitly and implicitly to suggest feminist politics, queerness, and rebelliousness in characters with varying access to musical performance. *Love Don't Cost a Thing* is the only film of the four in which the girl is not the protagonist, although Christina Milian, the actor who plays Paris, is a real-life singer. Although her interest in music is marginalised in this film, the film nevertheless draws on R&B conventions and the star image of the actor. She is also the only one of the four who plays acoustic rather than electric guitar. In *Juno*, classic and recent punk are cited visually and in dialogue to suggest a more radical persona while the genteel folk soundtrack offsets any political or aggressive connotations that allusions to punk may offer the protagonist, while also avoiding any progressive and/or feminist politics historically associated with folk music. In all four of these films, guitars are important to characters' self-expression, agency, and identity construction. However, songs in the soundtrack and various narrative events often undermine characters' implied musical tastes, politics, and identities in ways that reveal a great deal about popular constructions of gender, race, ethnicity, and sexuality in relation to music. In addition, two of these films suppress the threat of the female guitar player by excluding performance scenes, placing male gatekeepers in the narrative, and engaging female characters in more traditionally feminine behaviour throughout the film.

Adolescent rebellion is central to representations of youth, being considered both a necessary step in the coming of age that nevertheless must be managed and contained, and an important commodity in its own right. In her book *Girls*, Catherine Driscoll explains how rebellion is associated with masculine adolescence in contemporary culture, while feminine adolescence is represented as more conservative and bound up in consumption (2002, p. 218). Similarly, while discussing the work of sociologist Barbara Hudson, Kimberley Roberts (2002) describes the gendered nature of the "lone wolf" narrative of adolescent rebellion. She explains that all adolescents are expected to rebel, but girls have the added pressure of simultaneously transforming into proper young ladies, developing adult social skills and emotional maturity, and conforming in a manner at odds with teen rebellion. Thus, Roberts asserts that "most teenage girls [are left] in a classic double-bind; they believe that their rebellious feelings make them improper as 'young women' and, conversely, that their status as young women requires them to leave rebellious adolescence behind before they have really experienced it" (p. 223). Since guitar playing (particularly electric) has been closely linked with teenage rebellion in popular culture for many years, this "double-bind" provides some insight into why representations of young women who play the guitar are so conflicted. On the one hand, teenage girls, both onscreen and off, have been playing guitar for many years as a form of rebellion and/or simply for the love of music. But on the other hand, most mainstream representations are still unable to endorse fully the control of such signifiers of traditionally masculine rebellion by young women. The protagonists of the four films I discuss in Part I do not subscribe to a consumerist ethos in relation to rebellion as Driscoll describes, nor are they able to rebel as straightforwardly as boy protagonists could.

Agency does shift over time, though, as traditional gender expectations weaken and change form. Mary Celeste Kearney (2002) suggests that an increase in the agency of teenage girls has accompanied the weakening of strict gender boundaries:

> [...] changes in our society's ideologies of gender and sexuality have blurred the boundaries between masculinity and femininity and thus transformed both the ways in which girls are socialized and the

expectations they have for the future. For example, the populariza-
tion of liberal feminist ideas about women's equality with men has
altered significantly the ways in which girls dress, behave, and interact with others. One effect of this phenomenon is that female youth
are no longer seen as abnormal for wearing clothing or participating
in activities traditionally associated with males. Furthermore, girls
are encouraged to develop into assertive and independent individuals capable of taking care of themselves.

(p. 129)

All of these changes are reflected to some extent in contemporary youth
films, with girls often exploiting the new possibilities as tools for self-
expression. Interest in listening to and playing music has become more
widespread for young women in these films, too. The liminality of adolescence provides great potential for situations in which the gender binary
is stretched, questioned, and ultimately shown to be a construction that
must be actively negotiated. In such an unstable existence, the status quo
is upheld not through passivity, but through conscious action. However,
the popularisation of feminism that Kearney mentions has influenced
filmic representations of teenage girls in conflicting ways. On the one
hand, gender boundaries have been permeated (though not completely
broken down in most cases), and girls in these films are freer to express
themselves in less traditionally feminine ways that disturb the binary
gender system and make for more varied explorations of identity. But on
the other hand, this has resulted in the achievements of feminism being
taken for granted, as discussed in the literature on postfeminism.[1] Girls
in teen films often perform popular feminism (though it is not always
identified as such) in a way that shows some resistance and rebellion,
but ultimately lacks serious political conviction because the needs of the
narrative shift their attention to romance.

Girls play the guitar in each of the films I discuss in Part I. In every
case it is important to note the specific contexts of their guitar playing
and whether they play electric or acoustic guitar, since gender and genre
connotations, agency, and power are connected to the acoustic guitar
and the electric guitar in different ways. In his discussion of the electric
guitar and "cock rock", Steve Waksman asserts that "[t]he association
of the electric guitar with excessive male physicality has been one of the
most prominent themes in the recent history of the instrument" (1996,
p. 9). He goes on to argue that this association has its origins in cross-
racial, or possibly racist, desire:

> [...] the electric guitar as "technophallus" was built out of a highly
> charged relationship between white and black men, within which
> white males sought to appropriate what they perceived to be the
> potency of black men. The electric guitar mediated this relationship

in at least two ways. Visually, it was used to accentuate the phallic dimensions of the performing male body. Aurally, the volume and distortion generated by the instrument had a similar effect, amplifying the physical presence of the performer.

(p. 9)

Waksman's argument highlights not only the electric guitar's perceived connection to male physicality, but also its visual and aural symbolisation of phallic power. This specifically white, male, phallic power thus becomes a symbol of both sexual and racial dominance. In addition, Waksman states that for musicians like the members of Led Zeppelin, "[p]art of the privilege of being a male rock star was the power to do so with impunity, even when the stakes involved something on the order of rape" (p. 17).

For these reasons and others, electric guitar playing has long been considered a masculine pursuit;[2] girls and women have been both passively and actively excluded. Mavis Bayton (1997) discusses the absence of women electric guitarists she observed in her study of women rock musicians in the 1980s and mid-1990s. Technology in general has long been considered masculine territory, and the electric guitar is no different. Bayton argues that girls are encouraged from a young age to engage in more feminine pursuits, and playing rock music involves being sweaty, messing up one's hair, cutting one's fingernails, and potentially developing muscles – all concerns identified (though not always agreed with) by her respondents. In addition, Bayton claims that girls and women are exposed to images of electric guitar players who are almost exclusively men and therefore do not tend to identify with and emulate guitar heroes in the same way as boys, more often being restricted to fandom. Social aspects are also a central factor. Pressure on girls to find a boyfriend; lack of money, time, space, transport, and access to equipment; and exclusion from groups of boys in which learning takes place, information is exchanged, and bands are formed are also key factors in male domination of the electric guitar. Women who want to have children can also be excluded by the demands of family and career. Finally, Bayton identifies how guitar stores are masculine spaces that can be intimidating to young women, and she argues that boys and men will actively exclude women from playing the electric guitar, and rock music in general, so that rock performance continues to express heightened masculinity for its performers. A 2010 article by Monique Bourdage suggests that little has changed, with many of the same prohibitive issues for female guitar players being identified. She also discusses the patronising and sexist design and marketing of guitars for girls, as well as the fact that in almost all cases signature model guitars feature male guitarists' names. As further evidence, Bourdage cites a study suggesting that only around ten percent of guitar sales in the United States in 2009 were to girls and women (p. 12). Finally, Sarah Thornton (1996) states the following regarding gendered conceptions of popular culture:

> Even among youth cultures, there is a double articulation of the lowly and the feminine: disparaged *other* cultures are characterized as feminine *and* girls' cultures are devalued as imitative and passive. Authentic culture is, by contrast, depicted in gender-free or masculine terms *and* remains the prerogative of boys.
>
> (pp. 104–105)

Although Thornton uses dance culture as her object of study, the historic coding of rock music as 'authentic' also makes this assertion relevant to the discussion of guitar playing.

This historical gendering of rock music and its technologies is significant in the ways it continues to affect girls' participation in musical cultures. However, simply looking at the issue through this lens can be problematic. Susan Driver (2007) criticises the phallocentricity of this sort of approach. While she considers the merits of Bayton's writing, she also argues that such "discussions of women's rock tend to reproduce assumptions about rock as a conventionally masculine preserve that ends up ghettoising women's talents and tastes" (p. 206). The result is that "women's differences stand out as exceptions to the systematic dominance of male-produced popular music", thus "reifying sexual differences between men and women as the primary focus of analysis" (p. 206). Driver argues that it is important to study what queer girls actually do within musical cultures, rather than focusing on exclusionary elements. While I agree with Driver's argument, it would be dangerous to ignore the ways that sexism and masculine coding still influence musical cultures and industries, as well as their representations in cinema. For this reason, I intend to critically analyse how filmic representations of girls who play guitars serve to reinforce or subvert these connotations and conventions, as well as consider how girls in these films participate in musical cultures in ways not directly related to a binary conception of gender. With all of this in mind, what does it mean for teenage girls to play the electric guitar in films? Furthermore, how does this meaning change when they perform publicly? I argue throughout Part I that gender and guitar playing are mutually constitutive in articulation with other elements of identity. Although identity and agency are always fluid and affected by multiple interactions, the agency of girls who play guitars has the potential to be greatly increased by the adoption of an instrument with strong connotations of masculinity, power, and heteronormativity. However, as I will discuss, this agency is often contained and undermined in youth films, both through narrative events and in the way the soundtrack can contradict or alter narrative implications of identity and agency.

In the first two chapters of this section, I consider *10 Things I Hate About You* and *All Over Me*, two films in which riot grrrl music plays a strong role in creating a general sense of progressive politics in the narrative and suggesting feminism, strength, and individuality in the lead characters. Riot grrrl was a feminist cultural network that sparked international interest in the early 1990s, particularly through the music made by some of the young women involved. Joanne Gottlieb and Gayle Wald (1994) neatly summarise the characteristics of riot grrrl music (and culture) that have allowed its songs and imagery to bring such potent meaning to cinema:

> Riot grrrls not only have reconfigured punk's energy and rebelliousness in specifically female and feminist terms, but have also drawn upon punk's D.I.Y. tradition to blur the boundaries between musical production and consumption. If, according to Frith and McRobbie's models, girls have traditionally participated in rock as consumers (either active or passive), then riot grrrls pose a challenge to these models, insofar as they potentially allow women—even the ones not up on stage playing guitars or drums—to assume the (masculine) role of subcultural producer.
>
> (p. 263)

This music's incorporation into popular culture during the 1990s made much of the English-speaking world (and beyond) aware of its politics. However, use of this music and allusions to the riot grrrl movement have the potential not only to bring feminist politics to a film and empower its female characters, but also to distract the perceiver from the more conservative gender politics present in other aspects of the film. I argue that the genre's presence in *All Over Me* achieves the former, while its use in *10 Things* performs the latter. In addition, I consider *Love Don't Cost a Thing* in Chapter 1, drawing parallels between the restriction of musical agency in it and in *10 Things*.

In the final chapter of Part I, I address musical taste, performance, and agency in *Juno*. In this film, the titular protagonist is shown to be a fan of punk rock through dialogue and mise-en-scène. However, the film's dramatic score mainly consists of genteel, quirky contemporary folk, which often serves to infantilise Juno (or conflate Juno with the baby growing inside of her) and contradict the rebellious connotations of the punk rock she professes to like, as well as her more masculine mannerisms. In addition, Juno's guitar playing – particularly that of the electric guitar – is limited. While riot grrrl music is not central to this film its influence still lingers, particularly in one scene where Juno and another character play Hole's 'Doll Parts'.[3] As in *10 Things I Hate About You*, the soundtrack of *Juno* undermines and contradicts the narrative's characterisation of the protagonist in ways that explicitly and implicitly influence the construction of the protagonist's gender.

Notes

1 See, for example, Yvonne Tasker and Diane Negra (2007) and Rosalind Gill (2007).
2 For a discussion of "technological tinkering" and the electric guitar that considers its relationship to masculinity, see Steve Waksman (2004).
3 While Hole was not part of the riot grrrl scene, the band was often discussed in relation to it due to having a female vocalist, Courtney Love, who sang about gender in a more challenging way than was often heard in mainstream music.

References

Bayton, Mavis (1997) 'Women and the Electric Guitar' in Sheila Whiteley (ed.) *Sexing the Groove: Popular Music and Gender*, London: Routledge, pp. 37–49.

Bourdage, Monique (2010) '"A Young Girl's Dream": Examining the Barriers Facing Female Electric Guitarists' in *Journal of the International Association for the Study of Popular Music*, Vol. 1, No. 1, pp. 1–16.

Driscoll, Catherine (2002) *Girls: Feminine Adolescence in Popular Culture & Cultural Theory*, New York: Columbia University Press.

Driver, Susan (2007) *Queer Girls and Popular Culture: Reading, Resisting, and Creating Media*, New York: Peter Lang.

Gill, Rosalind (2007) 'Postfeminist Media Culture: Elements of a Sensibility' in *European Journal of Cultural Studies*, Vol. 10, No. 2, pp. 147–166.

Gottlieb, Joanne and Gayle Wald (1994) 'Smells Like Teen Spirit: Riot Grrrls, Revolution, and Women in Independent Rock' in Andrew Ross and Tricia Rose (eds) *Microphone Fiends: Youth Music & Youth Culture*, London: Routledge, pp. 250–274.

Kearney, Mary Celeste (2002) 'Girlfriends and Girl Power: Female Adolescence in Contemporary U.S. Cinema' in Frances Gateward and Murry Pomerance (eds) *Sugar, Spice, and Everything Nice: Cinemas of Girlhood*, Detroit, MI: Wayne State University Press, pp. 125–142.

Roberts, Kimberley (2002) 'Pleasures and Problems of the "Angry Girl"' in Frances Gateward and Murry Pomerance (eds) *Sugar, Spice, and Everything Nice: Cinemas of Girlhood*, Detroit, MI: Wayne State University Press, pp. 217–233.

Tasker, Yvonne and Diane Negra (eds) (2007) *Interrogating Postfeminism: Gender and the Politics of Popular Culture*, London: Duke University Press.

Thornton, Sarah (1996) *Club Cultures: Music, Media and Subcultural Capital*, Middletown, CT: Wesleyan University Press.

Waksman, Steve (1996) 'Every Inch of My Love: Led Zeppelin and the Problem of Cock Rock' in *Journal of Popular Music Studies*, Vol. 8, No. 1, pp. 4–25.

Waksman, Steve (2004) 'California Noise: Tinkering with Hardcore and Heavy Metal in Southern California' in *Social Studies of Science*, Vol. 34, No. 5, pp. 675–702.

Filmography

10 Things I Hate About You (1999, USA) directed by Gil Junger, music by Richard Gibbs, music supervision by Alfonso E. Chavez, Buena Vista Home Entertainment.

All Over Me (1997, USA) directed by Alex Sichel, music by Miki Navazio, music supervision by Bill Coleman, Alliance.

Ghost World (2001, USA) directed by Terry Zwigoff, music by David Kitay, music supervision by Melissa Axelrod and Christine Bergren, Icon Home Entertainment.

Juno (2007, USA) directed by Jason Reitman, music by Mateo Messina, music supervision by Peter Afterman, 20th Century Fox.

Love Don't Cost a Thing (2003, USA) directed by Troy Beyer, music by Richard Gibbs, music supervision by Michael McQuarn, Warner Home Video.

Pretty in Pink (1986, USA) directed by Howard Deutch, music by Michael Gore, music supervision by David Anderle, Paramount Home Video.

Some Kind of Wonderful (1987, USA) directed by Howard Deutch, music by Stephen Hague and John Musser, music supervised by Tarquin Gotch, Paramount Pictures.

1 The Girl Can't Have It

Restricted Musical Agency in *10 Things I Hate About You* and *Love Don't Cost a Thing*

In this chapter, I will be discussing two films in which girls have limited and problematic musical agency and no access to public performance. Although the girls I will discuss in these films do play the guitar, both of them are denied the opportunity to perform publicly within the film, and in both cases the romantic relationship takes precedence. The first film I will discuss, *10 Things I Hate About You* (Gil Junger, 1999), is a youth film adaptation of Shakespeare's *Taming of the Shrew* set in modern-day Seattle. In *10 Things*, Kat Stratford (Julia Stiles) is a rebellious high school senior whose younger sister, Bianca (Larisa Oleynik), is more traditionally feminine and popular. Knowing that Kat has no interest in dating, the girls' overprotective father has ruled that Bianca cannot date until Kat does. This provides a challenge for the boys who are interested in Bianca, including Cameron (Joseph Gordon-Levitt), who recently transferred from another school, and Joey (Andrew Keegan), the wealthy school hunk/underwear model. Thus, Cameron uses Joey by convincing him to pay school delinquent Patrick Verona (Heath Ledger) to ask Kat out on a date. While Cameron knows that this is in Joey's interest, he hopes to win Bianca's heart first. Shockingly, Verona ends up falling for Kat, the girl whom no one else is willing to date, and Bianca eventually picks Cameron over Joey.

The film initially shows Kat to be a rebel, a ruthless individual who terrifies boys and, as the guidance counsellor reveals, once kicked a classmate in the crotch. Rejecting femininity is a possible source of rebellion for teenage girls, and Kat is characterised as a muddled, pop-cultural version of what it means to be a feminist. As opposed to the perky, sun-dress clad, adoration hungry Bianca, Kat plays football, wears less traditionally feminine clothes, is concerned with scholarly pursuits, and always seems to be angry. While all of these traits seem to imply a feminist character, much of Kat's implied feminism is manifested as general grumpiness and a loathing of boys. It turns out that Kat was popular at school until she dated and slept with Joey in the ninth grade because "everyone else was doing it". He later broke up with her when she was unwilling to repeat the act, and from that point onwards she swore she would never again give in to peer pressure. Kat's experience with Joey is presented as the chief motivation behind her unwavering individualism. Throughout the film, allusions to riot grrrl and related musical genres draw on popular media representations to suggest an alternative to traditional femininity and a musical agency that are tenuous and ultimately undermined in the narrative.[1]

A detailed comparison of *10 Things I Hate About You* and its source text is beyond the scope of this discussion; furthermore, this has already been done by Robert L. York (2006). It is interesting, however, to consider a few of York's observations. With regard to the film's simplification of the plot of *The Taming of the Shrew*, York states the following:

> The consolidation of this labyrinthine information in *10 Things* keeps the source at arm's length while simultaneously borrowing its basic skeletal structure. The improbability and comedy belying both narratives share qualities, and the factor of money, Petruchio's desired dowry and Patrick's acceptance of money to date Kat, reinforces both a Shakespearean complexity and a teen-driven motivation—especially in an apparently affluent high school.
>
> (pp. 71–72)

While York initially deals with these differences descriptively, he eventually concludes that the film is an unworthy Shakespeare adaptation. He argues that "[w]hile this cursory adaptation of the play indicates that Shakespeare can offer credibility to even the slightest of ideas, the filmmakers' trivialisation of their source contravenes any notion that their work does anything to repay the favor" (p. 87). Instead of engaging with the film on its own terms and considering significant issues such as identity and agency, York chooses to judge the film based on its lack of fidelity, a criterion now considered archaic in adaptation studies, as well as its status as a popular teen film. While York does describe the music at several points, he never touches on the cultural meanings contained in the music or the gender implications of Kat's guitar playing.

The opening credits suggest, both visually and aurally, a simplistic binary of teenage girl identities: conformist, cheery, traditionally feminine ones, and Kat. The bouncy pop of 'One Week' by the Barenaked Ladies sets *10 Things* up as a typical teen film as it plays over the squiggly, animated opening credits and shots of the Seattle skyline.[2] The song takes on a source as a Volkswagen convertible in which four teenage girls bop merrily along to the music approaches and stops in the foreground. After a few seconds, the hard rock of Joan Jett's 'Bad Reputation' creeps in and takes over the soundtrack as another car pulls up alongside the Volkswagen. When the girls look to their left, the camera follows their glances to the source of the song – a beat-up, two-tone car where Kat, solemn-faced and dressed in black, is the lone traveller. The lyrics "I don't give a damn 'bout my reputation," as well as the vocal delivery and punky sound of the music, tell the perceiver that Kat is a rebellious loner compared to the other girls at whom she glares condescendingly. It is eventually revealed, however, that Kat is not as anti-social as she is initially portrayed. She enjoys literature and music, and although she spends much of her time alone, she ultimately wants to fit in. While Kat does criticise patriarchal society early in the film, her protests are later contradicted both by the music and by her actions.

The inclusion of the Joan Jett song in the opening sequence is also important for the cultural links it brings to the film. In her discussion of riot grrrl, feminism, and lesbian culture, Mary Celeste Kearney (1997) explains that journalists often referred to older artists such as Kim Gordon of Sonic Youth and Joan Jett as ancestors of the riot grrrl community. Journalists also connected riot grrrl bands to contemporary all-female hardcore groups such as Hole and L7, who had different agendas than the riot grrrl bands and less hostility towards the corporate music industry. By the end of the 1990s, mainstream media had distilled riot grrrl into an easily identifiable set of images and sounds that circulated in popular culture. That the media had to borrow these signs from more clearly defined genres was largely due to the way riot grrrls dealt with representation of themselves. In addition to a media blackout during which they refused interviews, Marion Leonard (1997) states that:

> Another way in which riot grrrls deferred reappropriation was in their refusal to invest in common semiotic signifiers. In order for the dominant culture to appropriate subcultural signs there has to be some consensus of opinion on what actually constitutes these symbolisations [...] Riot grrrls did not offer clear symbols which could be extracted, thus undermining their subcultural currency and working against the dynamism of the network. This is not to say that riot grrrl is devoid of any symbolic systems, but rather to comment that participants frustrated attempts to precipitate certain essences from the fluidity of its underground network.
>
> (pp. 245–246)

While this lack of easily recognisable signifiers may have caused difficulty for the media and cultural producers in pinning down a coherent riot grrrl style, the ambiguous nature of the network was dealt with by filling in the gaps. The resulting oversimplification and misrepresentation of riot grrrl fit perfectly with the fairly transparent symbolic systems of musical, visual, and verbal representations in mainstream cinema. In *10 Things*, riot grrrl politics are conflated with alternative music and vague non-conformity to conjure ideas of feminism and difference. The location of this film is also significant since Olympia, Washington is considered one of the birthplaces of riot grrrl. The proximity of Seattle,

Washington to Olympia connects riot grrrl music to the less political yet also 'angry' and 'alternative' genre of grunge.

Riot grrrl music is directly referenced in a scene where Verona, armed with illicitly obtained details of Kat's interests, goes to Club Skunk to ask her out. With a cut to a narrow, colourful corridor, Letters to Cleo's live performance of 'Come On' becomes audible. Verona turns the corner and walks towards the camera as the post-grunge alternative pop of the song fills the narrow space. When Verona passes the camera the perceiver suddenly adopts his point of view and audition, seeing others' reactions to his presence in combination with the music as he makes his way down the corridor. At once it is evident that this is a space of female agency, suggestive of a riot grrrl club. Verona receives glances that appear to be either bemused or disgusted as he passes a succession of young women on his way to the main room. But this hostile reception is short-lived and obviously meant to convey an initial threat that relies on stereotypes of hostile feminists for effect.

As Verona enters the main room of the venue, the camera once again leaves his body and follows him from behind. After the initial intense scrutiny no one really takes notice of him, although the male bartender does know him by name and asks why he is there. When Kat spots Verona at the bar she gives a disgusted look and questions his motives, but she also dares him to ask her out again. Verona then makes a transparently scripted remark that Letters to Cleo "are no Bikini Kill or The Raincoats, but they're not bad." Kat sceptically asks, "You know who The Raincoats are?" To which Verona replies, "Why, don't you?" and flashes a smug smile. Kat's resulting annoyed facial expression reveals that she is aware of what Verona is trying to do, but his attempt to impress her is ultimately successful. Verona then confidently exclaims, "I was watching you out there before. I've never seen you look so sexy." Predictably, the music ends mid-sentence and leaves his audacious words hanging in the silence, followed by widespread giggling.

In this scene, Verona exploits riot grrrl for financial gain, since he is being paid to pursue Kat. He name-drops Bikini Kill, one of the best known riot grrrl bands, and The Raincoats, a band often cited as a major riot grrrl influence. His transparently insincere attempt to impress Kat does not seem to bother her in the long run, though. The crowd at Club Skunk is inconsistent as well: the giggling in response to Verona's suggestive remark seems to contradict the suspicious glances he received on entering the venue. While the gauntlet of stares in the entrance corridor plays on popular media's equation of riot grrrl ideology and feminism with man-hating, the rest of the club scene contradicts the rather intimidating entrance. Musically, the performance by Letters to Cleo, never named but understood to be Kat's favourite band, is more alternative pop than riot grrrl. We only really hear Kat listening to bands with a similar feel throughout the film. In addition, she has a poster of

Juliana Hatfield on her bedroom wall and has "Poe" (not the writer, as evidenced by the distinctive logo) written on her binder at school. Both are female singer-songwriters who became popular during the mid-1990s glory days of alternative music. Although Kat also has some posters of female punk bands on her wall, such as Seven Year Bitch, it seems like the filmmakers' strategy may have been to draw upon a mélange of sounds and images from various contemporary genres associated with less straightforwardly mainstream alternative female artists to construct a strong female lead character. While such a spread of musical interests is probably a realistic representation of a teenager's musical taste, this conflation of alternative music with riot grrrl culture and thus feminism is not entirely accurate.

In his chapter 'Youth, Excess and the Musical Moment', Scott Henderson (2006) discusses the use of music and its political ramifications in *10 Things* and *Tank Girl*:

> Through their use of textual excess in the construction of these 'musical moments', *10 Things I Hate About You* and *Tank Girl* may be positioned as progressive texts in terms of their construction of femininity. The links between music and identity position their main female characters in opposition to the conventional feminine role rather than providing the social integration so central to both the classical musical and to the contemporary teen film.
>
> (p. 147)

The main musical moments Henderson refers to in *10 Things* are a scene where Verona sings 'Can't Take My Eyes Off You' in the school stadium and the final scene of the film where Letters to Cleo play Cheap Trick's 'I Want You to Want Me' on the roof of the school. In the former scene, Verona sings and dances to impress Kat while the school marching band provides musical backing. His performance, although definitely out of character, is not so out of place in this type of film.[3] Teen films have a history of unlikely musical moments that disrupt the narrative. Some notable examples are Duckie's outlandish miming and dancing to Otis Redding's 'Try a Little Tenderness' in *Pretty in Pink* and Ferris' commandeering of a parade float and performances of 'Danke Schoen' and 'Twist and Shout' in *Ferris Bueller's Day Off* (John Hughes, 1986). Due to the huge influence of John Hughes' films (*Pretty in Pink*, although directed by Howard Deutch, was written by Hughes), such moments have occurred repeatedly in the teen genre. But these occurrences do not necessarily mark a text as progressive.

In addition, Henderson claims that the performance of 'I Want You to Want Me' by Letters to Cleo crosses gendered genre boundaries and therefore reasserts the progressive construction of Kat's identity (p. 156). But in the wake of riot grrrl bands and the increased presence of female performers in rock bands overall, it is unclear what makes the performance of a popular classic rock song by a female singer progressive. Since before the dawn of punk, women have written and played much more assertive and subversive music than Cheap Trick covers. This song reflects, rather, the desire Kat feels for Verona when he buys her a Fender Stratocaster to make up for the pay-off scandal, and it re-enforces his feelings for her. The female vocals shift the "want", "need", "love", and "beg" of the song's lyrics to Kat's perspective rather than making the overall performance somehow subversive. The vocals start when Verona silences Kat's castigation with a kiss, and the song carries on through part of the end credits, with a sweeping view of Letters to Cleo performing high atop the school roof. This scene is an effective end credit turned music video sequence, but it seems to have no real narrative impact other than re-enforcing the romantic plot resolution. Henderson claims that in this scene "the use of a female singer to perform a masculine rock song repositions subjectivity", and goes on to assert that "the gift of the guitar, and Kat's musical aspirations, place this resolution on her terms" (p. 156). However, Kat is passive with regard to her musical aspirations. It is Verona who acts on her desires and buys the guitar.

Kat has a distinct lack of musical agency throughout the film, despite the mention of feminist bands in dialogue and the narrative foregrounding of her musical taste. After a party, she drunkenly declares to Verona her desire to start a band, and in the same breath sarcastically exclaims, "my father would loooove that!" This statement suggests that the judgement of her father is never far from her thoughts, and the mention of it pretty much dismisses the likelihood that she will act on her desire. Thus Kat's agency is directly obstructed by her familial patriarch, and indirectly constrained by patriarchy more generally. She never takes any steps towards the realisation of her dream of starting a band. In one scene,

Figure 1.1 Kat is silenced and surveilled.

Kat strums silently in a guitar store while Verona watches from behind, and though she can hear herself through headphones, her playing makes no sonic impact on the film. Her musical expression is muted. Instead, a Joan Armatrading song entitled 'The Weakness in Me' functions as source scoring. The vocals and overall melancholic feeling of the song seem to convey a sense of yearning that shifts the subjectivity to Verona. The song starts on a close-up of Verona after he once again accepts money from Joey and bridges a cut to Kat in the guitar store. The lyrics "I have a lover who loves me, how could I break such a heart" foreground his sense of guilt as he stands behind Kat and secretly watches her play.

Unlike Verona, who sings in the stadium, Kat is never given the opportunity to perform. Her only 'performance' is a drunken table dance at a party, during which a crowd of male students ogle and cheer. While this may be considered a form of empowerment when viewed through a postfeminist lens, it does not contribute to Kat's musical agency overall. In the end, it is Verona who enables Kat to play music by giving her a guitar to make up for his dishonest behaviour. This is the rock 'n' roll equivalent of apology flowers. Whereas girls in some other youth films play a role in their own musical exploration and performance, Kat must ultimately wait for her boyfriend to provide the means, at least as far as performance is concerned.

This lack of musical initiative and Kat's attendance at the prom (for which she previously expressed hatred) would make it seem less likely that she resists social integration in the way Henderson suggests. In fact, social integration is made explicit by an overhead shot of Kat and Verona at the prom, both in traditional formal wear, dancing in a sea of similarly dressed students. And since Verona somehow convinced Kat's favourite band to play at the prom, all of the students are dancing to the music she likes, and they seem to be enjoying it. While one may be

Figure 1.2 Verona gives Kat the gift of musical agency.

tempted to read this as a victory for Kat's music and thus for Kat, the fairly standard pop rock is easily contained within the context of the prom – an institution that enforces traditional gender roles, serves as a dress rehearsal for marriage, and acts as a rite of passage into conventional adulthood. The prom scene, Kat's table dance, and another scene in which she flashes her breasts at a teacher to distract him while Verona sneaks out of detention, would give the impression that she is not as feminist or independent as the film initially suggests.

Kat's character is feminist in a merely superficial sense. While much of the film's audience may have understood Kat to be rebellious, nonconformist, and political, her musical characterisation is confused and contradictory. Theo Cateforis argues that Kat is "bolstered by the liberatory powers of a rebellious musical stance, but because she must also carry the brunt of the teen movie's soundtrack, she is forced to conform to the film's obvious commercial designs" (2009, p. 185) The use of music by alternative female artists of the 1990s and earlier performers connected to riot grrrl in the mainstream media brings to Kat's character already tenuous connotations of feminism that are ultimately undermined by the film's musical choices and other narrative events. Thus, the diluted form of progressive, feminist politics presented musically in *10 Things* becomes a generic residue of angry teen rebellion that is basically wiped clean by the film's final kiss.

Another film in which a girl's musical agency is limited and subservient to the narrative focus on the romantic relationship is *Love Don't Cost a Thing* (Troy Beyer, 2003), a remake of the teen film *Can't Buy Me Love* (Steve Rash, 1987) with an African-American protagonist and a mostly non-white lead cast. The film's protagonist, Alvin Johnson (Nick Cannon), is a 'nerd' who spends all his free time working on a car engine and hanging out with his similarly unpopular friends. After the beautiful, wealthy cheerleader Paris Morgan (Christina Milian) wrecks her parents' SUV, Alvin offers to pay for the new parts and repair the vehicle; in exchange, he asks Paris to pretend to be his girlfriend. Paris agrees to this, even though she is dating a professional athlete. Alvin hopes this arrangement will make him popular at school, which it naturally does. However, this newfound status gives Alvin a bloated ego, and perhaps unsurprisingly, Paris ends up falling in love with the person he used to be. The 'real' Alvin seems to have disappeared, though, abandoning his old friends in the process. After plenty of narcissistic behaviour and some humbling embarrassment, Alvin reverts to his old personality and finds Paris waiting for him, having all but abandoned her popular cheerleader persona.

Paris is played by Christina Milian, a Cuban-American R&B and pop singer-songwriter, record producer, dancer, and actor – so it is no surprise that her character has an interest in music.[4] When Alvin visits Paris at her house and walks in uninvited, he hears her playing an acoustic guitar.

This is followed by a cut to Paris sitting with a guitar in a room that looks too bare to be her bedroom. The initial view is in soft focus – Paris and her surroundings are blurred like a dream. Everything about this space is softened; there are pillows everywhere. It is all very cool, neutral, and impersonal, and the invasive Alvin's beige clothing fits perfectly into the room's colour palette. This is an alternate, stylised world, devoid of the personal decoration so important to teens' self-identity, where Paris appears as a pop star in a video. Annoyed by Alvin's recent adoption of a cocky attitude, she greets him coldly. Paris initially refuses to play her guitar for him, mentioning that she is still learning and her lyrics do not yet fit the melody, but she finally agrees to play while Alvin reads the lyrics that she has written. The lyrics are about self-empowerment, but Paris never really follows the path that her words lay out. She does not even speak or sing the words to her own song at any point in the film.

After Paris plays some of her song, Alvin asks her to get dressed and follow him. At this point, a more complete yet still lyric-less (only humming is heard) version of her bluesy R&B song begins and bridges a cut to an overhead shot of cars on the motorway. The music continues to score the entire next scene, which takes place in a club where musicians, poets, dancers, and other artists perform. As we soon find out, this is a trip into Paris' dream world as imagined by Alvin. It is in this club that Paris discloses her desire to be more than just a cheerleader and girlfriend of a professional athlete. She dreams about going somewhere where nobody knows her and "just bein' this girl with, like, crazy cool dreads and a guitar". However, she immediately dismisses the possibility of this happening. When Alvin suggests that she play her guitar at that club, she says "I can't." Alvin then corrects her, saying, "you mean you won't."

In this scene, Alvin learns of Paris' love of music and aspirations of transformation and performance. The desires she states at the end of the scene are underlined by the presence of her song throughout the clip. Unlike rock clubs usually visited by white teens in films, this is a more mature urban space where an open-mic night features performers from a variety of races, ethnicities, and ages. In a way, Paris' aspirations are for a less teen-identified performance context than those of most other youth film characters. In her desire to leave behind the cheerleader image, she also wishes to progress into young adulthood. But Paris' dreams of having "crazy cool dreads" and performing in a club are never to be realised within the limits of the film.

The end of the film contains the usual romantic plot resolution that basically negates any desire for agency Paris may have had throughout the film. When this ending is compared to the alternate ending included on the DVD, however, it takes on new meaning. In the ending chosen for the film, Alvin finally admits he was trying to be someone he is not and stands up to one of the school's basketball players who is picking on his friends during the game. After this public display and a standing ovation from the audience, Alvin walks out of the gymnasium, followed after slight hesitation by

Paris (who has been cheerleading at the game). When Paris runs outside, her famous boyfriend Drew appears out of nowhere and tries to get back together with her. But she dismisses Drew, saying "I have other dreams." She then runs to Alvin and tells him that she understands what he's going through because she has been pretending to be someone else for as long as she can remember. Alvin then silences her speech with a kiss, just as Verona does in *10 Things I Hate About You*. As the camera zooms out, he comically grabs her behind and she laughs. Paris' song begins once again with the kiss and bridges the fade to black, carrying on over the credits.

The song, this time complete with Paris' lyrics, is entitled 'We Rise'. It is performed by Rama Duke and co-written by the film's director and co-writer, Troy Beyer. In this ending, Paris' musical dreams are an afterthought, merely suggested by the presence of her song. When Paris tells Drew she has other dreams, it recalls her speech from the club scene. But despite the presence of the song, the film's romantic resolution takes precedence, and with the kiss the "other dreams" to which Paris alludes are transferred to her relationship with Alvin. Even though she leaves her famous boyfriend and gives up her popular cheerleader persona, it is uncertain if she will ever get the courage to play her music in public.

Interestingly, the film's alternate ending continues on from this and has a different focus. This ending, instead of climaxing in a comic bum squeeze that negates any serious revelations of the two characters, cuts from the couple kissing outside the school to another kiss inside the club from the earlier scene. Paris – now with dreads – pulls away from Alvin after the kiss and walks up onto the stage. A Princeton jacket hangs on Alvin's chair – proof that he has achieved his goal of getting into the prestigious university. Paris sits down in front of a microphone with her

Figure 1.3 Crazy cool dreads: an alternate ending.

guitar and gets ready to perform. While the audio track for this scene is obviously unfinished (only the actors' movements and room tone are audible), it does revert the meaning of Paris' "other dreams" back to her performance and personality transformation. Presumably, 'We Rise' would have come in somewhere near the end of this scene and bridged a fade to the credits, although this is just my guess. The alternate ending foregrounds Paris' personal achievements most of all. Thus the only public performance is cut out of the film, which, as I discuss in Chapter 3, is also the case with *Juno* (Jason Reitman, 2007).

Without the alternate ending, though, Paris is simply portrayed according to R&B genre conventions for women. In her article on the representation of black womanhood in R&B and rap videos, Rana A. Emerson states that an "emphasis on appearance and physical attraction confirms the notion of the excessive sexuality of the Black woman" and "[i]t supports the ideological controlling image of the hypersexual 'sapphire' or 'jezebel,' effectively undermining Black womanhood and humanity" (2002, p. 129). Although Paris' identity is not limited to her looks, her appearance is emphasised by her clothing and is central to the film's plot – after all, the popularity that Paris wishes to escape is mainly based on her appearance. Emerson goes on to argue, however, that music video portrayals are often more complex than the sexist imagery would suggest:

> [...] in the videos analyzed, glamour and style are not the only salient attributes possessed by Black women artists. Instead, a sexualized image often occurs simultaneously with themes of independence, strength, a streetwise nature, toughness, and agency. Most of the time, the same artists express themselves in a single video as sexy and savvy, glamorous and autonomous.
>
> (p. 129)

But this level of complexity does not really apply to the characterisation of Paris that finishes with the kiss in the film's chosen ending. Without being able to express herself through performance, Paris' musical identity is only tied to her stylish and sexualised appearance, which is similar to that of Christina's public persona. The film's alternate ending steers Paris' musical persona towards a bluesy-folk mode via her hair, clothing, and solo acoustic guitar, and this brings with it different genre connotations that further complicate her identity. Despite the fact that Christina is a performer in the real world, the film does not allow Paris the agency of performance.

In both *10 Things I Hate About You* and *Love Don't Cost a Thing*, the musical agency of the girls I have discussed is limited in a way that cannot be disconnected from their gender and heterosexuality. While Kat is the protagonist of *10 Things*, her musical performance is regulated by males. Initially it is her father who keeps her from starting a band by mobilising the authority that is his birthright in a patriarchal society. In the masculine space of the guitar store Kat wears headphones while playing, suggesting that she does not feel confident enough to submit her playing to the scrutiny of males who lay claim to the mastery of the electric guitar. It is ultimately Verona who must provide Kat with the guitar in a rite of passage that suggests a passing of Kat from her father to her boyfriend. This reading is further strengthened by the fact that the narrative is driven by the need to gain the father's permission to date. With this passing of masculine authority Kat is given permission to play, but only after forming a stable heterosexual couple in which masculine authority can be sustained. In the case of Paris, the alternate ending of *Love Don't Cost a Thing* provides a useful counter-scenario of what could be. However, instead of Paris's "other dreams" referring to her desire to be a performer, the dreams instead concern having a different boyfriend. While the film suggests that Alvin may be supportive of her future transformation, the film's romance-focused ending, with Paris in a cheerleader outfit rather than with "crazy cool dreads and a guitar", serves to keep her in her place in the patriarchal order. This is not simply because she is a cheerleader, but rather because she verbally rejects her cheerleader image as false – a rejection that is somewhat negated by ending with an image of the cheerleader as the ideal romantic achievement for Alvin. Not only does the boy get the girl, the nerd gets the cheerleader.

Notes

1 This argument, and my analysis of *10 Things*, was originally developed for papers I presented at the 2008 Screen Conference and the 4th Annual Film and Music Conference, National Media Museum, Bradford, in 2008. Theo Cateforis (2009) presents a very similar argument, so I will engage with his article only where our conclusions differ or where his perspective adds to my own analysis of the film.
2 'One Week' appears twice in *American Pie* (Paul Weitz, 1999), another popular teen film released in the same year. This intertextual connection further constructs *10 Things* as a typical teen comedy from the outset.
3 While Cateforis (2009) discusses this type of performance by male characters in a number of teen films, he does not consider Verona's performance in *10 Things*.
4 It is worth noting that Christina's original surname was Flores, but she adopted her mother's maiden name to land a wider range of acting roles (Soren Baker, 2005, p. 3).

References

Baker, Soren (2005) 'As This Moon She Rises Higher' in *Los Angeles Times* [Internet], Available from: http://articles.latimes.com/2005/mar/03/news/wk-movies3 [Accessed 6 September 2010].

Cateforis, Theo (2009) 'Rebel Girls and Singing Boys: Performing Music and Gender in the Teen Movie' in *Current Musicology*, Vol. 87, Spring, pp. 161–190.

Emerson, Rana A. (2002) '"Where My Girls At?": Negotiating Black Woman-hood in Music Videos' in *Gender & Society*, Vol. 16, No. 1, pp. 115–135.

Henderson, Scott (2006) 'Youth, Excess and the Musical Moment' in Ian Conrich and Estella Tincknell (eds), *Film's Musical Moments*, Edinburgh: Edinburgh University Press, pp. 146–157.

Kearney, Mary Celeste (1997) 'The Missing Links: Riot Grrrl – Feminism – Lesbian Culture' in Sheila Whiteley (ed.), *Sexing the Groove: Popular Music and Gender*, London: Routledge, pp. 207–229.

Leonard, Marion (1997) '"Rebel Girl, You Are the Queen of My World": Feminism, "Subculture" and Grrrl Power' in Sheila Whiteley (ed.), *Sexing the Groove: Popular Music and Gender*, London: Routledge, pp. 230–255.

York, Robert L. (2006) '"Smells Like Teen Shakespirit" Or, the Shakespearean Films of Julia Styles' in Kevin Wetmore, Jennifer Hulbert, and Robert York (eds), *Shakespeare and Youth Culture*, Gordonsville, VA: Palgrave MacMillan, pp. 70–100.

Filmography

10 Things I Hate About You (1999, USA) directed by Gil Junger, music by Richard Gibbs, music supervision by Alfonso E. Chavez, Buena Vista Home Entertainment.

American Pie (1999, USA) directed by Paul Weitz, music by David Lawrence, music supervision by Gary Jones, Universal Home Entertainment.

Can't Buy Me Love (1987, USA) directed by Steve Rash, music by Robert Folk, music supervisor not listed, Buena Vista Home Video.

Ferris Bueller's Day Off (1986, USA) directed by John Hughes, music by Arthur Baker, Ira Newborn, and John Robie, music supervision by Taquin Gotch, Paramount Home Video.

Juno (2007, USA) directed by Jason Reitman, music by Mateo Messina, music supervision by Peter Afterman, 20th Century Fox.

Love Don't Cost a Thing (2003, USA) directed by Troy Beyer, music by Richard Gibbs, music supervision by Michael McQuarn, Warner Home Video.

Pretty in Pink (1986, USA) directed by Howard Deutch, music by Michael Gore, music supervision by David Anderle, Paramount Home Video.

2 Queer Agency and the Reappropriation of the "Technophallus" in *All Over Me*

In Chapter 1 I discuss how girls' musical agency often takes a back seat to the heterosexual relationship at the centre of mainstream teen films. In this chapter I focus on *All Over Me* (Alex Sichel, 1997), an independent film with a lesbian protagonist, to understand how girls' musical agency is affected when successfully coupling with the male love interest is no longer the primary narrative goal. As was the case with *10 Things I Hate About You* (Gil Junger, 1999), riot grrrl music and guitar playing are important to construction of the protagonist's identity in *All Over Me*. This film tells the story of Claude (Alison Folland), a teenage girl struggling to come to terms with her sexuality and the fact that her best friend, Ellen (Tara Subkoff), will never be in love with her. Though previously inseparable from Claude, Ellen becomes distant when she enters into a drug-addled and abusive relationship with the thuggish Mark (Cole Hauser). Claude was initially satisfied with spending time in her bedroom with Ellen in a platonic friendship, but she now must confront the reality of their weakening bond. Since they both play the electric guitar, Claude tries to start a band with Ellen, but Ellen shows her obvious disinterest by rushing through the songs as they play together. As a result of spending more time on her own, Claude befriends the pink-haired Lucy (Leisha Hailey) after seeing her in a guitar store and later watching her band, Coochie Pop, perform at a club. Claude initially resists Lucy's advances because she is still in love with Ellen. However, Claude and Ellen's friendship weakens further as Ellen's drug problems worsen, and the two finally part ways after Claude reports Mark's involvement in the murder of her friend Luke (Pat Briggs) to the police.

After some time and patience, Lucy does become the focus of Claude's romantic interest. Significantly, Lucy is played by real-life musician Leisha Hailey of The Murmurs, who is joined in a fictional band by Mary Timony of the band Helium. Leisha's musicianship brings credibility to the role and makes Lucy appear more natural and justified as a young female musician in a youth film. Overall, *All Over Me* gives its lead and supporting young women more musical agency than most other youth films. This is largely made possible by the film's construction of Claude and Lucy as outsiders. Outsider status is partially emphasised by the girls' interest in alternative music, which is often used to code both boys and girls as outcasts in youth films. In addition, as lesbians, both Claude and Lucy are immediately outsiders in the typical youth film context. This whole film could be considered an outsider in the world of youth movies, not only because of its exploration of lesbian identity and the musical agency it allows its female characters, but also because it is set in Hell's Kitchen, a Manhattan neighbourhood with a historically gritty reputation, instead of some leafy suburb. Claude's queer identity, I will argue, is tightly bound to her relationship with music and actually enables her considerable musical agency rather than stereotypically marking her as a quirky character, an object of heterosexual male fantasy, or a social outcast.

All Over Me manages to avoid some of the representational pitfalls typical of youth films through its use of music and other narrative elements. While this film deals with female friendship and lesbian sexuality straightforwardly, it must nevertheless navigate the complications of representing a queer character in a still homophobic society. Timothy Shary (2014) discusses the shift in representations of homosexuality in cinema of the 1980s and 1990s:

> Teenage homosexuality (and bisexuality) in American cinema up to the 1990s was handled in often vague if not symbolic terms, and when it was handled, the characters in question were almost always troubled and trying to deny their nonheterosexual impulses, lest they face the consequence of ridicule, condemnation, or even death.
> (p. 266)

Shary goes on to state that "many queer youth depictions by the '90s tended to deal with tensions around both sexual experience and romantic longing," and therefore queer characters were being treated more similarly to non-queer teens (p. 268). In addition, he argues that more queer characters were appearing in films of the 1990s, sometimes as stereotypes, but more often in sympathetic roles. In *All Over Me*, Claude is a fully-developed, well-rounded character who faces the romantic trials of many filmic teens, although her situation is more complicated due to the context. While Claude is somewhat troubled and confused, she does not attempt to hide or deny her lesbian sexuality. But she is cautious about divulging this information, because as Shary observes, doing so may lead to scorn or even death – a threat made very real with the murder of Claude's gay friend Luke. Thus a tragic gay character is depicted, but he is not the sole bearer of queer representation in the film.

Expanding on work by Yvonne Tasker, Mary Celeste Kearney (2002) asserts that while films about preteen girls show the benefits of female friendship, films about teenage girls tend to insist that the destruction of same-sex friendships is necessary for entry into (heterosexual) womanhood. As such, these films often involve brutal feuds between former friends. Kearney suggests that this "unwillingness to explore the homosociality of female youth and its possible effects [...] arises from the fear that girls' same-sex bonds might be understood as homosexual and therefore as offensive" (p. 133). But she states that films such as *The Incredibly True Adventure of Two Girls in Love* (Maria Maggenti, 1995), *Girls Town* (Jim McKay, 1996), *Foxfire* (Annette Haywood-Carter, 1996), and *All Over Me* "provide new images of female adolescence that are as disturbing in their depiction of the various problems teenage girls face as they are inspiring in their themes of female empowerment and solidarity" (p. 134). In *All Over Me* a same-sex friendship is broken up, but in this case there was homosexual desire involved, and the resulting same-sex relationship entered into by the protagonist is a romantic one. The friendship also dissolved because of Ellen's boyfriend Mark's involvement in Luke's murder – a more serious offence than those that usually divide friends in youth films. Rather than simply conforming to the typical mainstream youth film treatment of same-sex friendships or subverting conventions, this film proudly flaunts its so-called 'transgression' by turning the heterosexual female friendship model on its head.

The opening credit sequence of *All Over Me*, featuring 'Hello' by Babes in Toyland, contrasts sharply with that of *10 Things I Hate About You* in its use of music, introduction of characters, and general setup of the film. It begins with a slow-yet-heavy drumbeat and a black screen, shortly followed by credits and a distorted, moody, grinding guitar. The sludgy, somewhat discordant music is soon combined with a shot of a large, urban playground with cityscape in the background. The screen then goes black again and the film's title appears. A sweeping view of a street accompanies the entrance of slightly deadpan female vocals before the camera locks on to two tall, foreboding apartment towers – possibly low-income housing projects. The vocals declare "I know somewhere we could go," inviting the perceiver into the urban setting, just before the guitar strikes hard with a cut to a black screen containing Alison Folland's name in white letters, followed by other cast members. The next line of the song, "better than you could ever know", elaborates on the original enticement. The invitation contained in this gritty song and cityscape is obviously something outside of the usual youth film experience and the combination of elements suggests a more working-class, less traditionally feminine protagonist than the opening of *10 Things*.

The song continues with a montage cutting between black screens with credits and scenes of children playing, as well as a lingering shot on a wall containing ornate graffiti reading "Hell's Kitchen" and "Drug". Next, Claude and Ellen sweep into view and are immediately identified as important characters connected with the music. Towards the end of the credits, from Claude's point of view, an electric guitar is shown propped up against cardboard boxes and other possessions waiting to be moved into an apartment. At this point, the music accelerates; churning guitar and drums evoke a speeding train that propels the perceiver towards the guitar, which Claude unhesitatingly and with a mischievous smile picks up and plays just as the song ends.

When compared with the title credits for *10 Things*, the differences in characters' musical agency are evident from the start. The colourful opening credits of *10 Things* and sweeping view of Seattle from a safe distance combine with The Barenaked Ladies' 'One Week' to introduce the film as light and fun. The source of the song is a car with four chirpy girls that is used to create a humorous juxtaposition with Joan Jett's 'Bad Reputation', which soon radiates from Kat's car. Such an introduction undermines the subversive potential of Kat's anger. The opening of *All Over Me*, however, establishes the film's mood using the kind of music that will later come to characterise Claude. Since the camera adopts Claude's point of view at the end of the sequence (which can retroactively give the impression that all shots without Claude and Ellen were from her point of view), the song is more decidedly associated with her character. The breaks between narrative visuals and black credit screens also serve to disrupt the artificiality of the opening sequence, thus providing a less comfortable entrance into the film's world. Therefore, the music combines with scenes of the city and children playing to suggest latent danger for the children – this sense of unease will transfer onto the events of Claude's coming of age story. But at the same time, Claude will gain agency that will carry her through her trials from this type of music.

With the song's power focusing on Claude as it ends, she unashamedly picks up the electric guitar, smirks, strikes a rock 'n' roll pose, starts to play, and spits her candy out onto the pavement in a gesture mocking masculine rock posturing. Claude's actions call to mind the gendered history of rock 'n' roll music, and her reappropriation of the "technophallus" comments on the masculine connotations that accompany playing the rock star. However, as Joanne Gottlieb and Gayle Wald (1994) assert, this act is always problematic for women:

> Women performers go through complicated contortions as they both appropriate and repudiate a traditionally masculine rock performance position which is itself premised on the repression of femininity, while they simultaneously contend with a feminine performance position defined primarily as the erotic object-to-be-looked-at.
>
> (p. 260)

In this scene, there are plenty of contradictions and complications to consider. Claude's general comfort with an electric guitar and more 'masculine' clothing make her posturing less of a contortion, particularly because she is visibly mocking male rock guitarists. And while these characteristics may complicate her status as "erotic object-to-be-looked-at", she is performing for Ellen, by whom she very much wants to be admired. Thus, Claude's bravado and knowledge of the guitar stake out a claim to musical agency very early in the film. A scene where Claude and Lucy interact during the performance of the latter's band works in similar ways – I will return to this scene shortly.

It turns out that the guitar on the pavement belongs to Luke, a young man who is moving into Claude's building and to whom Claude is instantly drawn. Luke's homosexuality is not stated outright and it is not clear at what point Claude recognises it. But the two become friends almost instantly, and along with giving Claude a lucky coin as a tip for the pizza she serves him, he also tells her about his friend's club where lots of female bands play. Just after this exchange, Luke gets into an argument with Mark, and it is later revealed that Luke has been murdered just outside of Claude's building. Along with the presumption of Mark and his friends' guilt, it is also suggested that the murder was at least partially motivated by homophobia. Since Claude suspects that Ellen has some knowledge of Mark's guilt, she proposes a road trip to California to escape Mark and his drug-aided control over Ellen. Ellen nastily declines the offer, however, and runs out of Claude's bedroom. 'Squeeze-box Days' by the Murmurs enters the soundtrack as Ellen rushes out. The slow, grinding guitar comes in as Claude digs out Luke's lucky coin, picks out a shirt to wear, and heads off to the club about which Luke told her. As previously mentioned, Leisha Hailey, who plays Lucy, is one half of the Murmurs. The lyrics of the song, which are about unrequited love, perfectly reflect what Claude is feeling at this moment in time. Additionally, for perceivers aware of the song's authorship, it sonically draws Claude to Lucy and to the club where she is playing. Claude feels threatened by the murder of Luke and somewhat distanced from Ellen because of her involvement in it. Perhaps she goes to the club not only because of her interest in starting a band, but also to seek out a safe space and supportive social environment.

The club that Claude enters is a very different venue from Club Skunk in *10 Things I Hate About You*. First of all, the sluggish drums, distorted guitars, and low-pitched, deadpan female vocals are in stark contrast to the cheery pop of Letters to Cleo's performance in Club Skunk. And the band, Coochie Pop, is made up entirely of young women. Lucy plays guitar in this band, and the singer is Mary Timony of Helium, who actually wrote and performed the song. The crowd in this club is different as well. The young women have more of an 'indie rock' look. They are dressed in a more casual style, wearing T-shirts and trousers in most cases, and many of them have short hair. The less traditionally feminine and at times more masculine appearance of this crowd connotes lesbian identity in some cases to be sure, but it also gives an overall feeling of antagonism towards the traditional gender roles that are still evident in most rock and dance clubs. The young women in Club Skunk, on the other hand, are much more feminine and sleek in appearance. Although Claude never performs in public, aside from her impromptu jam on Luke's guitar, it is important that Lucy plays guitar on stage – this ensures that the band is connected to the protagonist. Whereas the bands featured in *10 Things* are real-life, nationally recognised bands loved by the main character, the local band performing in *All Over Me* is within reach for Claude (even if some of its members are well-known musicians).

Both this scene and Claude's ironic masculine posturing while playing Luke's guitar have a serious impact on the way performance, gender, sexuality, and music interact in the film. As previously discussed, Claude's knowing criticism of tired rock 'n' roll clichés subverts presumptions of male hegemony in rock music, as well as filmic representations of musical performance. The Coochie Pop gig further complicates matters, and problematises Laura Mulvey's (1975) seminal theorisation of the male gaze. As Susan Driver states with regard to Claude's gaze:

> Claude becomes a desiring spectator gazing in on the "to-be-looked-at-ness" (Mulvey, 'Visual Pleasure' 487) of the straight female characters. Yet Claude's spectator position is not male; it crosses gender boundaries, at times holding a distance of sexual objectification and at other times emotionally engaged as a nurturing friend and daughter.
>
> (2007, p. 111)

Here Driver considers the dynamics of Claude's gaze with regard to Ellen. But at the gig, Lucy is the object of Claude's gaze. From the moment Claude enters the venue she focuses on Lucy. Having seen each other and briefly interacted in a guitar store, Claude is now pleasantly surprised to see Lucy on stage. After a minute or two, Lucy sees Claude and acknowledges her presence with an excited smile.

Thus the gaze is returned, shared between the two characters in a shot-reverse-shot sequence. Of course, the dynamics between Claude and Lucy are not just visual. Music plays an important role in this scene, and Lucy's role as a guitarist in an all-female band puts her in a position of musical agency not typically occupied by girls in films. This performance dynamic, combined with the gaze, disrupts the perceiver's position due to the sharing of the experience between Claude and Lucy. The band's music and what it represents (feminism, female agency, queerness) shapes the nature of the interaction between the two characters, and strongly encourages the direction of audience perception. The interaction not only connects Claude with the band on stage, but it also situates the possible identifications of perceivers within the context of lesbian desire and female musical practice. The male hegemony and masculine/phallic connotations normally attached to rock music and the electric guitar are heavily disrupted in this film, allowing the female characters to possess a great deal of musical agency. This space of female agency is particularly remarkable in contrast to a scene with Mark and Ellen in Claude's bedroom that is cut to just after Claude enters the gig. When Ellen jokingly calls Mark crazy he grabs her head with both of his hands and insists that she never call him that again. This heightens the threat of male violence that is always present in scenes with Mark and makes the relatively safe and supportive female-centred space of the gig all the more meaningful.

The active/passive masculine/feminine split in both rock performance and audiovisual representations has been heavily debated, and conclusions tend to be context dependent. In his discussion of the instabilities of the male pin-up, Richard Dyer (1992) says the following about looking, power, and gender:

> The idea of looking (staring) as power and being looked at as powerlessness overlaps with ideas of activity/passivity. Thus to look is thought of as active; whereas to be looked at is passive. In reality, this is not true. The model prepares her or himself to be looked at; and, on the other hand, the image that the viewer looks at is not summoned up by his or her act of looking but in collaboration with those who have put the image there. Most of us probably experience looking and being looked at, in life as in art, somewhere among these shifting relations of activity and passivity. Yet it remains the case that images of men must disavow this element of passivity if they are to be kept in line with dominant ideas of masculinity-as-activity.
> (pp. 109–110)

Thus, despite its artificiality, this active/passive dichotomy still informs the way one understands power relations with regard to photographs and audiovisual media. Although Dyer is considering still photographs, he relates these ideas to the way people look at each other as well, suggesting that men are conditioned to stare while women avert their eyes, or at most glance fleetingly and then look away. This tendency, which Dyer points out is always the case in depictions of young love in films and television, serves to (re-)establish male dominance (pp. 103–104). But in the case of a live performance – in the real world or in a film – this relationship becomes more complicated. While the audience members are doing the looking, the performers (those being looked at) are certainly not passive. They are constantly returning the look, moving around the stage, and perhaps most importantly creating sound that aurally and physically impacts the audience. When considered in terms of rock music's dominant masculine history, this fits with Dyer's observation about male pin-ups: they are always active or suggestive of activity. This is particularly why riot grrrl networks and music are important for redressing power imbalances.

The predominantly female and completely feminist riot grrrl networks and musical communities give power to women, even when men are involved. In *All Over Me*, young women are looking and being looked at, playing instruments and listening. Renee T. Coulombe (1999) describes this dynamic between audience and performer at riot grrrl gigs:

> Seeking out local artists, or finding those who have created their own uncensored communication channels, encourages a dynamic performer/audience relationship – one that I would label "feminist." The "classical music" heritage that we in the West enjoy carries with it stigmas of power/performance vs. passive/audience in its concert structure. But this construct pre-empts many other relationships that are possible between performer and audience. Some are more ambiguous: in music the edge separating performer and audience, music and words, power and vulnerability can be more slippery, less definite, intuitive. Active and passive can become one, with all participants in the musical experience being performer, listener.
>
> (p. 258)

This relationship between audience and performer attempts to level the playing field, eliminating power imbalances that usually exist between all-male rock bands and female, as well as male, audience members. Coulombe later elaborates on how this dynamic at riot grrrl gigs breaks down the boundary and accompanying power imbalance between artist and audience. This argument reflects the dynamic that Claude experiences in the club. However, the dynamic that Coulombe describes as "feminist" is not necessarily so, since it exists in other music subcultures as well. It does provide an opportunity for progressive politics, however. In the case of riot grrrl, the fluid relationship between performer and audience exists because of the political aims of the music. Thus, riot grrrl performer/audience dynamics work to destroy the conditioned shyness of female looking that Dyer describes, as well as further exposing the artificiality of the active/passive split and encouraging participation.

The reason this club is such a haven for Claude is that the music is primarily a vehicle for expressing feminist politics and the experiences of young women using a medium about which many teenagers and young adults are passionate. As Joanne Gottlieb and Gayle Wald (1994) explain, the music is actually an organising tool for riot grrrl networks, which reach far beyond the bands themselves:

> By organizing around a certain musical style, riot grrrls seek to forge networks and communities of support to reject the forms of middle-class, white, youth culture they have inherited, and to break out of the patriarchal limitations on women's behavior, their access (to the street, to their own bodies, to rock music), and their everyday

pleasures. Riot Grrrl—the name refers to the movement-at-large—
has forged salient connections between musical subculture and explicitly feminist politics; these qualities in turn transform or revise
previous paradigms of rock production and consumption.

(p. 253)

In Claude's case, the limitations to which Gottlieb and Wald refer are all
broken. While patriarchal society still imposes limitations on Claude,
direct paternal control does not exist. Her father is no longer around
and her mother's hapless suitor only seems concerned with trying to win
Claude's favour. (However, a more vile character is suggested when he
tells Claude how mature she is when her mother is not home.) Claude
freely travels the streets, listens to and plays rock music, and generally
does what she wants. By the end of the film, she has also gained control
over her sexuality and taken possible steps towards performing music
publicly. Riot grrrl networks and music facilitate all of these achievements. Without the music and the venue, Claude would not meet Lucy
or have access to the musical opportunities that are opened up to her.

Claude and Lucy officially meet and talk to each other for the first
time after the Coochie Pop gig. The two girls then head to Lucy's bedroom, where they bond over their common love of music. The scene cuts
back and forth between the two girls in Lucy's bedroom and Ellen and
Mark in Claude's bedroom. Lucy and Claude seem to be getting on well,
but before long Claude's inner struggle resurfaces. This is catalysed by
a song from one of her favourite artists, Patti Smith – a poster of whom
also hangs on the wall of Claude's bedroom. After playing a few songs
on her stereo, Lucy invites Claude to play some music because her parents are away and no one will complain about the noise. Claude puts on
'Pissing in a River' by Patti Smith, though she is aware of the feelings
the song will betray – she even says "I'd better not" before playing it. As
she sways to the moody music, Claude mouths the words that reflect her
confusion about the present situation with Lucy and her feelings about
Ellen: "Should I pursue a path so twisted?/Should I crawl defeated and
gifted?/Should I go the length of a river?" Claude's emotional reflection
climaxes with the line "Everything I've done I've done for you" – an
obvious allusion to her devotion to Ellen.

As the song provides continuity on the soundtrack from its position as
source scoring, the film cross-cuts between Claude and Lucy in Lucy's
bedroom and Ellen and Mark in Claude's bedroom. Tensions boil between Ellen and Mark as Ellen ingests several lines of cocaine and Mark
repeatedly tells her she has had enough. Eventually Mark picks Ellen up
and throws her out of Claude's room. The connection between the two
locations is strengthened by the presence of the Patti Smith poster on the
wall of Claude's bedroom. As Claude's distress mounts, she breaks into
tears and sways mournfully. It is as if Claude can see and hear what Ellen

and Mark are up to in her bedroom through the eyes and ears of the vigilant Patti Smith – who is present both visually and aurally. Claude becomes almost omniscient through the song's inexplicable (albeit conventional in terms of film music practice) presence in her bedroom, where Ellen and Mark are arguing. With cuts to Claude's bedroom, the level of the music drops as if coming from nearby, even though Claude's bedroom is nowhere near the source of the music (Lucy's bedroom).

This scene clearly demonstrates Claude's intimate relationship with music. She uses the Patti Smith song to express her own emotions and work through her confusion. The explicit connection to a strong female musician and use of music to express identity are not often available to teenage girls in films. However, in her previously mentioned discussion of female friendship and adolescent empowerment in youth films, Kearney (2002) confirms this as a trend in some independent films of the 1990s:

> The use of feminist music and the portrayal of female musicians in films focusing on teenage girls are notable attempts to move beyond the formula of studio-produced female teenpics, which continue to rely predominantly on male-created music for their soundtracks and portray male figures as girls' primary role models and objects of desire.
>
> (pp. 138–139)

It is perhaps not surprising that independent films, especially those considered by Kearney that were written and/or directed by women, would grant their female leads musical agency equal to or greater than their male counterparts in Hollywood films. And when young women are idolising women rather than men, the idea of becoming a musician seems more feasible.

Claude's musical agency exists from the outset – she owns and plays an electric guitar and tries to start a band with Ellen. She is also helped along by Luke, a gay musician, who tells her about the club. Finally, she is able to meet Lucy, develop a relationship with her, and play guitar with her near the end of the film. The relationships Claude develops show that her sexuality and love of music are closely intertwined. Mavis Bayton (1998), in her study of women in the popular music industry, asserts the following about lesbian musicianship and agency:

> Joining an all-women band gave lesbians a chance to break the heterosexist discourse of rock and pop by, for instance, writing and performing love songs addressed to women. Moreover, lesbians had liberated themselves from the need to prove their femininity and conform to heterosexist expectations—the role of wife or girlfriend, and so on. Without these commitments lesbians were (and still are) freer than the average woman to engage in rock music-making if desired.
>
> (p. 73)

Thus, while Claude's sexuality may complicate her life in many ways and actually endanger her as it did Luke, it also facilitates her participation in the local music scene. Driver (2007) discusses the crucial role queer music can play in the lives of queer girls, both in terms of identity construction and the creation of queer spaces:

> Being able to have access to queer music through online musical dialogues, friendship networks, and live events helps queer youth to counter the heteronormative ethos of their social environments. Music's ability to cross boundaries, to be a potential source of personal pleasure and subversion, even in the most restrictive and hostile of locations, is especially useful for fostering counter-public queer cultures that validate and nurture youth. Not only does music provide an embodied and interactive medium, it is also open-ended and ambiguous, generating complex expressions of queer identity and politics.
>
> (p. 198)

All Over Me perfectly illustrates Driver's argument, with Claude finding friendship, love, and strength, as well as further developing her own identity, through entering and participating in a space queered by music.

Eventually Claude figures out how to move on from her infatuation with Ellen, and music proves to be an avenue through which Claude and Lucy can develop their relationship. The film's soundtrack contains riot grrrl, punk, alternative, and hardcore songs performed almost exclusively by female artists. This focus on female performers reflects the centrality of women to the narrative, but the outsider status of these genres and their use in real-life music scenes also signify feminism and lesbian sexuality. Club performance and bedroom guitar playing act as a space in which Claude and Lucy can freely explore their feelings for one another and their common interests. The music, which would usually code social 'otherness' in youth films, serves to naturalise what would also be coded as sexual 'otherness'. And unlike the musical rebelliousness ultimately undermined in *10 Things I Hate About You*, the cohesive soundtrack of *All Over Me* works together with the narrative action towards a more progressive representation of strong, musically accomplished girls.

Kearney (2002) suggests that this progression is due in no small part to the breaking down of gender boundaries more generally:

> Given these films' message that female youth need to develop and exhibit attributes traditionally associated with femininity *and* masculinity to survive in today's society, their representations of teenage girls subvert the two-gender system that grounds the ideologies of not only patriarchy and heterosexuality but also liberal and cultural feminism. In doing so, such films signify an important turning point

not only in the media's representation of girlhood and female empowerment but also in our society's understanding of gender and subjectivity.

(p. 140)

While *All Over Me* does in fact "subvert the two gender system", one could go even further and argue that the meaning associated with traditionally feminine and masculine attributes is changed in a less heteronormative context. To consider Claude's actions in terms of 'masculine' and 'feminine', even when referring to society's understanding of these terms in the traditional sense, seems to place false constraints on the fluidity of her identity. Although I have discussed Claude's agency in contrast with male teenage protagonists, I have done so to compare male and female characters, rather than 'masculine' and 'feminine' ones. Admittedly, though, the terms 'male' and 'female' can be just as restrictive.

Near the end of the film Claude and Lucy play their guitars together in Claude's recently redecorated bedroom and are nearly caught kissing when Claude's mother enters the room. Although Claude has not yet come out to her mother, she is much more comfortable with her sexuality than she was at the start of the film. Unlike when Claude and Ellen played earlier in the film, the guitars are amplified this time, highlighting the perfection of the new pairing and suggesting that Claude's life is finally 'plugged in'. This scene further emphasises the strong ties between music, sexuality, and agency that exist in *All Over Me*, as well as in the lives of real teenagers.

Figure 2.1 Claude and Lucy: finally plugged in.

References

Bayton, Mavis (1998) *Frock Rock: Women Performing Popular Music*, Oxford, UK: Oxford University Press.

Coulombe, Renee T. (1999) 'The Insatiable Banshee: Voracious Vocalizing… Riot Grrrl… and the Blues' in Elaine Barkin and Lydia Hamessley (eds), *Audible Traces: Gender, Identity and Music*, Zürich: Carciofoli Verlagshaus, pp. 257–272.

Driver, Susan (2007) *Queer Girls and Popular Culture: Reading, Resisting, and Creating Media*, New York: Peter Lang.

Dyer, Richard (1992) *Only Entertainment*, London: Routledge.

Gottlieb, Joanne and Gayle Wald (1994) 'Smells Like Teen Spirit: Riot Grrrls, Revolution, and Women in Independent Rock' in Andrew Ross and Tricia Rose (eds), *Microphone Fiends: Youth Music & Youth Culture*, London: Routledge, pp. 250–274.

Kearney, Mary Celeste (2002) 'Girlfriends and Girl Power: Female Adolescence in Contemporary U.S. Cinema' in Frances Gateward and Murray Pomerance (eds), *Sugar, Spice, and Everything Nice: Cinemas of Girlhood*, Detroit, MI: Wayne State University Press, pp. 125–142.

Mulvey, Laura (1975) 'Visual Pleasure and Narrative Cinema' in *Screen*, Vol. 16, No. 3, pp. 6–18.

Shary, Timothy (2014) *Generation Multiplex: The Image of Youth in Contemporary American Cinema*, Revised Edition, Austin, TX: University of Texas Press.

Filmography

10 Things I Hate About You (1999, USA) directed by Gil Junger, music by Richard Gibbs, music supervision by Alfonso E. Chavez, Buena Vista Home Entertainment.

All Over Me (1997, USA) directed by Alex Sichel, music by Miki Navazio, music supervision by Bill Coleman, Alliance.

3 Silent Punk and Audible Folk
Musical Sleight-of-Hand in *Juno*

The final film I examine in which guitar playing and musical agency are affected by soundtrack choices and the protagonist's gender is *Juno* (Jason Reitman, 2007). While there is no riot grrrl music in the soundtrack, the film uses allusions to Juno's taste in punk rock to suggest similarly rebellious (although not necessarily feminist) attributes in the protagonist. The film follows 16-year-old Juno MacGuff (Ellen Page) through an unplanned pregnancy, a tenuous relationship with her good friend and one-time lover Paulie Bleeker (Michael Cera), and her dealings with the adoptive couple, the saccharine, yuppyish Vanessa and Mark Loring (Jennifer Garner and Jason Bateman). When Juno finds herself pregnant after having sex with Bleeker only once, she visits a clinic to terminate the pregnancy. However, after being informed that foetuses have fingernails and panicking in the waiting room Juno runs out of the clinic and decides to put the baby up for adoption. Having seen Mark and Vanessa's ad in the *Penny Saver*, Juno meets up with the couple and eventually bonds with Mark, a commercial composer, through his love of 1990s alternative rock and horror films. This relationship, which coincides with Juno's deteriorating friendship with Bleeker, becomes partially responsible for Mark's eventual decision to leave Vanessa. It turns out that Mark never wanted to have a baby in the first place, and he decides to walk out on Vanessa, the adoption, and the couple's yuppie lifestyle. In the end, Juno and Vanessa decide to go through with the adoption, and Juno and Bleeker ultimately profess their love for one another.

Juno is an indie/grunge-attired, self-consciously quirky and sarcastic teenager who plays guitar and declares a love for 1970s US punk. However, throughout the film Juno mainly plays folk music on her acoustic guitar and is largely accompanied in the score by twee anti-folk, though the "anti-" prefix seems somewhat inappropriate in this context.[1] As I will argue, these elements of Juno's characterisation undermine her implied musical agency, taste in aggressive music, and sarcastic, tomboyish personality. *Juno*'s treatment of abortion, pregnancy, and sexuality has been hotly debated by critics and academics alike, but scholars' arguments have largely ignored the role the film's music plays in the perceiver's understanding of Juno and her actions. Jessica Willis (2008) states the following about sexuality and agency in the film:

> [...] Juno is shown as agentive in the decisions she makes about her body, sexual desire, and modes of self expression; her classification as a girl who identifies as a "freak," cares little about what other people think of her, and dresses in grunge style clothing connote an independent self-confidence that is apparent in all of her intimate relationships.
>
> (p. 242)

Willis goes on to say, however, that the depiction of Juno's sexual desire in the film "raise[s] questions about the extent to which constructs of girlhood are still intricately tied to social ideas about purity, innocence, and vulnerability to sexual corruption even if and when that sexual corruption comes from within oneself" (p. 242).

Willis structures her argument around the discourse of 'protection', one of three recent prominent discourses of girlhood that she argues shape representations of young female sexuality.[2] This discourse "emphasizes girls as innocent and vulnerable subjects in need of protection from a violent and unsafe world" (pp. 244–245, footnote 8). Such representations are harmful, Willis claims, because the denial of young female sexuality severely limits the expression of identity for young women. However, she argues that in *Juno* a focus on sexual innocence is replaced by an emphasis on nature:

> The film reinstates a traditional discourse cautioning girls that sex and sexual desire are dangerous. While Juno as a character resists normative framing of youthful sexuality through her direct and open display of desire, her story simultaneously reproduces traditional discourses of femininity linking female sexuality to pregnancy and the female body to "nature." This narrative of girlhood not only connects female sexuality to pregnancy, but also reasserts a construction of the female body within nature that does little to disrupt conventional discourses of femininity.
>
> (p. 248)

Thus, Juno's sexual desire is contained by its function as the means to pregnancy (and, importantly, childbirth). But what Willis ignores is the role that music plays in highlighting both the innocence of Juno's character and the connotations of nature connected with the pregnancy.

Juno's soundtrack consists largely of acoustic folk songs, 10 of which are written and performed by Kimya Dawson (including two with Antsy Pants and one written and performed with Adam Green as The

Moldy Peaches). Some of these songs were recorded specifically for the soundtrack while others were pre-existing (*Juno Soundtrack Commentary*, n.d.). Dawson's songs on this soundtrack are cute folk tracks that typically contain whimsical lyrics about love. Her childlike vocal delivery and lyrics, as well as song titles like 'Tire Swing', 'My Rollercoaster', 'So Nice So Smart', 'I Like Giants', 'Tree Hugger', and 'Anyone Else But You' convey ideas of youthful innocence and 'puppy love'. These songs are so abundant on the soundtrack that they also colour the perceiver's impressions of other songs in the film, such as two similarly folky songs by Belle and Sebastian, and the Velvet Underground's 'I'm Sticking with You' – sung by drummer Moe Tucker in a voice as childlike as Dawson's. A coherent audio-visual style connects these and other songs to the audio-visual world created by Dawson's music, and the overall innocent aesthetic produces meaning forcefully enough to supplant the lyrical content and musical connotations of non-Dawson songs. This use of Dawson's music and its context within the film have an infantilising effect that limits Juno's musical agency and contains the progressive potential of her implied musical taste. The childlike vocal delivery of this music could also reflect the presence of the baby; regardless, it conflates Juno with her baby, arresting Juno's teenage autonomy.

A cohesive musical groundwork is laid out early in the film. After narrating a brief flashback to the moment of conception that contains a barely audible Astrud Gilberto song, Juno walks into the rotoscoped opening credit sequence. In animated form, Juno strolls through town while 'All I Want is You' by Barry Louis Polisar plays on the soundtrack. The traditional sounding acoustic folk of this song mixes with images of Juno walking/gliding past houses, shops, and trees. The autumnal scenes, strummed acoustic guitar, and naïve lyrics about love and desire all work together to conjure nostalgic ideas of youth and innocence. In fact, Barry Louis Polisar is a performer of children's folk music who tours schools throughout the US and Europe (*Barry Louis Polisar: Books and Music for Children*, n.d.). In this sequence, a close shot of Juno's black Converse All Stars highlights her awkward stance, suggesting youthful insecurity, and the inclusion of many trees and colourful leaves closely ties Juno to nature. Juno's diminutive stature is also exaggerated by the giant jug of Sunny Delight from which she drinks, the relative towering height of the boys who jog past, and the many overhead shots of her. The connotations of youthful, folksy, quirky innocence suggested by the music and visuals in this opening credit sequence attach themselves to Juno – who is the focus of the entire sequence – for the rest of the film. Frequent recurrences of similar acoustic folk throughout the film recall connections made in the opening credit sequence and re-enforce Juno's ties to innocence and nature.

More folk music is heard almost immediately after the opening credit sequence when Juno enters a shop to take her third pregnancy test of the day. After a humorous, wise-cracking exchange with the store clerk, Juno heads to the restroom. The strumming of an acoustic guitar starts immediately as she sits down on the toilet, accompanied by a few high-pitched chimes, and continues until she walks out into the store and the pink plus sign indicating pregnancy appears on the test stick, at which point the music slows to a stop. This music – a piece of original score by Mateo Messina entitled 'Up the Spout' on the soundtrack album – works differently than much of the other music in the film. While this composed score creates stylistic continuity with most of the songs in the film's soundtrack, it also serves a specific narrative purpose. The music's somewhat dire tone and absence of lyrics connect the perceiver with Juno's subjectivity as she waits for the results of the test. In contrast, the previously described songs with a lighter tone and whimsical vocals serve to distance the perceiver from Juno's subjectivity, or at least suggest a less mature and cognisant subjectivity. Even though this emotional fit could be attributed to the fact that the music was composed for the scene, pre-existing songs can perform a similar function when selected to do so.

Immediately following this scene, Juno leaves the shop and walks home. As she exits with a distraught look on her face, 'Tire Swing' by Kimya Dawson appears on the soundtrack. Dawson's childlike voice and melancholic lyrics about discovering that someone has a new girlfriend serve only to elicit sympathy for Juno. Instead of focusing on her current emotional state and conveying a sense of nervous anticipation like the earlier score, 'Tire Swing' encourages the perceiver to feel sorry for this poor pregnant girl. With a cut the camera tracks Juno from behind, this time hiding under her hood, and again a group of boys jogs past, surrounding her and emphasising her size. To further accentuate her despair, at the end of this sequence Juno pretends to attempt to hang herself from the tree in her front yard with a liquorice rope. The lyrics, which cease to make any sort of sense after the first line or two, further distance the perceiver from Juno's subjectivity. The inclusion of 'Tire Swing' in this scene does not allow access to the protagonist's head, nor does it work in some contrary way to aid in Juno's musical agency. While the earlier original score did serve the typical function of conjuring specific emotions, it also connected with the character's subjectivity very carefully and allowed her mind to dictate feeling in a mature manner. 'Tire Swing', on the other hand, simply suggests that Juno is an unfortunate little girl for whom pity should be felt.

Near the end of this song, Juno enters her bedroom and the camera pans over various artefacts, including naked baby dolls and a photo of Juno, Bleeker, and Juno's friend Leah (Olivia Thirlby) playing music. Juno is standing with an electric guitar and Bleeker is seated with an acoustic guitar. The appearance of this photo at this point in the film is significant. Since Juno has just learned that she is pregnant, her bedroom full of nostalgic items takes on new meaning – these possessions signify

a childhood to which she can never return. The highlighting of Juno's innocence throughout the film always also suggests its inverse – innocence
lost. As Willis points out, "[t]his thematic loss of innocence associated
with the end of virginity, the literal changing of the seasons, and the
physical capability to conceive is, thus, particular to Juno's female subjectivity" (p. 248). Baby dolls are children's toys that must be left behind,
and in this case, so is the band in which Juno played. Throughout the
film it is understood that a rock band is no place for a pregnant young
woman, and later in the film Bleeker even suggests that they get the band
back together *after* Juno has the baby (as Willis points out, Bleeker also
suggests the same about himself and Juno getting back together romanti-
cally). Although Juno does play electric guitar with Mark in one scene
(and not while she is visibly pregnant), she does not play with Bleeker
until after the baby is out of the picture.

Throughout the film Dawson's songs, whether recorded for the film or
pre-existing, serve some functions typical of composed dramatic score.
This is also the case with some of the folk tracks by other artists. Often
used to bridge cuts, these songs are especially prevalent during scenes
of transit. Whether Juno is driving somewhere in her van, walking, or
riding her bike, these folk songs again lend a youthful innocence and occasional angst to Juno's agency. Although often impulsive in her actions,
the musical continuity colouring Juno's travels tends to constrain this
agency due to the above mentioned connotations of nature and innocence that the music conveys.

I am not trying to argue here that the presence of folk music alone limits
Juno's agency. Female folk singers, and those female singer-songwriters
who do not exactly play folk but do share some idiomatic traits with
folk singers, have historically found this type of music a crucial outlet
for the exploration of topics central to women's everyday lives, as both
Charlotte Greig (1997) and Sheila Whiteley (2000) have pointed out.
Greig argues that childbearing is one topic that affects women uniquely
and thus its audibility in popular music should be commonplace:

> So much of our adult lives is taken up with our emotional responses
> to the question of childbearing and motherhood – whether or not we
> actually have children, the question always hangs over our heads –
> that you might expect to find a wealth of popular songs dealing
> with this whole drama in all its complexity: songs about pregnancy,
> childbirth, about motherhood, about turning away from all this,
> about remaining single, about abortion, and so on.
>
> (p. 169)

Greig goes on to state that due to strict conventions in pop songs, pregnancy and motherhood were not very prominent in mainstream music
with the exception of some material by singer-songwriters since the

1970s, although more recent female pop singers have included these top-ics in their work (p. 169). For Whiteley, folk music is one of the genres where women have been successful in contemplating motherhood, which sits among many other topics of great concern to women:

> The continuing history of women as providers and mothers is but one thread in the rich tapestry of folk. The traditional handing-down of ballads and songs which focus on both the everyday and the ex-traordinary dimensions of women's life experiences range from the starkly autobiographical to the humorous and poetic.
>
> (p. 73)

Based on Whiteley's assertions, folk could be employed in cinema as a relevant genre to explore motherhood and many other important issues that women deal with in their everyday lives. But in *Juno*, folk music is not used to explore childbearing, or abortion, or motherhood. While the songs do convey some sense of youthful angst and insecurity, the lyrics mostly deal with love and/or are pre-occupied with whimsical wordplay. Therefore, it is not the overall use of folk music that limits Juno's agency, but rather the types of songs that are used. Crucially, tension exists in the film between these folk songs and not only other types of songs on the soundtrack but also Juno's explicitly stated and not so implicitly sug-gested taste in music. It is this tension that disrupts the portrayal of Juno as an independent character with strong musical agency.

The film gives little indication that Juno is interested in folk music until the very last scene. Instead, dialogue and mise-en-scène suggest that Juno listens to punk rock and plays the electric guitar. As previously mentioned the photograph in Juno's room shows her playing the electric guitar, although she does own and later plays an acoustic guitar. When Mark asks Juno who her favourite musicians are, she replies that it is "a three-way tie between the Stooges, Patti Smith, and the Runaways". All three artists are best known for playing heavier proto-punk or garage rock. While a vinyl copy of Patti Smith's 1975 debut album *Horses* is vis-ible in Juno's room when she calls the clinic, only those familiar with the album's cover could recognise it in the blurred background.[3] Further-more, stickers with logos of the bands Bad Religion, the Ramones, and the Dead Kennedys are visible inside Juno's school locker during a scene where she drops her book and is harassed by a 'jock' who secretly has a crush on her. Again, all three of these are punk rock bands, and in the case of Bad Religion and the Dead Kennedys, overtly political ones.

Juno's musical taste is further emphasised when she visits Mark and Vanessa's house for the first time. After Juno goes upstairs to use the cou-ple's bathroom, she encounters Mark in the hallway. As they are about to go back downstairs, Juno catches a glimpse of Mark's guitar, which she instantly recognises as a Gibson Les Paul. The two begin to bond over a

Figure 3.1 Juno and Mark have an illicit jam session.

shared interest in music after Mark agrees to let Juno hold the guitar. Indeed, Juno's fascination with Mark's "technophallus" foreshadows, and perhaps is partially responsible for, the physical relationship the characters later narrowly avoid. When Mark states that 1993 was the "best time for rock 'n' roll", Juno vehemently disagrees, insisting that 1977 was far superior. This assertion is further evidence of Juno's taste in punk rock since 1977 is considered a landmark year for that genre. After a cut to awkward conversation downstairs between Vanessa and Juno's father while the couple's attorney looks on, guitar playing and singing can be heard coming from upstairs. Vanessa, annoyed by the delay in adoption planning, goes upstairs to find Juno and Mark playing 'Doll Parts' by Hole. Since Juno obviously knows the song, this must be a shared interest for herself and Mark, once again attesting to Juno's love of edgy rock music and suggesting a rebellious, if not explicitly feminist, nature.

Juno only expresses herself through recorded music on a single occasion once the relationship between her and Mark escalates to a nearly romantic level. She brings along a few CDs when she last visits Mark, knowing that Vanessa will not be home. After Mark takes Juno to the basement and shows her a comic book featuring a pregnant super hero, Juno tells Mark which track number to play from one of her CDs. The song turns out to be 'All the Young Dudes' by Mott the Hoople, which Mark instantly recognises. Juno acknowledges the difference between this song and the music she normally talks about by saying, "this one is actually kinda slow, but it's Mott the Hoople, so it's still totally rad and hardcore." After Mark remarks that he danced to this song at his prom, Juno puts her arms around him and they start to dance. In fact, she probably did choose a slow song with the hope of initiating some romantic encounter, since she is shown putting on what appears to be lipstick (the only time in the film, although the director's comments on the DVD reveal that this is not lipstick but rather Lip Smackers lip gloss) before going to see Mark. As they dance, Mark declares his intentions to leave Vanessa, and Juno becomes very distraught. Although she is ultimately unhappy with the outcome of her visit, Juno uses recorded music in this scene to achieve a goal, albeit one she may not fully have intended. This is one of the few instances in the film when she exhibits such musical agency, and yet this song does not carry any of the aggressive, angry, or political connotations that the bands Juno claims to like would transfer to her character if they were to appear on the soundtrack.

Juno only plays guitar in one scene other than the aforementioned performance of 'Doll Parts' on Mark's electric guitar. At the end of the film, after the baby has been delivered and summer has arrived, Juno rides her bike to Bleeker's house with her acoustic guitar strapped to her back. The bike ride is scored by the second appearance of Kimya Dawson's 'Tire Swing'. Unlike the first placement of this song just after Juno confirms her pregnancy, this use of the song has carefree connotations as Juno zooms along on her bike and her voice-over exclaims how great Bleeker is as a boyfriend. The song starts when 'SUMMER' appears over a scene of the school's track team running on a path. The re-appearance of 'Tire Swing', like the dawn of summer, brings the movie almost full circle. The song ends when Juno sits down with Bleeker, also holding an acoustic guitar, in front of his house. Juno is once again free to be a teenager, and she joins Bleeker in a performance of The Moldy Peaches' 'Anyone Else But You' to consummate this return to youthful innocence. The sexual connotations of the word 'consummate' are intentional in this case, because the two scenes in which Juno plays the guitar can easily be read as metaphors for a sexual encounter.

In the first instance, when Juno plays 'Doll Parts' with Mark, the encounter is much more illicit. As Vanessa waits downstairs, eager to work out the details of the adoption, Mark and Juno sing the words "yeah, they really want you, they really want you, they really do/Yeah, they really want you, they really want you, but I do, too." Removed from the context of the song and situated in this atmosphere of taboo sexual tension, the lyrics take on a new meaning, developing the feeling of desire between the two characters that will later come to fruition. In addition to the lyrical meaning taken out of context, the original is a much darker song than 'Anyone Else But You', and its performance by a married man and a pregnant teenage girl is a further representation of the apple of carnal knowledge that folk seems set up to oppose throughout the rest of the film.

On the other hand, Juno and Bleeker's performance of 'Anyone Else But You' is a back-and-forth duet that still has romantic connotations, but its sweet folk and silly lyrics about youthful desire come after the pregnancy is out of the way as if it never occurred. The young couple are now back together after avoiding each other for the better part of the pregnancy, but rather than playing in their old band, which included another member, they engage in this tender duet. Thus, Juno's two musical performances in the film could be perceived as expressions of sexual desire, with the transgressive nature of the former being erased by the youthful naïveté of the latter. This final performance serves to 'redeem' Juno's character and reinstate her into adolescence.

Although Juno's guitar playing is limited in the film, a look at the deleted scenes on the *Juno* DVD reveals a public performance that did not make the final cut (much like the alternate ending of *Love Don't Cost a Thing* discussed in Chapter 1). This scene, had it been included, would have provided an example of greater musical agency for Juno. In the deleted scene entitled 'Café Triste', Juno plays a solo electric set in a café in front of a small audience, which includes Bleeker and Leah. She sings a wryly cross song about having sex with Bleeker, getting pregnant, and Bleeker being angry with and avoiding her. After the song, Juno tells the audience that it was about a good friend of hers who is "a track and field enthusiast and may or may not be in the room right now". This song, with such lines as "I made zub zub with my best guy friend/And now I'm knocked up to no end" and "he filled me with baby batter", is not only an aggressive musical display by Juno, but also more lyrically graphic than other songs on the soundtrack. In this humorous and affective deleted scene, Juno uses music to express her anger and confusion directly in a manner unlike any performance in the actual film. In addition, Juno's sober facial expression, dry vocal delivery, and aggressive lyrics deflect any potential sexual objectification of the type that is common in scenes of women performing onstage. The inclusion of this scene in the final cut

Figure 3.2 'Café Triste': Juno's excluded performance.

of the film would have significantly changed Juno's musical agency and undermined the more innocent connotations of the overall soundtrack.

Another deleted scene that would have changed the musical characterisation of both Juno and Leah is an expanded version of a scene where Juno writes a note to Vanessa stating that she still wants her to adopt the baby, even though Mark is leaving. This rather anarchic scene, simply titled 'Montage', contains the following series of events (among others): Leah hits the mailbox of the girl Bleeker asked to the prom with a baseball bat while Juno drives her in the van, Juno and Leah buy giant slushy drinks, the two girls drop off the note at Mark and Vanessa's house only after throwing one of the slushies at the entrance sign of the upscale housing development where the couple live, the girls buy enough small boxes of Tic Tac candies (Bleeker's favourite) to fill two plastic bags, and all of the Tic Tac boxes spill out of Bleeker's mailbox when he opens it the next morning. All of this happens while the pop-punky garage rock of 'He's Out There' by Miss Ludella Black binds the montage together and adds a sense of youthful menace to the proceedings. The song stops temporarily with a cut to Mark and Vanessa looking sombre just before they hear a knock on the door and discover the note that Juno has left for Vanessa. It then starts back up and continues for the rest of the montage. The song's lyrics, with the repeated line "he's out there", are about a former lover going out with someone else while the singer is left alone. Lyrically, the song reflects Juno's thoughts about Bleeker and the possibility that he may be dating another student – an idea further emphasised by the destruction of the mailbox. This montage, which begins with Leah twirling a baseball bat and smiling fiendishly as she walks down her front steps, suggests a more playfully sinister and mildly delinquent disposition for both Leah and Juno. Musically it broadens the characters' personalities and disrupts the emotional earnestness that is otherwise insisted upon by the part of the film into which this montage would have fit.

While these deleted scenes have no impact on one's perception of the theatrical release if they have not been seen, they do shed some light on what remains in the film and what, more importantly, is missing. In the film, Juno's guitar playing is limited to two performances that serve romantic functions and do not possess the progressive potential of the deleted club scene. Scenes where girls play guitar publicly are very rare in both mainstream and indie cinema, and the omission of this scene is something of a missed opportunity for *Juno* to redress the exclusion. Despite its lack of solo performances by Juno, the film contains a scene where Bleeker plays what sounds like 'Anyone Else But You' on his acoustic guitar alone in his room. The music bridges a cut to Juno contemplating what to do in her van and starting to write the aforementioned note to Vanessa, and again bridges a cut to Mark and Vanessa, ending before they speak to each other and receive the note from Juno. The scenes connected by this music in the theatrical release were also included in the deleted 'Montage' but take on different meaning due to the change of music. Instead of the previously discussed 'He's Out There' with all it brings to the montage, Bleeker's playing foreshadows the romantic plot resolution and return to childhood innocence that comes with the duet of the very same song in the final scene. Whereas the montage would have further developed Juno's individuality, the choice of Bleeker's playing keeps the focus on romance.

It is interesting to consider how some of the musical choices in *Juno* came to be made since the process has been so well publicised in this instance. Firstly, the majority of the film's soundtrack was the result of a suggestion by Ellen Page. In an interview with Ellen Page and Kimya Dawson, director Jason Reitman explains how he asked Page what kind of music she thought Juno would listen to, and her reply was "The Moldy Peaches" – a band consisting of Kimya Dawson and Adam Green (*Juno Soundtrack Commentary*, n.d.). Reitman had never heard any of Dawson's music before, but his listening to it resulted in a soundtrack full of the artist's songs, both newly recorded and pre-existing. Furthermore, despite releasing a children's album entitled *Alphabutt* in 2008, Dawson herself points out in a 2008 interview with Dead C that "the songs on the soundtrack are pretty tame" compared to other, less innocent and occasionally raunchy songs in her catalogue. She also states that some of the songs picked for the film have less substance than most of her other material. Since songs that were more substantial and less innocent would have had a similar musical aesthetic to the songs chosen for the soundtrack, the decision to use the more juvenile-sounding tracks suggests a conscious attempt to avoid subversive, or at least more mature, musical characterisation. Finally, when director's and writer's comments are enabled on the DVD, during the deleted scene 'Montage' that was discussed earlier, Reitman states, "originally this sequence was cut to kind of an aggressive punk song," to which the film's writer Diablo Cody replies, "one of my few remaining musical notes". This comment by Cody and all of the allusions to Juno's character liking punk rock in both dialogue and visuals suggest that the punk side of Juno likely came from Cody and was toned down by musical choices made for the theatrical release. This mixing of musical influences in the making of the film created a tension between what is implied and what is heard.

Willis (2008) comes to conclude that *Juno* re-asserts sexual norms and limits agency while pretending to be something more progressive, or at least different:

> Juno's character is understandable as a metaphor for conditions of female sexuality that continue to limit girls' full expressions of sexual desire. Like the character of Juno, girls today are caught between increased expectations of agency on the one hand and continuing

restrictions of their sexual expressions of desire on the other. In conceptualizing Juno's agency it is important to recognize the material and social ways in which Juno's agentive "choice" is constrained. [...] The central paradox within *Juno* is that it celebrates agency for girls while simultaneously linking that agency to their physical desirability and role as potential reproducers.

(p. 254)

Juno's soundtrack significantly enforces this sexual conservatism and limits the possibilities of what a teenage girl can do, while it masquerades as a celebration of agency and quirkiness. Juno's potentially subversive love of punk rock is undermined by the ubiquitous naïve folk of the soundtrack which neither engages with the central concerns of the film nor contributes to Juno's musical agency. The tension between silent punk and audible folk gives the impression that something out of the ordinary is going on, but ultimately the omnipresence of the folk – as well as its visual counterparts in nature and childhood iconography – saturates the film with its musical signification. Moreover, as far as guitar playing is concerned, Juno's two performances do link her musical agency to desirability and reproduction, just as Willis suggests. In the first instance, she is the mother of the child Mark will adopt, as well as a potential lover for Mark. In the second, she is the mother of Bleeker's baby, as well as Bleeker's past and (presumably) present lover. While *10 Things I Hate About You* and *All Over Me* do illustrate to varying degrees Catherine Driscoll's (2011, pp. 12–13) assertions that the content of teen films has always been significantly shaped by the desire to instruct, protect, and manage youth, *Juno*'s soundtrack most directly reflects these aims by insuring that Juno retains her 'innocence', and that her more masculine and less traditionally feminine tendencies are contained. To put it another way, the soundtrack of *Juno* and the restriction of musical performance in both *Juno* and *10 Things* serve to manage the stability of the gender binary and ensure its continuing influence on representations of youth.

Notes

1 These contradictions are considered by Michael Newman (2011) in his discussion of *Juno*, but I also discuss this at length in my PhD thesis (Timothy McNelis, 2010).
2 The other two discourses focus on 'girl-power' and the 's-hero' or 'super-girl-hero'. Willis argues that 'protection' is the "most deeply-rooted" discourse of the three (p. 244).
3 The appearance of Patti Smith in both *Juno* and *All Over Me* shows her significance as a role model for girls and a point of reference as an important female musician/artist (potentially suggesting a kind of feminism, even if it is not explicit).

References

Dead C (2008) 'Dawson's Crack: Interview with Kimya Dawson' in *Monster Fresh* [Internet], Available from: http://www.monsterfresh.com/2008/03/19/dawsons-creak-interview-wkimya-dawson/ [Accessed 18 August 2014].

Driscoll, Catherine (2011) *Teen Film: A Critical Introduction*, Oxford, UK: Berg Publishers.

Greig, Charlotte (1997) 'Female Identity and the Woman Songwriter' in Sheila Whiteley (ed.), *Sexing the Groove: Popular Music and Gender*, London: Routledge, pp. 168–177.

Juno: Music From the Motion Picture (n.d.) *Juno Soundtrack Commentary* [video: m4v] [Internet], Available from: http://www.rhino.com/juno/# [Accessed 24 September 2009].

McNelis, Timothy (2010) *Popular Music, Identity, and Musical Agency in US Youth Films*, PhD Thesis, University of Liverpool.

Newman, Michael (2011) *Indie: An American Film Culture*, New York: Columbia University Press.

Polisar, Barry Louis (n.d.) *Barry Louis Polisar: Books and Music for Children* [Internet], Available from: http://www.barrylou.com/ [Accessed 24 September 2009].

Whiteley, Sheila (2000) *Women and Popular Music: Sexuality, Identity and Subjectivity*, London: Routledge.

Willis, Jessica (2008) 'Sexual Subjectivity: A Semiotic Analysis of Girlhood, Sex, and Sexuality in the Film *Juno*' in *Sexuality & Culture*, Vol. 12, No. 4, pp. 240–256.

Filmography

10 Things I Hate About You (1999, USA) directed by Gil Junger, music by Richard Gibbs, music supervision by Alfonso E. Chavez, Buena Vista Home Entertainment.

All Over Me (1997, USA) directed by Alex Sichel, music by Miki Navazio, music supervision by Bill Coleman, Alliance.

Juno (2007, USA) directed by Jason Reitman, music by Mateo Messina, music supervision by Peter Afterman, 20th Century Fox.

Love Don't Cost a Thing (2003, USA) directed by Troy Beyer, music by Richard Gibbs, music supervision by Michael McQuarn, Warner Home Video.

Part II

Listening to the Other
Cultural Borrowing and Critical Reflection

Introduction

Performance is one of the many ways that teenagers engage with music. They also have an intimate relationship with recorded music, using it to construct self-identity in both the private and public realms. This can involve alteration of one's personality based on an understanding of songs and their place in popular culture. For my analyses in Part II, I am particularly interested in songs that carry connotations of the racial Other. More specifically, I will focus on white characters' use of 'black music'[1] in *Ghost World* (Terry Zwigoff, 2001), *Save the Last Dance* (Thomas Carter, 2001), *Bring It On* (Peyton Reed, 2000), *Mean Creek* (Jacob Aaron Estes, 2004), and *Napoleon Dynamite* (Jared Hess, 2004). In some instances, the use of these songs not only involves white characters borrowing 'black culture', but also literally borrowing or stealing the music from African Americans.

In order to understand how film constructs, upholds, and circulates concepts of race and ethnicity, one must consider how racial and ethnic differences are constructed. In US youth films these differences are often constructed in relation to whiteness, since most of these films have few non-white characters of central importance to the narrative. Sharon Willis argues that 'blackness' is constructed as racialised in opposition to 'whiteness' (1997, p. 3). Thus, 'whiteness' is devoid of meaning – white is represented as a non-race. While Willis is considering the binary division most visible in Hollywood film, her claim is no less true with regard to other racial and ethnic groups, whether physically present in films or culturally invoked through music, clothing, dance, or ways of speaking. Ella Shohat and Robert Stam argue that representations of oppressed communities are "allegorical; within hegemonic discourse every subaltern performer/role is seen as synecdochically summing up a vast but putatively homogenous community" (1994, p. 183). Thus, members of these groups are rendered as unproblematically representative of the whole. Conversely, Shohat and Stam claim that representations of dominant groups "are seen not as allegorical but as 'naturally' diverse, examples of the ungeneralizable variety of life itself" (p. 183). It is the presentation of whiteness as devoid of racial meaning that allows it to be the only site for true diversity in such representations. Richard Dyer (1997) considers how 'whiteness' is constructed within visual media in Western culture. He argues that whiteness is moulded by 'white' people, and thus is inscribed with ideological power and freedom far beyond constructions of other races and ethnicities in the Western world, which are also usually conceived by 'white' people. Like Willis, Dyer argues that "[a]s long as race is something only applied to non-white peoples, as long as white people are not racially seen and named, they/we function as a human norm. Other people are raced, we are just people" (p. 1).

In 'Eating the Other: Desire and Resistance', bell hooks (1992) analyses the relationship white consumers have with 'black culture', considering such factors as desire, commodification, and power relations. For hooks, the desire involved in 'eating the Other' is potentially very positive and productive, as long as it avoids uncritical fetishisation:

> Within a context where desire for contact with those who are different or deemed Other is not considered bad, politically incorrect, or wrong-minded, we can begin to conceptualize and identify ways that desire informs our political choices and affiliations. Acknowledging ways the desire for pleasure, and that includes erotic longings, informs our politics, our understanding of difference, we may know better how desire disrupts, subverts, and makes resistance possible. We cannot, however, accept these new images uncritically.
>
> (p. 39)

Therefore, self-reflective cultural borrowing – and representations of this practice that consider the power dynamics involved – can be a progressive means of breaking down perceived racial boundaries and focusing on shared interests rather than differences. Throughout Part II, I interrogate how white characters engage with black music and the effects of this cultural borrowing on identity construction, agency, and the filmic narrative as a whole. I argue that an examination of the political implications of this type of cultural borrowing, with a focus on film music, can illuminate the processes through which racial discourses are constructed. Films that deal with these depictions in a critical manner provide tools for perceivers to question their own understanding of race and how it is used in popular culture.

In his study of American teenagers and consumption, Murray Milner, Jr. (2006) mainly focuses on social use when discussing popular music. He argues that teenagers primarily use music to assert generational difference and to form genre-based friendships and cliques (although he fails to acknowledge much of the important – if problematic – literature on musical subcultures, scenes, tribes, etc.):[2]

> Music sets off teenagers from adults, but also distinguishes various adolescent subcultures. Country and western, ska, west coast rap, east coast rap, classic rock, acid rock, hard rock, and techno rock, not to mention older forms like jazz, rhythm and blues, and swing, are only a few of the distinctions that were significant in the last decades of the twentieth century. Most large high schools have some devotees to each of these genres and often this shared appreciation will serve as the basis for friendships and cliques.
>
> (p. 52)

Although a substantial review of sociological youth studies is beyond the scope of my research, it does seem to me that Milner is overemphasising the genre-based subculture formation that actually takes place in modern high schools. Despite this emphasis, Milner goes on to stress that teens do use music to create links across social boundaries because music is more widely available than certain types of clothing or other commercial goods that carry status in the teen world (pp. 55–56). While the reality of teenage listening is likely to involve more genre hopping than the term 'subculture' would suggest, teenagers undoubtedly bond over shared musical taste. Thus, recorded music is vital to intimate friendships and other social interactions.

For my research, the most important point to take from Milner's observations is that teenagers use music to create their own sense of self and express this identity through interactions with others. Reed Larson's (1995) study of adolescents' private media use focuses a great deal more on music and its role in identity construction. After pondering why "adolescents' quest for a more secure and authentic self involves use of a public, shared medium" (p. 547), Larson suggests the following about how adolescents use music to construct the self and make sense of their relationships with others:

> [...] the secure self adolescents seek is not solely a static icon of who they are, but rather a dynamic personal imagery that helps them regulate their internal life. Popular music is crafted to generate powerful images and emotions that adolescents can use to make sense of and cope with their stressful lives. The strong passions awakened by a song provide a personal refrain around which a provisional identity might cohere [...] A retreat to one's bedroom and headphones after school returns one to a forum of emotional images for reassembling a sense of personal stability after surviving the slings and arrows of the day. The predictable selves that come alive in music are a vehicle

for navigating the unpredictable and sometimes uncontrollable cas-
cade of adolescent daily life.

(p. 548)

Private listening is important because it enables adolescents (this includes teens) to develop their own 'unique' identities and yet still have
a connection to their peers' identities and everyday social interactions.
Songs are such powerful tools for teenagers because they provide an
emotional escape from, and way to make sense of, the trials of everyday
life while simultaneously enabling a shared experience with many others
of a similar age.

One method that teenagers use to (re)create their internal and pro-
jected identities involves drawing on perceived traits of Other cultures
through such forms as popular music, television, clothing, and vernac-
ular. In Part II, I primarily focus on white teens' use of black music in
films, as well as considering how characters employ this music in service of their own agency. S. Craig Watkins (1998) shrewdly states that
"one of the most striking ironies of late twentieth-century capitalism is
the simultaneous structural and economic displacement of black youth
along with the emergence of a voracious appetite for the cultural performances and products created by them" (p. 71). Youth films both cater
for and dramatise this appetite of white youth for a certain type of black
youth culture. This fascination of white teens with African-American
art forms involves a complex mix of desire, disapproval, and disavowal.

The quest to find one's self is a theme central to most youth films, and
unsurprisingly the desire to try on new personalities leads protagonists
to musical exploration. Regarding white audiences' attraction to black
culture, hooks (1992) states the following:

> Within current debates about race and difference, mass culture is the
> contemporary location that both publicly declares and perpetuates
> the idea that there is pleasure to be found in the acknowledgment and
> enjoyment of racial difference. The commodification of Otherness
> has been so successful because it is offered as a new delight, more
> intense, more satisfying than normal ways of doing and feeling.
> Within commodity culture, ethnicity becomes spice, seasoning that
> can liven up the dull dish that is mainstream white culture.

(p. 21)

This notion of ethnicity adding 'spice' to the otherwise insipid banquet
of mainstream white culture reflects back on the idea that whiteness is
conceived of by white people as bland, devoid of meaning and 'flavour'
(Dyer, 1997; Willis, 1997). For many white teens, the fascination with
black music is an easy and attractive way of accessing a colourful
palette with which to paint the perceived blank canvas of one's identity.

Of course, the metaphors of 'spice', 'flavour', and 'colour' are problematic and hide a history of oppression, marginalisation, fetishisation, and essentialist thought. I am merely reflecting the way these terms have been employed in popular racial discourse. Nevertheless, these terms are used to express a real desire, both cultural and physical, for the Other.

hooks (1992) also stresses the dangers of and prejudices lying beneath these practices of cultural representation through popular entertainment:

> When race and ethnicity become commodified as resources for pleasure, the culture of specific groups, as well as the bodies of individuals, can be seen as constituting an alternative playground where members of dominating races, genders, sexual practices affirm their power-over in intimate relations with the Other.
>
> (p. 22)

This scenario presents the cultural borrowing as a sort of colonising consumption, the 'Eating the Other' to which hooks refers. Members of the dominant group get to live a fantasy of the exotic Other without confronting the realities, both positive and negative, of inhabiting Other bodies. Similarly, for Stuart Hall (2003), the desire that underlies this process is an integral part of complicated racist identification:

> We think about identification usually as a simple process, structured around fixed "selves" which we either are or are not. The play of identity and difference which constructs racism is powered not only by the positioning of blacks as the inferior species but also, and at the same time, by an inexpressible envy and desire; and this is something the recognition of which fundamentally displaces many of our hitherto stable political categories, since it implies a process of identification and otherness which is more complex than we had hitherto imagined.
>
> (p. 92)

This is not to say that all cross-racial desire is racist in nature, but that this type of identification can be slippery if engaged in uncritically. However, cultural borrowing can also serve to build progressive links between youth. hooks asserts that "cultural appropriation of the Other assuages feelings of deprivation and lack that assault the psyches of radical white youth who choose to be disloyal to western civilisation" (p. 26). While not all rebellious teens could be described as 'radical', hooks' statement does provide an explanation for why some white teens who feel they exist outside of the mainstream develop an interest in black music.

In what ways, then, do white characters use black music (and other elements of culture), and how does this cultural borrowing change their trajectory through film narratives and affect perceivers' understanding

of them? Krin Gabbard (2004) addresses these questions with particular attention to music in *Black Magic: White Hollywood and African
American Culture*. He argues throughout the book that film music
presents elements of African-American culture, often in the absence of
African-American characters. Two concepts that often crop up in discussions of black music are 'authenticity' and 'masculinity'. Gabbard elaborates on how this cultural borrowing affects white characters:

> Whether or not they are on the screen [...] African Americans radi-
> cally transform the lives of white characters, usually providing them
> with romance and gravitas. And although it's seldom acknowledged,
> representations of black masculinity now provide the model for
> most of what is considered white masculinity, especially among the
> working classes.
>
> (p. 6)

Often without the presence of black characters, stereotypical traits of black
culture are transferred onto white characters for emotional impact and
'spice'. Imagined excessive black sexuality, necessary in moments of passion but avoided at other times when it would be too transgressive for white
protagonists, is also drawn upon using popular song. Gabbard later asserts
that this mix of desire and disdain has long been exploited in popular
entertainment, explaining how "working-class white men at the minstrel
shows could indulge their contempt for African Americans at the same
time that they took vicarious pleasure in the supposed transgressiveness,
carefree abandon, and unlimited sexual license of black men" (p. 210).

Gabbard also provides an interesting discussion of how racial connotations of music help to create shifts in mood on three separate occasions
in *Pleasantville* (Gary Ross, 1998), a film in which a present-day teenage
brother and sister are transported into the world of a 1950s sitcom. In
this film, a shift from white pop to black-influenced rock 'n' roll and
finally to black rhythm and blues music[3] accompanies and helps connote
a shift from innocence to sexual awareness in 1950s teens (pp. 94–95).
Later in the film, two jazz songs are used to signify an acquisition of
knowledge about literature that never existed within the world of the
sitcom (all library books are empty inside until the brother and sister
divulge the details of their stories) (pp. 95–99). The first song, 'Take
Five' (from the album *Time Out*), is performed by the Dave Brubeck
Quartet, of which all but one member was white. The next song, 'So
What' (from the album *Kind of Blue*), is performed by the Miles Davis
Sextet, of which all but one member was black. Gabbard describes what
he considers the motivation behind this song placement to be:

> The coffeehouse hipness that Gary Ross heard in "Time Out" still
> clings to the song and marks it as an artefact of the 1950s. "So What"

has acquired more of what we might call "timelessness" and plays a much more convincing role as *Pleasantville*'s signifier of profound transformation. More importantly, as black music, the Miles Davis recording carries with it an aura of the forbidden and the transgressive that *Pleasantville* needs as it moves the narratives of the civil rights movement to a small town devoid of African American faces.

(p. 98)

Gabbard's discussion of the two examples above, as well as another in which 'Teddy Bear' (performed by Elvis Presley) is followed by 'At Last' (performed by Etta James) to signify sexual passion (p. 101), cleverly illustrates the power of black music to bring a wealth of meaning to white characters and their narrative, particularly in the absence of black bodies. Conversely, Michael D. Dwyer (2012) argues that lip-synching to 'oldies' by white youth in Reagan-era teen films represents a conservative backlash against the displacement of heterosexual, white males in popular music genres such as disco. According to Dwyer, even when these songs were by African-American artists, they were used to represent a nostalgic desire to return to traditional family values, rather than the rebellion associated with white teens' interest in black music during the 1950s and early 1960s. In the 1990s and 2000s, political shifts and the increased mainstream popularity of contemporary black music meant that the engagement of white youth with such music must be considered in a different socio-political context.

The makers of youth films use black music to bring connotations of masculinity, authenticity, romance, threat of racial violence, sexuality, and feelings of great loss to the narrative. All of these connotations are employed to different ends in the films I analyse throughout Part II. It is important to think about the different ways songs create meaning based on whether a character is performing or listening to the music. The position of songs as source music, source score, or dramatic score can also change how these texts affect the perceiver's understanding of characters. Whereas characters use some songs to manage their feelings, exude 'coolness', or generate cultural/subcultural capital, other music plays in the soundtrack (often source score or dramatic score) to establish an urban setting with the looming threat of racial violence.

In Chapter 4, I consider how songs can be used to transfer specific racially coded ideas to characters and how characters can use music to construct identity based on these mediated concepts, using *Ghost World* as a case study. Enid (Thora Birch), the film's protagonist, uses different types of recorded music to continually construct and re-construct her identity, and in so doing stumbles upon an old blues song that brings ideas of black masculinity and authenticity into the story. In Chapter 5, I use *Save the Last Dance* to examine how characters can engage more deeply with the musical culture of the racial Other, how their critical awareness of racial issues is influenced by this use of music, and in what ways this engagement can benefit their own musical agency. In this film, Sara (Julia Stiles) uses hip hop music and dance to adapt to life in a new high school, find romance, and eventually dance her way into the prestigious Juilliard performing arts conservatory. This cultural borrowing results in increased agency for Sara, but she is also forced to contemplate her privileged position in society, which raises many interesting questions about the implications of her cross-racial desire and the agency she is able to gain through black music and dance as a white girl.

Building on discussions of borrowing, identity, and agency in Chapters 4 and 5, Chapter 6 is used to examine some of the more nuanced implications of cultural borrowing through a comparison of three films. *Bring It On* raises ethical questions about cultural theft from a privileged position when a squad of mostly white high school cheerleaders discovers that they are performing routines stolen from a primarily African-American/Latina squad from another school. In *Mean Creek*, a more limited and less critical type of cultural borrowing is represented through the interaction of one character and one song. George (Josh Peck) listens to rap music while filming with a camcorder, and his own narration gives us insight into why this outsider may identify with this music. Finally, with *Napoleon Dynamite*, I consider how a particular type of whiteness is highlighted through engagement with black culture. The protagonist of this film borrows black music and dance with unclear motives and in the process asserts his particular nerdish whiteness through a critique of ubiquitous cultural borrowing.

Notes

1   In *Popular Music in Theory*, Keith Negus (1996) presents a critical overview of the arguments surrounding the term 'black music'. He concludes that 'black music' is an important category because of the social struggles it represents, and asserts that "[w]hile there is racism, social segregation and economic inequality, the term 'black music' will continue to have a resonance as a signifier of a culture created out of these experiences" (p. 112). In this chapter, the term 'black music' refers to music with African-American roots or music that carries cultural connotations of 'blackness', whether that be through production, mediation, or consumption. In this sense the term 'black music' will carry the memory of struggle Negus emphasises, but it will also carry the assumptions about a mediated racial group that I wish to tease apart and consider more carefully.

2   For a useful overview and discussion of this terminology, see Hesmondhalgh (2005).

3   Music progresses from 'Mr. Blue' performed by Pat Boone to 'Be-Bop-a-Lula' performed by Gene Vincent to 'Lawdy Miss Clawdy' performed by Larry Williams.

References

Dwyer, Michael D. (2012) 'The Same Old Songs in Reagan-Era Teen Film' in *Alphaville: Journal of Film and Screen Media*, No. 3, pp. 1–14.

Dyer, Richard (1997) *White*, London: Routledge.

Gabbard, Krin (2004) *Black Magic: White Hollywood and African American Culture*, New Brunswick, NJ: Rutgers University Press.

Hall, Stuart (2003) 'New Ethnicities' in Linda Martin Alcoff and Eduardo Mendieta (eds), *Identities: Race, Class, Gender, and Nationality*, Oxford, UK: Blackwell, pp. 90–95.

Hesmondhalgh, David (2005) 'Subcultures, Scenes or Tribes? None of the Above' in *Journal of Youth Studies*, Vol. 8, No. 1, pp. 2–40.

hooks, bell (1992) 'Eating the Other: Desire and Resistance' in bell hooks *Black Looks: Race and Representation*, Boston, MA: South End Press: Chapter 2.

Larson, Reed (1995) 'Secrets in the Bedroom: Adolescents' Private Use of Media' in *Journal of Youth and Adolescence*, Vol. 24, No. 5, pp. 535–550.

Milner, Jr., Murray (2006) *Freaks, Geeks, and Cool Kids: American Teenagers, Schools, and the Culture of Consumption*, London: Routledge.

Negus, Keith (1996) *Popular Music in Theory: An Introduction*, Cambridge, UK: Polity Press.

Shohat, Ella and Robert Stam (1994) *Unthinking Eurocentrism: Multiculturalism and the Media*, London: Routledge.

Watkins, S. Craig (1998) *Representing: hip hop culture and the production of black cinema*, Chicago, IL: University of Chicago Press.

Willis, Sharon (1997) *High Contrast: Race and Gender in Contemporary Hollywood Film*, Durham, NC: Duke University Press.

Filmography

Bring It On (2000, USA) directed by Peyton Reed, music by Christophe Beck, music supervision by Billy Gottlieb, Universal Home Entertainment.

Ghost World (2001, USA) directed by Terry Zwigoff, music by David Kitay, music supervision by Melissa Axelrod and Christine Bergren, Icon Home Entertainment.

Mean Creek (2004, USA) directed by Jacob Aaron Estes, music by tomandandy, music supervision by Robin Urdang, Palisades Tartan.

Napoleon Dynamite (2004, USA) directed by Jared Hess, music by John Swihart, music consultancy by Tracy Lynch-Sanchez, Paramount Pictures.

Pleasantville (1998, USA) directed by Gary Ross, music by Randy Newman, music supervision by Bonnie Greenberg, New Line Cinema.

Save the Last Dance (2001, USA) directed by Thomas Carter, music by Mark Isham, music supervision by Michael McQuarn, Paramount Home Video.

4 Consumption, Authenticity, and Identity Experimentation in *Ghost World*

In *Ghost World*, a recent high school graduate named Enid (Thora Birch) struggles to figure out how best to progress into an adult world where she sees no plausible fit. Although Enid and her best friend Rebecca (Scarlett Johansson) were non-conformists in high school, Rebecca becomes increasingly caught up in domesticity and a conventional adult lifestyle after graduation, whereas Enid continues to resist this brand of adulthood. Rebecca gets a job, dresses more conservatively, and obsesses over finding an apartment and the accompanying housewares, while Enid chases tangents and cultivates an unstable and ultimately damaging friendship with a 40-something man named Seymour (Steve Buscemi), who develops a dependency at odds with her experimental approach to life.

Ghost World begins with the opening dance scene from a Bollywood film named *Gumnaam* (Raja Nawathe, 1965); masked men and women in black suits and bright dresses dance to 'Jaan Pehechaan Ho' – a twangy, surf-tinged rock 'n' roll song performed by Mohammad Rafi. The music bridges a cut to an average-looking neighbourhood and continues as the camera pans over the windows of several apartments, showing the mundane yet slightly bizarre activities of some local people. It is then revealed that Enid is playing the Bollywood film in her bedroom and imitating the dance moves in her graduation gown. This short opening sequence establishes Enid as an intriguing and adventurous character in contrast to her dull neighbours. Far from being the typical teen character who only listens to pop music while dressing for the prom, Enid actively seeks out different musical forms. According to Jason Sperb (2004), this opening also establishes one of the film's key themes. Sperb suggests that "opening *Ghost World* with clips from *Gumnaam*, instead of images of Enid or of another one of the film's characters, emphasises the film's pre-occupation with simulation, with facades that mask depth" (p. 210). As I argue throughout this chapter, there is a depth to Enid's engagement with music, although her search for identity, depth, and authenticity in music ultimately fails to meet her expectations or provide a satisfactory portal into a more meaningful version of her life. Enid's most significant interaction with a recording, however, is heavily articulated with connotations of authenticity and originality related to archaic black music, specifically the blues.

Enid 'tries on' different musical personae (as she does clothing styles) throughout *Ghost World* in the hope of finding some meaningful form of self-expression. In her exploration of musical genres, Enid becomes obsessed with Seymour's taste in old jazz and blues records, largely due to the 'authenticity' these artefacts seem to exude. This musical soul-searching proves hollow, however, and her attempts to gain agency through music are ultimately unsuccessful. Sperb (2004) argues that, although Enid somewhat recognises the emptiness of texts that are mere simulations of some mythical authentic experience, she "embraces these texts because, as a teenager in America, simulation constitutes her only point of reference for history or authenticity..." (p. 210). Despite her knowledge of the empty promise this authenticity contains, Enid continues to search for a musical experience with some real depth throughout the film, "to uncover depth beneath the cultural simulation, or to ascribe and impose depth on the world around her" (p. 211).

I will first discuss Enid's use of punk rock to rebel against what she perceives as Rebecca's pull towards traditionally vapid adulthood. While sitting in a diner, Rebecca reads apartment listings to Enid, who seems to have no interest in searching for somewhere new to live. Enid's facial expression grows suspicious when Rebecca tells a fellow student that they will probably move downtown, apparently having never discussed this with Enid. After Rebecca suggests that they buy nice clothes and pretend to be yuppies to get the perfect apartment, Enid glares at her sceptically. With a cut to Enid's bedroom, 'What Do I Get' by the 1970s English punk band The Buzzcocks blasts from her cassette deck as she dyes her hair green. Enid has decided to go for what she later describes as a "1977 original punk rock look" – complete with black leather jacket – and she uses this song to soundtrack her transformation. Fittingly, the song's lyrics reflect Enid's dissatisfaction with her current lifestyle and future prospects.

Figure 4.1 Enid tries on "a 1977 original punk rock look".

Enid's musical rebirth is short-lived, however. Rebecca gets upset about the new look because she fears it will hurt their chances of getting the ideal apartment and Enid's likelihood of landing a job. Enid is also insulted in a comic book store by three young men who mock her new look and make anti-Semitic remarks. This nasty reception and Rebecca's dissatisfaction result in Enid's abandonment of the punk image. The use of punk to rebel is a typical strategy of white, middle-class teenagers in the present-day United States (despite punk's working-class subcultural roots), and while Enid may feel she is combating society, this act of rebellion situates her comfortably in a white, middle-class, possibly suburban context. In adopting a genre heavily associated with rebellious youth, Enid is simultaneously attempting to resist entry into an uncertain adulthood and to avoid what she sees as the only path available – a capitalist society in which individuals attempt to attain happiness through consumption. Ironically, by searching for meaning in objects and style, Enid is engaging in classic consumerist behaviour, although this is somewhat complicated by the very real and justified feelings of anger and confusion she is attempting to address. In tapping into the historical meaning of punk music and identifying with its community of fans, Enid's approach is more social than the individual attention to fashion might suggest. Nevertheless, Enid's strategy partially reflects uncritical consumption, in terms of both music and clothing. Fitting with the film's critique of modern culture, she fails to locate any depth of meaning in the experiment. Rather than gaining respect from her peers, Enid's attempt to rebel is met with cynicism. Even though she claims that everyone is too stupid to 'get' her new look, their opinions are obviously important to her. Enid's failure to sustain the 'punk look' reflects the history of punk as a subculture. This type of rebellion is probably sought out because it enables one to fit in with an alternative group while appearing to act as an individual. However, Enid has no punk community with which to connect. Without the social support, she decides the punk image is not worth maintaining.

When Enid gets home from the comic book store, she starts to play 'What Do I Get' again, but the song, like her punk image, no longer fits. After rummaging through a pile of cassettes on her bedroom floor, she decides to play an old country-blues record that she bought from Seymour. The slow, archaic, acoustic blues of 'Devil Got My Woman' by Skip James begins with a cut to a warped record spinning on a tiny phonograph. Enid is then reflected in her bathroom mirror, having dyed her hair black again. Her facial expression suggests an immediate and intense fascination, and identification, with what she is hearing. After Enid walks from the bathroom into her bedroom, she is shown from behind with the record spinning over her shoulder. A reverse shot then shows her from the front, contemplating the song. The shot-reverse shot is a technique typically used to naturalise a conversation between two people, but in this case it structures an interaction between Enid and the phonograph/record/song. This strategy

Figure 4.2 Enid hears 'Devil Got My Woman' for the first time.

turns the act of listening into a dialogue between Enid and both the music on the record and the physical record itself. Next, the camera rotates nearly 180° around the front of Enid, emphasising her enthralment with the song and mimicking the spinning of the phonograph, creating an analogy between Enid and the record. After another cut to a close-up of the needle on the record, there is a fade to Enid reclining in front of the phonograph that shows the passage of time. She has obviously been listening to the same song repeatedly and moves the needle back yet again as the music ends.

In her discussion of records in girls' rites-of-passage films, Robynn J. Stilwell (2006) describes this scene in the following way:

> The circularity of the experience is emphasized, from the obviously repetitive motion of Enid placing the needle at the beginning of the track once again, to the spinning of the record accentuated by the warp, to the track of the needle in the groove, echoed by the camera's motion, spiralling in on Enid's moment of self-discovery.
>
> (p. 159)

This circularity not only reflects Enid's repeated playing of the record, but it is also symbolic of her quest for identity. Enid cycles through music and clothing styles, always returning to try on a new persona when the previous one fails to satisfy.

This song strongly resonates with Enid's quest for a meaningful musical identity and helps her connect with Seymour's record listening and collecting practices. She seems to desire Seymour's stability of image and his separation from conventional society. Both Sperb (2004) and Tim Anderson (2008) emphasise the bridge this song (and the record that contains it) builds between Enid and Seymour. Anderson asserts that "the record suggests a mysterious depth that Enid does not initially ascribe to Seymour's sad-sack profile" (p. 68). For Sperb, Seymour "also represents a part of the album's past", and his character "symbolizes Enid's desired journey from surface to depth, from simulation to origin" (p. 215). While Enid may connect this song's perceived authenticity, mystery, and depth to Seymour (more on this later), she must also identify with some element of the song on a personal level since she plays the record many times throughout the film. Enid uses the song, just as she uses Seymour, to escape briefly the boredom and superficiality she experiences in everyday life. However, this journey leads to a dead end. Seymour 'owns' this music in a way that is less straightforward for Enid. This has much to do with the fact that Enid is a young woman and Seymour is an older man who partakes in the typically masculine-coded tradition of record collecting. This is not to say that women do not collect records, but rather that the myth of the lonely male collector with an encyclopaedic knowledge of music still dominates the discourse.

Seymour is, in his own words, a "bookish fellow", a 40-something man who often wears a green cardigan and is an obsessive collector of old jazz and blues records. His bedroom contains countless old 78-RPM records, music-related paraphernalia, an old phonograph, and pictures of long-dead musicians. While Enid admires Seymour for his musical knowledge and position on the cultural margins, he enjoys no such adoration from others. Will Straw (1997), in his discussion of gender and record collectors, describes the fine line separating nerdish collectors from hip connoisseurs:

> Hipness and nerdishness both begin with the mastery of a symbolic field; what the latter lacks is a controlled economy of revelation, a sense of when and how things are to be spoken of [...] It is within social constructions of hipness that values we might call masculinist and strategies whose effect is to reproduce social stratification interweave in interesting ways.
>
> (p. 9)

Straw argues that the purveyors of hipness act as gatekeepers who exclude females from the social aspects of record collecting culture. This could be considered a form of Pierre Bourdieu's concept of 'cultural capital' (as I discuss in the General Introduction), used to ensure that men dominate the field of popular music knowledge. Unlike the hip gatekeepers described by Straw, Seymour has no mastery of social situations. In one scene, Seymour and Enid go to a bar to hear an old, African-American guitarist perform. After the set, Enid convinces a woman standing at the bar to sit down next to Seymour in an attempt to encourage romance.

When the woman refers to the guitarist's music as 'the blues', Seymour corrects her by pointing out that his playing was more in the "ragtime idiom". He then provides her with an awkward description of the difference between ragtime and the blues. Bewildered by Seymour's lack of social skills and infatuation with taxonomy, the woman ultimately loses interest in him.

Seymour is not only defined by the act of collecting, however. The genres of music he collects and the medium he collects them on are just as significant. Jazz and the blues are regarded as traditionally African-American genres that are associated with the culturally-defined concepts of 'authenticity' and 'masculinity'. The music projects these traits onto Seymour in a way that positions his relative 'whiteness' with respect to other white characters. Sharon Willis (1997) argues that:

> [...] contemporary representations of "race" emerge in a culture marked by the difficulty that "whiteness" has had in seeing itself as racialized. Since this culture is thoroughly racialized, this means that whiteness has had a hard time seeing *itself* at all. Where it can juxtapose itself to "blackness," blackness becomes the bearer of racial meanings so that whiteness can emerge as free from meaning.
>
> (p. 3)

It is precisely due to this lack of meaning that whiteness can be used as a blank canvas in films. However, in *Ghost World* whiteness *is* visible and *has* meaning. Discourse around musical genres plays a substantial role in creating this meaning. For example, in his discussion of the film *The Bridges of Madison County* (Clint Eastwood, 1995), Krin Gabbard (2001) describes how the singing of black vocalist Johnny Hartman is used to "endow Clint Eastwood's actions with real masculine authority at the same time that it heightens the film's romanticism" (p. 306). Gabbard illustrates how white popular conception of black masculinity works a great deal in the construction of Eastwood's onscreen persona. However, in *Black Magic*, Gabbard (2004) suggests a form of black masculinity particularly attractive to men like Seymour:

> Fans of blues and jazz tend to be less interested in black athletes or in the more provocatively masculine music of African American youth culture, such as rap and hip hop. The favored form of black masculinity for jazz and blues collectors can be understated, ironic, instinctual, learned, witty, slightly transgressive, and maybe even a bit pathetic, as in the delicate tenor voices of some early blues singers.
>
> (p. 218)

This more nuanced description of a particular type of black masculinity seems to be a good fit for Seymour's character. His music helps emphasise his implied intelligence, suspicious world-view, and sense of superiority. Furthermore, these connotations challenge racist ideas about black music being music solely of the body (and not the mind).

Ghost World's presentation of musical taste also draws on shared cultural knowledge of music genres to contrast different shades of whiteness and highlight ties between race and gender. For example, Seymour and Enid are put into stark contrast with the suburban, white femininity of the character of Dana (Stacey Travis). Dana and Seymour begin dating after she answers his personal ad in the newspaper regarding a 'moment' they shared during a random encounter. A particularly interesting example of music's ability to shape the perceiver's understanding of a character occurs when Seymour and Dana are on their first date. This scene is full of cultural signification and thus necessitates a thorough description. It starts with Seymour and Dana sitting on metal and wicker chairs at a glass dining table adorned with lilies and matching candleholders. Dana's clothing and the apartment's decor are coloured with a variety of pastels. The space is painted in various light shades of pink and green, and Dana is wearing a pale yellow dress with a matching short-sleeved sweater, accessorised with a pearl necklace. Perhaps the appearance of both Dana and her apartment could best be described as aspirational, since all of her possessions seem to be upper-range department store purchases. Dana, who is not exceptionally wealthy, works in real estate, and her taste seems to reflect a desire for socioeconomic mobility. In contrast to Dana, Seymour is dressed understatedly in a dark plaid shirt and dark trousers. He is visibly uncomfortable in Dana's domestic space.

When the scene begins in Dana's apartment, fairly standard jazz – what could be described as 'dinner music' – is playing. This is followed by a cut to Enid sitting on her bed waiting for Seymour to call and tell her how badly the date went. Once again, Enid is listening to 'Devil Got My Woman' in her dark yet tastefully tacky teenage bedroom filled with old toys and kitsch. With a cut back to Seymour and Dana, now standing and eating ice cream out of stemmed crystal bowls, the song 'Solid (As a Rock)' by Ashford and Simpson starts to play on the radio. As Dana turns up the volume, she says "I love this song...doesn't it make you wanna dance?" She has already begun to dance, in what might facilely be described as a white, middle class, 'soulless' manner. When she tries to convince Seymour to dance he declines, and when she forcefully separates him from his ice cream bowl he looks at his watch and suggests that they will be late for the movie if they do not leave soon. A final cut back to Enid, still listening to 'Devil Got My Woman', solidifies the meaning of the scene in Dana's apartment and tells the perceiver quite a lot about the three characters. This works in relation to several other scenes in which Dana's and Seymour's tastes in music, film, clothing, and decoration are contrasted.

In this scene, 'Solid (As a Rock)' seems to convey 'soullessness' or whiteness in collaboration with various components of Dana's character

Figure 4.3 Seymour freezes with his ice cream.

due to the earnestness and positivity of the song, as well as the absence of those elements that signify black authenticity and masculinity in the music Seymour loves. Through music and visuals, Dana's white, suburban, middle-class femininity and consumerism are constructed in opposition to Seymour's white yet pseudo-black and lower-middle-class masculinity and authenticity. The scenes shared by Seymour and Dana sharply contrast with those with Enid, who is listening to 'Devil Got My Woman' on the record she bought from Seymour. She intensely identifies with this song and listens to it obsessively throughout the second half of the film. It is interesting to note, however, that two African-American artists perform the song used to emphasise Dana's whiteness. As opposed to the endless possible variations of whiteness represented in mainstream US films, the single approved version of blackness promoted by this film suggests that Ashford and Simpson are too white to be hip. This use of 'Solid as a Rock' also articulates certain ideas related to gender. Most music consumption in this film is measured in relation to Seymour. While the film portrays Enid as musically discerning and reserved in a manner similar to Seymour, Dana is a source of humour because she lacks taste as defined by Seymour and dances to un-hip music. In other words, Dana's stereotypically feminine relationship with music (i.e., it is something to dance to) is appalling to Enid and Seymour – a fact made all too clear when Seymour freezes with his ice cream bowl. Not coincidentally, the woman who talks to Seymour in the blues bar is also made to look foolish by dancing enthusiastically to an unabashedly inauthentic blues-rock band (four young white men playing hard rock and singing about picking cotton) that follows the old African-American guitarist.

While music is a powerful tool for conveying such identity connotations, the technological means of listening are just as important as the music itself, as Pamela Robertson Wojcik (2001) suggests in her discussion of the cinematic "trope of the girl and the phonograph". Enid listens to music in the form of videocassette, audiocassette, and record. Considering the film's release date (2001), all of these media are archaic to some extent. Vinyl was still preferred by some audiophiles and music enthusiasts for audio, visual, aesthetic, and ideological reasons, and videocassettes were still cheap and available in 2001.[1] Audiocassettes, however, were out of fashion by that time, especially for teenagers living in the United States. A few compact discs are visible in a pile on Enid's floor, but she does not play any throughout the film. The conspicuous absence of compact discs in Enid's listening practices puts her at odds with modern times. It is important, too, that she plays records on a small, portable phonograph. Her turntable is the size of a 45 and so the LP that Enid repeatedly plays hangs well over the edge and wobbles due to its terribly warped condition. This results in an awkward visual impression, suggesting that the record is too big for her phonograph to handle and that this misshapen record is inferior to those in Seymour's pristine collection. However, this image could also reflect Enid's strong belief in the beauty of imperfection (or at least imperfect people), which is both explicitly stated and implicitly suggested throughout the film. In combination with the previously discussed analogy between Enid and the record in the scene where she first hears 'Devil Got My Woman', this image of the warped record on the tiny phonograph further emphasises her incongruous relationship to the modern world, what Stilwell (2006) refers to as "a mark of otherness, retrograde technology and nostalgic authenticity in the plastic, conformist world she scorns" (p. 166).

The infantile connotation of Enid's small phonograph is later highlighted when she finds and plays a 45-RPM record from her childhood. The song, 'A Smile and a Ribbon', is sung by a little girl who plans to wear a smile on her face and a ribbon in her hair to look special and be noticed more than the other children. While listening to the song, Enid takes a contemplative look at her bright orange 'Computer Station' T-shirt and sets it back down. Enid's father's partner Maxine (Teri Garr), whom Enid hates, works for Computer Station and offered to get her a job there, which she initially turned down. It becomes obvious that Enid eventually took the job when she appears wearing the shirt and a nametag, but this is never brought up in dialogue. Lyrically, the song reflects Enid's desire to be different, to do something more important and fulfilling than the activities undertaken by the 'ghosts' who surround her. The song's message is the antithesis of the conformity, or even assimilation, that she sees in the Computer Station T-shirt. In addition, the voice and musical style further infantilise Enid's listening practices and highlight her inability to act on her desires.

The film is ultimately ambivalent with regard to Enid's use of music in service of agency. As with Seymour's listening practices, Enid's repeated playing of 'Devil Got My Woman' lends a masculine authenticity based on popular conceptions of the blues to her character. And although she fails to find satisfaction in her musical choices, her exploration of Bollywood music, punk rock, and old blues songs represents an agency not often available to young women in films. Searching for and choosing songs from different genres of music to construct one's identity is important for real world teens, but this process is often absent from youth films.

Robertson Wojcik (2001) describes how female use of phonographs in films "comes to signify transgressive female desire and lack" (p. 448). She also claims that, especially in youth films, "the phonograph marks awakening sexual desire" (p. 441). However, Robertson Wojcik asserts, this potentially empowering representation is often accompanied by more transgressive behaviour for which the character is later punished. This is surely the case in *Ghost World*, since Enid eventually sleeps with Seymour and is punished at the end of the film with the loss of an art college scholarship. Seymour's confusion about the sexual encounter results in him moving back in with his mother and seeing a therapist. Enid ultimately decides her only option is to escape her problems, and the film ends with her boarding an old bus on a discontinued line to some unknown location. Sperb (2004) asserts that the ambiguity surrounding Enid's final journey and "the oppressive hyperreal world from which she flees" reflect "the failure, as with 'Devil Got My Woman', to quantify and materialise genuine human experience" (p. 217). Regarding Enid's search for meaning in music from the past, Sperb goes on to say that "despite Enid's best efforts, the past is still in the temporal past, with only representations, simulations, to spatially reconstruct it for her" (p. 217). Enid uses music to propel herself through the narrative but never finds the sort of experience or comfort she craves.

For Anderson (2008), the significance of Enid's use of records lies in the fact that she employs them more proactively than Seymour does; whereas Enid uses records to progress through life, Seymour refuses to confront the painful realities of his life. While this may be true with regard to Seymour, the claim that Enid uses the records to progress is somewhat dubious. She does move on within the course of the film but ultimately chooses to escape. If the film's ending presented an ultimate goal or endpoint, then perhaps it could be said that Enid has progressed. But as it stands, she tries to progress but eventually seems to give up. Seymour also fails to move beyond his life as a lonely collector because he never moves beyond his fascination with a particular version of archaic black culture. Although he is a grown man, his fascination with black music serves a similar function to that of teenage boys who draw on black culture. With regard to this desire for the Other, Norman K. Denzin (2002) posits the following:

> The white late adolescent male seeks the deep emotionally rich self of the gifted black athletic male. White youth culture 'symbolically appropriates aspects of black culture through style and music [and sports]' (Tucker, Jr., 1993, p. 206). But while the white man's self superficially crosses over into the terrain of black male culture, the self that is realized risks being superficial and emotionally barren.
>
> (p. 58)

While the type of masculinity accessible through the music Seymour listens to is of a different variety, the end result of his consumption is the same. Seymour never finds the authentic experience he seeks and may continue to seek for the rest of his life. Instead, he is to remain unsatiated, always returning like an addict for another empty fix of authenticity.

Gabbard (2004) is more sceptical about the presentation of Enid's musical exploration, considering her relationship with 'Devil Got My Woman' as the only musical engagement of any merit:

> The film begins with Enid mimicking the manic dancing of Lakshmi Chayya in the 1965 Bollywood film *Gumnaam* as it plays on her television. Later she appears to be listening to heavy metal rock. Otherwise, she ridicules punk rock, Reggae, and a local band called "Alien Autopsy." Her attraction to Bollywood music is presented not necessarily as heartfelt but as part of her rebel's devotion to anything exotic or unusual as well as her keen sense of kitsch. Only when she encounters Seymour does Enid drop her adolescent nihilism and, at least temporarily, take music more seriously.
>
> (pp. 221–222)

While the film presents 'Devil Got My Woman' as the closest thing to an authentic musical experience, the song still fails to deliver an authentic life experience just as resolutely as any of Enid's experiments. Gabbard's argument that Enid's erratic musical engagement is presented as not "heartfelt" and is simply based on a fascination with the exotic belittles her active identity development that is also present in the narrative. Unfortunately, this argument also echoes typically dismissive judgements of teenage girls' engagement with music as frivolous fandom in comparison to the serious devotion of teenage boys and men to cerebral music. Enid becomes fascinated with 'Devil Got My Woman' because she identifies with the song in some way, much as she does with other music in the film. The fact that this particular song is more of a focus has much to do with the previously discussed 'authenticity' in Skip James' performance and the narrative necessity of the connection the song creates with Seymour. It is true that Enid is shown to be obsessed with the song and deeply moved by it, but this does not mean she was not taking music seriously before this song came into her life. Gabbard simply states that Enid "ridicules punk rock", but her temporary transformation into a punk would suggest she is taking it very seriously. In fact, the only reason she dumps the punk image so quickly is that her friends and acquaintances mock her.

In the end, it is the process that is important to Enid's identity construction, as well as her ability to control this process and identify with songs to which she feels a strong connection. Interestingly, Enid's use of music takes on a more 'feminine' character when compared to Seymour's 'masculine' record collecting habits. This engagement with music both allows her to move forward (as opposed to stagnating like Seymour) and prohibits her from ever finding music that complements the person she wishes to become. Stilwell (2006) recognises a trend in this type of identity journey for teenage girls in cinema and the role records play in it:

> [...] it is striking how often the record functions as a ritual object in the narrative, key in the girl's transformation into *herself*. The picture may not be as consistent as the lonely, object-and-system-oriented male collector, but there is a constellation of issues that are engaged with varying intensities. As a ritual object, the record is inscribed with power, but it is an ambivalent power. Since it is more than an item to possess or a weapon to wield, its use is individual to each girl. The importance of records, as artefacts to venerate and relics of sound and self with which to resonate, is central to the symbolic narratives of girls finding their voices.
>
> (p. 166)

In the case of records, girls are finding their own voices through a medium traditionally associated with male collection, but as Stilwell suggests, their connection to specific records is more personal and emotional than that of the stereotypical male hoarder. Of course, the correlation between filmic representations of youth engaging with records and what transpires in the real world is a problematic one to make. Not all males who collect records lack emotional connections to particular records or songs, and there are no doubt a fair number of female record hoarders. Nevertheless, this type of representation is important because it provides a fresh and empowering tool for teenage girls' constructions of self-identities, even if they have always used records for this purpose in the real world.

With regard to race, both Enid and Seymour look to black music for some sort of truth and authenticity. 'Devil Got My Woman' does lend a sort of magic to a film almost exclusively populated with white faces, following Gabbard's (2004) thesis laid out in *Black Magic*, which I discussed in the Introduction to Part II. But as bell hooks (1992) asserts, the critical engagement of white listeners with black music, and a critically reflective desire associated with this practice, can be positive and productive. In *Ghost World*, Enid and Seymour discuss racism in relation to the piccaninny-esque logo historically used by the fried chicken chain where Seymour works. Enid questions why Seymour chooses to live in the past and whether things were really better then, when racism was more overtly acceptable. Seymour concedes that things were not necessarily better back then. After this conversation, Enid borrows a large poster containing the old racist logo to take into art class as a statement on the acceptable use of racism in advertising in the past. Although her peers are confused and offended, her art teacher is impressed and chooses to enter this in a local exhibition, which results in the outrage of people who see the piece and do not understand its context. This in turn results in Enid losing her scholarship to the art college she was considering attending. Thus, both characters engage with meanings attached to the archaic form of blackness represented by 'Devil Got My Woman', the rest of Seymour's record collection, and many of the artefacts in Seymour's bedroom. This critical engagement with black culture still keeps it at arm's length, in much the same way that Enid and Seymour keep the world they live in at arm's length – both ultimately reject their world. Seymour regresses into a sort of second childhood, while Enid chooses instead to escape the mundane and superficial world she sees around her. Her musical agency is stunted by her inability to connect her musical interests with the society in which she lives. Enid is an outsider without any true friends, and the film sustains her authenticity and mystique by keeping her outside of any social group.

Note

1 Since 2001 the popularity of vinyl has grown exponentially in the US, which could alter one's reading of the film, but here I am considering the meaning of records and collecting around the time of the film's production.

References

Anderson, Tim (2008) 'As if History was Merely a Record: The Pathology of Nostalgia and the Figure of the Recording in Contemporary Popular Cinema' in *Music, Sound, and the Moving Image*, Vol. 2, No. 1, pp. 51–76.

Denzin, Norman K. (2002) *Reading Race: Hollywood and the Cinema of Racial Violence*, London: Sage.

Gabbard, Krin (2001) 'Borrowing Black Masculinity: The Role of Johnny Hartman in *The Bridges of Madison County*' in Pamela Robertson Wojcik and Arthur Knight (eds), *Soundtrack Available: Essays on Film and Popular Music*, Durham, NC: Duke University Press, pp. 293–316.

Gabbard, Krin (2004) *Black Magic: White Hollywood and African American Culture*, New Brunswick, NJ: Rutgers University Press.

hooks, bell (1992) 'Eating the Other: Desire and Resistance' in bell hooks *Black Looks: Race and Representation*, Boston, MA: South End Press: Chapter 2.

Robertson Wojcik, Pamela (2001) 'The Girl and the Phonograph; or the Vamp and the Machine Revisited' in Pamela Robertson Wojcik and Arthur Knight (eds), *Soundtrack Available: Essays on Film and Popular Music*, Durham, NC: Duke University Press, pp. 433–454.

Sperb, Jason (2004) '*Ghost* without a Machine: Enid's Anxiety of Depth (lessness) in Terry Zwigoff's *Ghost World*' in *Quarterly Review of Film and Video*, Vol. 21, No. 3, pp. 209–217.

Stilwell, Robynn J. (2006) 'Vinyl Communication: The Record as Ritual Object in Girls' Rites-of-Passage Films' in Phil Powrie and Robynn Stilwell (eds), *Changing Tunes: The Use of Pre-Existing Music in Film*, Aldershot: Ashgate, pp. 152–166.

Straw, Will (1997) 'Sizing Up Record Collections: Gender and Connoisseurship in Rock Music Culture' in Sheila Whiteley (ed.), *Sexing the Groove: Popular Music and Gender*, London: Routledge.

Willis, Sharon (1997) *High Contrast: Race and Gender in Contemporary Hollywood Film*, Durham, NC: Duke University Press.

Filmography

The Bridges of Madison County (1995, USA) directed by Clint Eastwood, music by Lennie Niehaus, music supervision by Peter Afterman, Warner Bros.

Ghost World (2001, USA) directed by Terry Zwigoff, music by David Kitay, music supervision by Melissa Axelrod and Christine Bergren, Icon Home Entertainment.

Gumnaam (1965, India) directed by Raja Nawathe, music by Jaikishan Dayabhai Panchal and Shankarsingh Raghuwanshi, Prithvi Pictures.

5 "I didn't move to Bosnia"
Critical Cultural Immersion in *Save the Last Dance*

In this chapter, the focus shifts from characters' distanced encounters with Other cultures through engagement with recorded music, to a more immersive experience of the culture of the Other. I consider how critical cultural borrowing and musical agency interact in *Save the Last Dance*, a film in which a white protagonist participates more directly with black music and dance. This film tells the story of Sara (Julia Stiles), a white teenage girl who must move in with her father in a working-class, predominantly African-American neighbourhood in Chicago after the death of her mother. Sara has a hard time adjusting to the changes until she is befriended by Chenille (Kerry Washington), an African-American girl at her new school. After Chenille takes Sara to a dance club called Stepps, Sara begins to embrace hip hop culture with help from Chenille's brother Derek (Sean Patrick Thomas). Derek gives Sara dance lessons so she can hold her own at the club and through the resulting closeness the two teens fall in love. Things get complicated, however, when the couple have to start defending their interracial relationship. The film highlights the differences between Sara and Derek's backgrounds and explores the challenges of growing up as a working class, inner city, African American, albeit through the lens of a white teenager from a very different background. By the end of the film, Sara reconciles her past and present by fusing hip hop and ballet into a contemporary dance piece for which she is accepted into the prestigious Juilliard performing arts conservatory.

The film begins with Sara on a train to Chicago; a flashback shows how her mother died in a car accident while rushing to watch Sara's ballet audition. Because of the guilt she feels over her mother's death, Sara gives up ballet. Sara's love of ballet moulds the perceiver's immediate understanding of her white, middle-class background due to its widely understood status as 'high art'. The opening scenes and flashback contain a dramatic, melancholic piano and string piece that emphasises Sara's sadness and the tragic nature of her mother's death.

When he first appears, Sara's father Roy (Terry Kinney) is smoking a cigarette on the train platform. His clothing and the image of him smoking on the dark platform could possibly suggest his profession as a jazz musician. It soon becomes clear that Roy is in fact a jazz musician when he brings Sara home. His tiny, dimly-lit apartment contains a trumpet, a microphone stand, and a great number of CDs and records against the backdrop of peeling paint. Even though Roy is white, his racial coding fits somewhere more 'black' on a racial/cultural continuum.[1] He is not simply a working-class white man, but a white jazz musician living in a mostly black neighbourhood. Although the film's soundtrack contains no jazz music, Roy's relation to the music complicates his racial identity and masculinity in a manner similar to that of Seymour in *Ghost World*. He takes on a certain cultured, urban hipness that once again suggests authenticity, despite his conscious cultural borrowing. A substantial scene where Sara sneaks into a club to hear Roy perform is contained in the 'Deleted Scenes' on the DVD release of the film. While the decision to cut this scene may have been made due to time constraints, it is interesting to note that it would have strengthened Sara's relationship with her father by foregrounding her desire to understand his musical (and occupational) world in a manner similar to her musical bonding with Derek. In addition, this scene highlights how Sara and her father both identify with African-American music and both adopt it as a form of expression.

Rap music is first heard in the film when Roy drops Sara off at her new school. The use of rap to introduce an inner-city school and its students, while often suggesting an element of danger, is a typical strategy that took on a somewhat sinister meaning in the 'hood' films of the early 1990s.[2] In *Hearing Film*, Anahid Kassabian (2001) discusses the different uses of rap in *Dangerous Minds* (1995) and *The Substitute* (1996) in relation to the films' protagonists. Both films feature a white teacher going into a predominantly non-white, inner-city high school and focus on the teacher's experiences with students these films present as 'troubled'. Kassabian argues that "while rap is used to differentiate Shale from the students [in *The Substitute*], it connects Lou Ann and her students [in *Dangerous Minds*], drawing them together in an affective and representational world more familiar to the students than the teacher" (p. 121). Kassabian asserts that the score in *Dangerous Minds* "[refuses] to police boundaries between Lou Ann Johnson and rap" and goes on to say that "the score suggests that the major project of assimilation rests on Lou Ann's shoulders, and that she needs to learn to live in her students' world" (p. 122). The relationship between Sara and rap in *Save the Last Dance* is similar to that which Kassabian describes in *Dangerous Minds*. However, Lou Ann is a teacher, an adult authority figure, and therefore she can never be fully incorporated into the students' social and cultural worlds. Since Sara is a student, this possibility exists for her, and it is realised – albeit problematically – by the end of the film.

When Sara's father drops her off at her new high school, the rap song 'You Don't Really Want Some' by Blaqout is playing outside as she opens the car door. The implied source of the music immediately situates it in the hands of the students we are about to see. This is not simply a rap song played over images of a group of African-American students to tell us that they are black and possibly threatening as convention dictates, although the visuals accompanying the music do not necessarily negate a similar interpretation. The volume jumps with a cut to some of the students in front of the school and continues at this increased level over several shots of different students wearing headphones, dancing, talking, smoking, and generally behaving like teenagers. The volume lowers again as Sara enters the school and fades out shortly after. Thus, the music is heard from Sara's point of audition, although the level is too continuous throughout most of the scene to reflect this realistically.

As Sara walks through the crowd outside, she passes a boy with a boombox – the obvious source of the music. While this music has a source belonging to a student and is not simply dramatic score, it still carries some of the stereotypical implication of threat in relation to the white, female protagonist due to most perceivers' familiarity with this type of scene. The lyrics of the song, which include "leave that thing on fire/'til you're ready to retire" and "you don't wanna see me/the black Ron Jeremy", carry obvious sexual meaning,[3] and as Sara passes the student with the boombox, he says to her "oh, what's up baby?" In the context of the rest of the film, 'You Don't Really Want Some' also serves as a challenge to Sara, both lyrically and through its cultural context. Although different from the intended lyrical meaning, in this scene the 'some' in the title could also refer to hip hop culture. Sara may not have chosen to move to this neighbourhood and attend this school, but she is here now. She has to stand up for herself and adapt to her new cultural surroundings. Thus, on a larger scale, the song asks if Sara is willing to accept and indeed participate in the musical and cultural world of the student body.

Nearly all of the rap music in this film has a diegetic source, whether visible or implied. This further emphasises the ownership of musical agency and highlights Sara's shifting perspective. When Sara first arrives in Chicago and attends the new school, she is lacking in musical agency. Her middle-class, possibly suburban or small town background is reflected in her love of ballet and her taste in music before she embraces hip hop. The only indication of Sara's musical taste that is given early in the film is during a scene in Roy's apartment. Sara is unpacking while listening to 'When It Doesn't Matter' by Angela Ammons. This is a pop-rock song with 'yearning' female vocals that would have fit comfortably on the *Dawson's Creek* soundtrack.[4] The lyrics refer to lost love and longing for someone who no longer cares. During this scene Roy tries to get Sara to eat a TV dinner and asks her to come to the jazz club with him, but the gap between them is made explicit when Sara says that her mom never let her eat "that stuff" and reminds Roy that she cannot stay out late because it is a school night. While the earlier flashback scenes of Sara and her mother at home show a more 'wholesome' domestic mother-daughter environment, it is obvious that Roy has played no part in raising his daughter. He has a refrigerator full of frozen dinners and beer. Although Roy's bachelor lifestyle is alien to Sara, the differences between the two characters are ultimately overcome when they learn to understand and accept each other for who they have become.

While the lyrics to 'When It Doesn't Matter' could reflect Sara's relationship with her estranged father and/or the loss of her mother, the style of the song contrasts the rap and R&B music that fills the rest of the compiled soundtrack in a way that mirrors Sara's initial isolation. This music, played as Sara unpacks belongings from her former home, anchors her in her old life, her childhood, which essentially ended with the death of her mother. In this scene, the old world (her music, her possessions, her mother's beliefs) clashes with the new (Roy's lifestyle, the city). The result is a highly emotional moment when Roy, frustrated by what he perceives as Sara's stubbornness, tells her to do whatever she wants and leaves for the jazz club. As often occurs in film scores, original, instrumental dramatic score takes over from the source music at this point to guide the perceiver's emotions down the appropriate avenue. There can be no musical ambiguity when it comes to emotional intensity.

The melancholic score continues as Sara unpacks her ballet slippers, breathes deeply, wraps them back up and places them in a box (with a teddy bear) that she puts on a shelf in her closet. The pop music from Sara's past gives way to composed score and the realisation that she must pack her childhood into a box and hide it in the closet. The music of her old life is not empowering in her new world. It facilitates no sort of social interaction. This is the last time she listens to this type of music in the film; it is as if she packs the music away with the other artefacts from her youth. But unlike the ballet slippers, the pop rock is never retrieved. When she finally does unpack the slippers and put them back on her feet later in the film, the initial optimistic composed score gives way to a rap song, further emphasising the cultural transformation Sara went through while the slippers rested in the box. This symbolic action suggests that her embrace of hip hop culture was a significant element in her maturation, and that she finally accepts her mother's death as an accident for which she was not responsible.

Sara's first real foray into hip hop culture occurs when Chenille invites her to Stepps after she discovers that Sara used to dance. However, as soon as Sara leaves her house it becomes clear that she is out of her element and in dangerous territory. It is dark. A police siren, a car alarm, and barking dogs can all be heard before she passes by two African-American teens who make lewd comments. She then walks under an elevated train bridge and is surrounded by homeless people warming themselves at garbage can fires. Sara's cultural distance from her new living situation is further emphasised when Chenille alters Sara's outfit to make her look less "country". However, Sara's main challenge arrives when the young women reach the club. 'Where You At?', a hip hop dance track by Fat Man Scoop, begins with a cut to the inside and raises the energy of the scene. Stepps is a members-only club where Chenille and her friends go to dance and where Derek's friend Snookie (Vince Green) spins records. Snookie, who is a misfit outside of the club, reigns over this musical space and places all of his friends on the guest list. As 'Where You At?' plays, shots of Chenille and Sara walking through the club are intercut with dancers showing off their moves. This scene foregrounds agency and power. Chenille forcefully squeezes a guy's crotch and makes him look like a fool after he grabs her from behind. Handheld, canted angle shots of club goers further emphasise their dancing skills. In part because she lacks cultural capital, Sara has no musical agency in this space. She is merely an observer.

Furthermore, there is an undercurrent of male dominance in this club. Although many important female rappers have made their way in hip hop, sexist attitudes still thrive in the rap industry, discourse, and song lyrics. In this club scene, the boys ask the girls to dance. Nikki is the only girl who asks a boy to dance, and Derek turns her down. Male power is enforced by the lyrics of 'Where You At?': "All the good lookin' women get your hands up! All the men who got money get your hands up!" With these words, men are encouraged to celebrate empowerment through wealth while women are encouraged to celebrate their attractiveness to men. Thus, as a girl with no hip hop dancing skills, Sara is doubly disadvantaged. The only way for women to obtain power in this setting is through dance, and ballet is of no use.

A few songs later Chenille is asked to dance by Kenny, the often-absent father of her child. 'Murder She Wrote', a dancehall/ragga song by Chaka Demus and Pliers, takes over the soundtrack and Sara watches her new friends dance sensually while leaning against the bar by herself. When Derek asks her to dance in a challenge to her previous boasting, she declines to avoid being exposed as incapable. But Derek insists, and Sara timidly attempts some steps until Derek takes over and starts to teach her. Although an accomplished ballet dancer, Sara can do nothing impressive in this context. The musical agency and dancing technique belong to her new friends, and she needs to embrace hip hop culture in order to flourish.

From this point in the film Sara moves away from her position on the margins of hip hop culture, and her cultural positioning becomes less fixed and more ambiguously signified. In a montage cut to 'You Know What's Up' by Donell Jones, Derek teaches Sara not only how to dance, but also how to express hip hop attitude in the way she walks, sits, and behaves in general. Although the cuts make the onscreen source of the music, Derek's radio, temporally impossible (thus positioning the cue as source scoring), one accepts that this is his music and that he is sharing his musical agency

Figure 5.1 Derek teaches Sara hip hop attitude.

with Sara. Though the music is Sara's gateway into hip hop culture, her transformation involves more than just a change in musical taste.

Soon after Derek's hip hop lesson, Sara listens to 'You' by Lucy Pearl featuring Snoop Dog and Q-Tip and talks on the phone to Lindsay, a friend from her old school. This is the first time she is shown listening to rap/R&B music on her own. Sara's conversation with Lindsay foregrounds some interesting issues regarding rap music and popular conceptions of inner-city violence. Rap music is often married to violence in the popular imagination and has been used as shorthand for gang violence in the media since the late 1980s. According to Norman K. Denzin (2002), "rap music and hip hop culture became signifiers of a new and violent racial order. In the minds of many, rap music meant racial violence. And this violence was spreading everywhere, threatening white America" (p. 171). This discourse of rap music and violence is deliberately evoked by some filmmakers through the cavalier employment of rap music and hip hop imagery in films.

In *Brothers Gonna Work It Out: Sexual Politics in the Golden Age of Rap Nationalism*, Charise L. Cheney (2005) describes the metamorphosis of gangsta rap's lyrical content from politically-charged narratives into decontextualised, co-opted rants:

> As a form of creative expression, gangsta rap spotlighted the socioeconomic conditions facing many young black men in urban America – black-on-black crime, drug trafficking, police harassment and brutality – at the same time that it tapped into fantasies that culturally resonated with many young heterosexual men regardless of race: rebelliousness, irreverence, fierce aggression, and the sexual

exploitation of women [...] However, what began as a playful celebration and/or dramatic critique of black life in America's inner cities quickly devolved into contemporary minstrelsy. The descriptive, anthropological narratives that characterized gangsta rap in the early years challenged misrepresentations of black men as pathological (violent, hypersexual, criminal) by providing a sociological context for understanding the psychology of some young black men living in postindustrial urban America.

(p. 6)

Cheney explains how widespread media and scholarly interest in gangsta rap have caused it to represent all rap music in the popular imagination. With the increased profitability of the genre, the bleak realities of inner-city life became detached from their socioeconomic context. As Cheney states, "the dialogic between reality and fantasy was reconfigured: gangsta rap was no longer oppositional as caricatures became the norm and stereotypes the rule" (p. 6). It is this oversimplified notion of rap that most often accompanies representations of African-American teenagers in youth films. Such restricted representations of hip hop culture, and of young African Americans in general, are largely the result of gang culture becoming a trendy topic in US cinema. According to Guthrie P. Ramsey (2003), early 1990s films such as *New Jack City*, *Boyz N the Hood*, *Strictly Business*, and *Juice* "have helped to create a highly recognizable hip-hop mode of representing a one-dimensional black youth culture" (p. 168). *Save the Last Dance* uses the vocabulary of these earlier films and triggers perceivers' memories of them to establish a simplistic atmosphere of young, urban, African-American violence.

Sara's phone conversation with Lindsay reflects the resulting stereotypes spread by such representations. When Sara tells Lindsay about Stepps, Lindsay asks, "Have you seen anybody get shot yet?" Sara replies, in a puzzled tone, "I didn't move to Bosnia." Lindsay goes on to say, "Jesus Sara, you're in the freakin' ghetto. Forget about the drivebys, how are you supposed to meet anybody?" After Sara tells Lindsay that she *did* meet someone, Lindsay asks, "They got white guys at your school?" Obviously, the thought of Sara dating a 'black guy' never crossed Lindsay's mind. All of Lindsay's racist assumptions and misunderstandings reflect back on the person one might assume Sara used to be. This scene shows that Sara, although never as naïve as Lindsay, has begun to acquire a new cultural perspective based on lived experience rather than one solely grounded in the racist pop-cultural stereotypes that inform Lindsay's world view. Sara has achieved this partially through the separation of negatively stereotyped images from rap music.

However, this gap between Lindsay's assumptions and Sara's reality is not as wide as Sara's attitude would suggest. While Sara did not witness a drive-by, she did have to flee Stepps after a brutal fight between Derek's

friend Malakai and another young African-American man who was deal-
ing drugs in the club. Furthermore, Malakai becomes both the target of
one drive-by and the agent of another later in the film. This violence somewhat contradicts attempts elsewhere in the film to separate hip hop culture
from stereotypes and place it in a 'real-life' context in which a white teenager finds hope. The fact that Malakai is played by Fredro Starr, a member
of the hardcore rap group Onyx, further connects his brutal actions to hip
hop culture. However, gun crime does exist in economically marginalised
urban areas. Sara's comment about moving to Bosnia thus reveals not
only a shift in cultural perspective but also a naïve ignorance of the harsh
realities that some young people face living in US cities.

Rap music's connotations of violence and masculine privilege are further emphasised in a scene where students are playing basketball. At the
start of the scene, the girls are playing basketball in gym class, and tensions
build between Sara and Nikki (Bianca Lawson), Derek's ex-girlfriend.
The rap song 'Simon Says' by Pharoahe Monch begins with a cut to the
boys playing basketball on an outdoor court. While the girls are playing
in the controlled, more domestic space of the school gymnasium, the boys
seem to be playing for fun on the concrete court. The song bridges cuts
back and forth between the outdoor court and the gym, even though
the source of the music, a radio, is clearly visible outside. The placement
of this song situates it as source scoring, since the music's visible source
makes its audibility in both locations impossible. Musical agency belongs
to the boys in this sequence due to the song's source, although the presence of the song in both locations connects and compares the two games.

The song starts with a cut to the boys' game. This choice, although
rationalised by the placement of the radio, emphasises the action and
street feel of the boys' game in comparison to the school-sanctioned girls'
game. Since the music continues over a cut to the girls and then back to
the boys, the aggressive rapping and simple bass line that calls the *Jaws*
(Steven Spielberg, 1975) theme to mind, combined with narrative action,
heighten the intensity in both locations. During the intercut scene of the
girls' game, Nikki shoves Sara, who then tackles Nikki onto a mat, and
the two proceed to exchange punches and slaps. The song continues over
a cut back to the boys' game as a car creeps up and the passengers open
fire, at which point the song drops out and is replaced by the sound of
gunshots. Malakai returns fire as all the other boys hit the ground, and as
the drive-by ends, a dire composed score fades in and emphasises the grav-
ity of Malakai's perilous lifestyle. Thus, the use of 'Simon Says' to score a
fight and a drive-by shooting, considering its source on the outdoor court,
draws on and reinforces ideas of black masculine violence in rap discourse.

As the only white character in this sequence of parallel violence connected to rap music, Sara's aggressive actions even become coded as black
and masculine. Behaviour that is uncharacteristic for Sara is presented as
natural when she is under the influence of inner city, African-American

teens. Since the musical agency belongs to the male students in this scene, it is their violence and its connection to rap music that codes Sara's behaviour. And while Malakai's main motivation for fighting is to gain respect, Sara and Nikki are apparently fighting over a boy – Derek. However, in the following scene, Nikki explains that Derek is not her only reason for hating Sara. She asserts that she is sick of white girls always taking whatever they want from the black community. This scene, as well as a later one in which Chenille tells Sara that Nikki was not completely out of line for resenting Sara's relationship with Derek, problematises race in a manner very uncommon in mainstream US youth films. While this film does not deal with contemporary African-American anger at past and present racism as unflinchingly as the explosive climax of Spike Lee's *Do the Right Thing* (1989),[5] it nonetheless makes more of an effort than most youth films to acknowledge the right for such anger to exist in the present. Sara is shocked by this anger and cannot understand why others are bothered by her relationship with Derek. Chenille's point is that Sara still does not understand her own privilege and the socioeconomic conditions of the people in her new community.

Since hip hop's origins were rooted in such conditions, parallels can be drawn between the content and culture of rap music and everyday life for black, inner-city youth. In *Black Noise: Rap Music and Black Culture in Contemporary America*, Tricia Rose (1994) states that "Rap music, more than any other contemporary form of black cultural expression, articulates the chasm between black urban lived experience and dominant, "legitimate" (e.g. neoliberal) ideologies regarding equal opportunity and racial inequality" (p. 102). Sara's implied upper middle class upbringing has given her tolerance and open-mindedness, but her view of society is still mediated by mainstream discourse via popular representations of hip hop culture and race relations. She does not understand why she is different from her African-American neighbours. Although Chenille later claims to have taken Nikki's side in the argument because she was angry with her baby's father, her initial point about Sara's lack of understanding of racial inequality is still valid. This is substantiated by the relative ease with which Sara 'escapes' the ghetto at the end of the film. Nikki's and Chenille's comments about Sara and Derek could be extended to include Sara's participation in hip hop culture and her eventual gain from it. In light of these considerations, even though rap music is coupled with violence in a few scenes, it is apparent that hip hop culture is not simply appropriated uncritically throughout the film.

Nevertheless, it is only Sara who ultimately benefits from hip hop. Although the other main characters enjoy dancing and listening to rap music in their everyday lives, Sara incorporates hip hop dance elements into her style to make her way into Juilliard. However, she does not simply co-opt hip hop music and dance. Sara immerses herself in the culture through listening to the music, dancing at Stepps, and dressing like her new friends. More than just a fetish, Sara's embrace of hip hop culture is a change in lifestyle. Derek takes an interest in Sara's love of dance, first with a surprise trip to the ballet and later by watching her ballet classes and encouraging her at the film's climactic Juilliard audition. But Derek has no desire to learn ballet. Furthermore, ballet is not as important of an element of Sara's social life as hip hop culture comes to be. Ballet is more like work, whereas hip hop is leisure and lifestyle that Sara uses to 'add flavour' to her 'serious' dance style.

Often naturalised in films, hip hop dancing is sometimes portrayed as a genetically inherited talent that all African Americans possess. This idea is related to an essentialism used to justify the argument that black music is 'of the body' while white music is 'of the mind'. Keith Negus (1996) asserts that this dichotomy is "based on the idea that black people are more 'natural', physical and spontaneous than white people, who in turn are more constrained by social conventions" (p. 102). However, hip hop dancing is presented in *Save the Last Dance* as an art form nearly equal to ballet in that it demands hard work for proficiency, although Sara's feet are only shown bleeding after ballet practice.

At the film's climax, after Sara performs a classical ballet dance at the Juilliard audition, she amazes the judges with the combination of hip hop moves and ballet in her 'contemporary' dance piece. The first half of the audition (classical ballet) is intercut with scenes of a drive-by shooting carried out by Malakai and his friends. Derek was asked to be involved in this retaliation for an earlier shooting but tries to convince Malakai not to take part. After Malakai ignores Derek's advice and drives off with his friends, Derek rushes to Sara's audition. The following sequence alternates between Sara dancing, Derek running and riding on a train, and Malakai shooting at his rivals. Dramatic score tightly follows each of the characters, with the consistent theme altering to establish mood: it connotes danger as Malakai shoots, apprehension as Derek runs, and hope as Sara dances. This sequence ends with Malakai and friends being arrested and/or taken away in an ambulance.

It is then time for Sara to perform her contemporary dance piece. The song Sara dances to, 'All or Nothing' by Athena Cage, is a mix of Western classical instrumentation, hip hop beats, and modern R&B vocals. After Sara falls on her first attempt, Derek runs into the auditorium and convinces her to try again when it seems she has lost all hope. She then performs the dance so flawlessly that one of the judges unofficially welcomes her to Juilliard. Of course, the dance is a metaphor for racial harmony more generally and for Sara's immersion into African-American hip hop culture more specifically. It is the mixing of racially coded dance moves that gets Sara into Juilliard. However, hip hop has the final word. In the last scene of the film and through part of the end credits, all of the main characters take turns dancing in the middle of the circle at Stepps.

Jade Boyd (2004) writes about agency and representation in *Save the Last Dance* with a focus on the role dancing plays in the film. She asserts that dancing is a means of agency, and that dance "has the ability to transform [the female body] from an object of repression, to a significant, beautiful and active subject" (p. 73). According to Boyd, this empowerment is where the allure of teen dance movies lies for many young women. However, she goes on to say that in this film any agency gained through dance is ultimately undermined during the Juilliard audition when Sara relies on Derek to convince her to try the dance again (p. 78). In addition, Boyd argues that the film's Juilliard climax simplistically and judgmentally juxtaposes blackness and whiteness as binaries, represented respectively by the drive-by shooting and ballet. For Boyd, the film (particularly the climax) commercialises hip hop culture and "transforms hip-hop dancing from an oppositional style [...] into an entertaining component of popular culture" (p. 78).

While I agree that Sara's need to be encouraged by Derek throughout the film does undermine her agency somewhat, I still feel that she empowers herself with hip hop music and dance to the extent that her agency cannot be dismissed so easily. Sara develops her hip hop skills from almost nothing at her first embarrassing dance attempt at Stepps to the level required to achieve her ultimate goal of getting into Juilliard. Regarding the film's commercialisation of hip hop culture, I believe that the forms of this culture included in the film became a profitable commodity many years ago. The idea that hip hop dancing is still an oppositional style is somewhat nostalgic. Although some forms may not have been co-opted as of yet, *Save the Last Dance* draws mainly on already commercial rap and dance styles to tell its story. Boyd's observation about the binarisation of race in the Juilliard/drive-by sequence is justified, however. This opposition is also clearly reflected in the different sections of composed score that accompany Malakai, Derek, and Sara before Sara's final dance.

With regard to Sara's use of hip hop culture, the film is respectful in that it calls her cultural borrowing to attention through her previously discussed fight with Derek's ex-girlfriend Nikki and subsequent conversation with Chenille about the problems with white women dating African-American men. Although Sara has used hip hop dancing and the musical agency she has gained through embracing rap and R&B to get into one of the most elite dance schools in the country, her new cultural perspective seems to have become a permanent part of her life. However, Sara's future is left up to speculation. While she will be attending Juilliard in New York City, Derek will be going to Georgetown University in Washington, DC. Their future together is not discussed in the film. In addition, will Sara continue going to hip hop clubs once she leaves Chicago? All of her ties to the black culture she has embraced may be severed when she goes.

Save the Last Dance is a film about a girl coming to terms with the death of her mother. It is a film about a white girl moving into a

Figure 5.2 Sara dances under the "L" track.

predominantly African-American neighbourhood and high school and embracing hip hop dance culture. It is also a film about an interracial relationship. But in addition, this is a film about a (white) girl who overcomes tremendous adversity (such as having to practice under an elevated railroad track with homeless people and garbage can fires) and escapes from the ghetto by dancing her way into Juilliard. The last summary may sound flippant and cynical, and yet the film conveys all of this. Sara triumphs to become the privileged, white, middle-class girl that she was all along.

My point is not to belittle the effort of the filmmakers to create what is one of the few mainstream youth films to present a considered analysis of racial relations without simply insisting on racial harmony or hopelessness. In addition, Sara has a great deal of musical agency in this film; she uses ballet and hip hop to achieve her goals. I wish to emphasise, however, that much like the politics of hip hop culture, the film's storyline and use of music include many contradictory messages regarding race, gender, and agency. On the one hand, Sara is forced to think about her white privilege in a way that she never did before. In the process, she immerses herself in hip hop culture and becomes close friends with African-American students, gaining first-hand experience rather than simply accepting highly mediated representations of African Americans. On the other hand, rap music is linked with violence on several occasions throughout the film, and Malakai's presence seems like an almost obligatory insertion of gang violence to satisfy film audience expectations. Surely there are ways of conveying hardships faced by black urban youth without falling back on gang violence, especially when it becomes juxtaposed with the 'pureness' and 'innocence' of a white ballerina. While *Save the Last Dance* may perpetuate some of the stereotypes it simultaneously fights against, it does present cultural borrowing in a critical manner, forcing perceivers of the film – a great many of whom are no doubt white and middle class – to think about modern race relations.

Notes

1 The idea of such a continuum is obviously problematic, and by using this term I am not suggesting that whites who engage with black culture have access to all of the richness and diversity this category takes in, nor am I arguing that they take on all of the historical and present discrimination that African Americans must face in their daily lives. Rather, I am suggesting that by adopting a certain fashion sense and consuming certain types of music, one can adjust the more fluid connotations of race, which are by no means essential, but instead linked to race through culture.

2 Examples include *Boyz N the Hood* (John Singleton, 1991), *New Jack City* (Mario Van Peebles, 1991), *Straight Out of Brooklyn* (Matty Rich, 1991), *Juice* (Ernest Dickerson, 1992), and *Menace II Society* (The Hughes Brothers, 1993).

3 Ron Jeremy is a famous American pornographic film actor.

4 *Dawson's Creek* (1998–2003) was a popular US teen TV drama with a predominantly white cast and a theme song ('I Don't Want to Wait' by Paula Cole) that had the same 'yearning' quality in the vocals.

5 After Radio Raheem (Bill Nunn), an African-American man from the neighbourhood, is killed by white police officers, Mookie (Spike Lee) throws a trash can through the window of the Italian-American owned pizzeria where he works, which sparks a riot that results in the burning down of the shop. This turn against his white employer with whom he was previously friendly due to his anger over the racist violence of the police has been a point of heavy debate, especially because the director's character sparked the riot. For an in-depth discussion of this debate see Willis (1997, pp. 163–167).

References

Boyd, Jade (2004) 'Dance, Culture, and Popular Film: Considering Representations in *Save the Last Dance*' in *Feminist Media Studies*, Vol. 4, No. 1, pp. 67–83.

Cheney, Charise L. (2005) *Brothers Gonna Work It Out: Sexual Politics in the Golden Age of Rap Nationalism*, New York: New York University Press.

Denzin, Norman K. (2002) *Reading Race: Hollywood and the Cinema of Racial Violence*, London: Sage.

Kassabian, Anahid (2001) *Hearing Film: Tracking Identifications in Contemporary Hollywood Film Music*, New York: Routledge.

Negus, Keith (1996) *Popular Music in Theory: An Introduction*, Cambridge, UK: Polity Press.

Ramsey, Guthrie P. (2003) *Race Music: Black Cultures from Bebop to Hip-Hop*, Berkeley, CA: University of California Press.

Rose, Tricia (1994) *Black Noise: Rap Music and Black Culture in Contemporary America*, Middletown, CT: Wesleyan University Press.

Willis, Sharon (1997) *High Contrast: race and gender in contemporary Hollywood film*, Durham: Duke University Press.

Filmography

Boyz N the Hood (1991, USA) directed by John Singleton, music by Stanley Clarke, music supervision by Raoul Roach, Columbia Pictures

Do the Right Thing (1989, USA) directed by Spike Lee, music by Bill Lee, Universal Studios Home Entertainment.

Ghost World (2001, USA) directed by Terry Zwigoff, music by David Kitay, music supervision by Melissa Axelrod and Christine Bergren, Icon Home Entertainment.

Jaws (1975, USA) directed by Steven Spielberg, music by John Williams, Universal Pictures.

Juice (1992, USA) directed by Ernest Dickerson, music by The Bomb Squad and Hank Shocklee, music supervision by Kathy Nelson, Paramount.

Menace II Society (1993, USA) directed by Albert and Allen Hughes (as The Hughes Brothers), music by Quincy Jones III, music supervision by Bonnie Greenberg and Jill Meyers, New Line Cinema.

New Jack City (1991, USA) directed by Mario Van Peebles, music by Vassal Benford and Michel Colombier, music supervision by George Jackson and Doug McHenry, Warner Bros.

Save the Last Dance (2001, USA) directed by Thomas Carter, music by Mark Isham, music supervision by Michael McQuarn, Paramount Home Video.

Straight Out of Brooklyn (1991, USA) directed by Matty Rich, music by Harold Wheeler, music supervision by Arthur Baker, The Samuel Goldwyn Company.

6 Cheerleaders, Bullies, and Nerds

Intersections of White
Stereotypes and Black Music
in *Bring It On*, *Mean Creek*,
and *Napoleon Dynamite*

As discussed in the previous two chapters, Enid and Sara engage with black music in very different ways in *Ghost World* and *Save the Last Dance*. While Sara immerses herself in contemporary hip hop culture, Enid becomes infatuated with a single archaic song as one step in her search for authenticity and meaning. Thus, Enid's engagement is much more distanced and shallow than Sara's. In this final chapter of Part II, I will be considering three films that show how certain teen film stereotypes – specifically the cheerleader, the bully, and the nerd – construct whiteness in relation to black culture. *Bring It On* (Peyton Reed, 2000), *Mean Creek* (Jacob Aaron Estes, 2004), and *Napoleon Dynamite* (Jared Hess, 2004) all contain interesting examples of white teens using black music to increase their narrative agency and enrich their identities. Through their use of variations on stereotypical white stock characters, these three films show how interracial cultural borrowing (or sometimes theft) alters particular types of whiteness. Furthermore, the way that each character engages with black music and the resulting changes to agency and identity construction provide further evidence of the instability of some aspects of racial identity.

In *Bring It On*, Torrance Shipman (Kirsten Dunst) is appointed captain of her mostly white (with one Asian American) cheerleading squad, The Rancho Carne High School Toros, when the previous captain known as 'Big Red' (Lindsay Sloane) graduates from high school. Torrance is shocked, however, when new cheerleader Missy Pantone (Eliza Dusku) takes her to an inner city school to show her the true origin of the squad's routines. It turns out that Big Red had been stealing routines from the East Compton Clovers, a primarily African-American and Latina/o cheerleading squad, and passing them off as her own creations. Throughout the rest of the film, Torrance and the other cheerleaders must struggle with the decision of whether to continue using the stolen routines to get to the national championships or try to learn all new routines and risk being unprepared.

The song used for both the Toros' and Clovers' versions of the routine is 'The 900 Number' (1987) by the 45 King (DJ Mark James), a hip hop song based around a highly distinctive saxophone sample. This sample originally comes from the intro to the soul classic 'Unwind Yourself' (1969) by Marva Whitney (backed by James Brown's backing band, the JBs). Furthermore, DJ Chad Jackson's 'Hear the Drummer (Get Wicked)' (1990) and DJ Kool's 'Let Me Clear My Throat' (1996) both re-sampled this same saxophone riff from 'The 900 Number'. As a piece of music that has been sampled (and profited from) several times over, this is an appropriate accompaniment to the stolen routine, whether the filmmakers were aware of its history or not. Of course, the practice of sampling is not considered theft by those who make, listen to, and study hip hop. Tricia Rose (1994) argues that:

> sampling, not unlike versioning practices in Caribbean musics, is about paying homage, an invocation of another's voice to help you to say what you want to say. It is also a means of archival research, a process of musical and cultural archaeology.
>
> (p. 79)

Thus, sampling involves a certain level of reverence. This practice of paying tribute and giving new life to a piece of music lies in complete opposition to the outright theft of the Clovers' routine. With knowledge of this particular sample's past, the musical choice casts a judgemental eye on the thieving Toros.

Even though Torrance is outraged when she finds out about the stolen routine, she goes along with the squad's decision to continue performing it because they do not have enough time to learn a new routine before the regional championships. The squad quickly change their tune, however, after the Clover cheerleaders show up at a Toros football game and mirror the squad's cheers from the stands. The embarrassment of this event leads the Toros to learn new routines for the championships, but the bitter rivalry that results from the theft follows both squads into the regional and national championships. Torrance tries to make up for the indiscretion by convincing her wealthy father to donate the money that the Clovers need to go to the national championships but cannot raise themselves. Isis (Gabrielle Union), captain of the Clovers' squad, refuses the money from Torrance, but the squad eventually convince a talk-show host (clearly based on Oprah Winfrey) to provide the necessary funds. The Clovers eventually go on to win the nationals, and towards the end of the film, a mutual respect develops between Torrance and Isis.

This finale is clearly a way of siding with the initially wronged Clovers, and there are no hard feelings between the two cheerleading squads in the end. In *Bring It On*, the fact that white characters have increased their agency through the theft of black music (and cheer routines) is made explicit, and the Toros' initial decision to continue using the stolen routines shows a clear exploitation of white privilege. Regardless of the eventual bonding between Torrance and Isis, Torrance and the rest of the cheerleaders in her squad never engage with black music or culture on any level other than the cheerleading routine. This superficial borrowing does not alter Torrance's identity in any way. In fact, Torrance is the only major character in the film for whom no indication of musical taste is given. Musical taste is clearly suggested for both of Torrance's love interests; Aaron (Richard Hillman), her older boyfriend who is now in college, has Matchbox 20, Sugar Ray, and Hootie and the Blowfish posters clearly displayed on his dorm room wall, and Cliff (Jesse Bradford), Missy's brother who later becomes Torrance's boyfriend, wears a Clash t-shirt and has various punk and proto-punk bands' posters on his bedroom wall, including Iggy Pop and Sid and Nancy. While Missy's posters are somewhat blurry in her bedroom, there is a Sleater Kinney poster visible (although the writing on the poster is not), which suggests a feminist, punky character. In comparison to these characters, Torrance is a blank slate, musically speaking. Pale, blonde, perky, and the head cheerleader, she embodies the stereotype of the popular, white teenage girl; her identity is not developed further by interests outside of cheerleading. The film's tone oscillates between ironic and sincere to knowingly send up cheerleading while still presenting racial inequality in a more serious light. Despite the film's message regarding white privilege and cultural theft, all of the Clovers cheerleaders remain minor, undeveloped characters.

In *Mean Creek*, a group of boys and a girl unintentionally kill a bully after a revenge prank goes too far. As the film begins, George Tooney (Josh Peck) is shown playing basketball by himself from the point of view of his camcorder. Sam Merric (Rory Culkin) then appears in front of the camcorder and picks it up to inspect it. Within a few seconds, George yells, runs over to the camcorder, and tackles Sam. He continues to beat Sam up and threatens to kill him if he ever touches his camera again. This violent reaction results in Sam's brother Rocky (Trevor Morgan) planning a prank to teach George a lesson. Rocky invites George on a boating trip to celebrate Sam's birthday with the intent of stripping George, throwing him into the river, and making him run home naked. The plan drastically backfires, however, after George antagonises one of the older boys who then knocks him into the river – where he drowns.

George is an overweight, crass bully with an explosive temper who likes to document his life and surroundings with his camcorder. His more creative, cerebral side is only shown twice in the film through a video he makes while waiting for the others to pick him up for the boat trip. Just before a scene in George's bedroom, the older boys pick up Sam and Millie (Carly Schroeder). At this point, a hardcore/punk song called 'On Edge' by Ethan Gold is playing in the car. The song ends with a cut to George fixing his hair in the mirror. He then picks up the camcorder from his bedroom floor and starts to film. 'Fear Not of Man' by Mos Def (1999) plays throughout this scene, following George around the first floor of his house with corresponding drops in volume, which suggest that the source of the song is in his bedroom. He first films his reflection in a mirror while viewing himself on his television. After stating, "My name is George," he points the camcorder towards the television and produces a black-and-white swirling effect, saying, "This is the inside of my mind." The shot then shifts to George's point of view via the camcorder as he films his mother exercising, the street that he lives on, and the surrounding countryside. George stops filming after the car pulls up outside, and with a shift to a passenger's point of view the music changes to 'The Sound of Settling' by Death Cab for Cutie, which plays on the car stereo.

On the surface, and for those unfamiliar with the often political lyrics of Mos Def, 'Fear Not of Man' sounds like a fairly average rap song. The rapping is laid-back and the music is melodic with a jaunty groove. This is not the type of rap often used to signify violence in films. Rather, George could be using this song to convey a relaxed-yet-assertive coolness as he prepares for the boat trip. The lyrics, such as "Fear not of men because men must die/Mind over matter and soul before flesh" and "The world is overrun with the wealthy and the wicked/But God is sufficient in disposin' of affairs," suggest a depth and spirituality usually hidden in his social interactions. Initially, George's use of the song gives the impression that he wants to feel cool and impress the older boys on the boating trip. But it also separates him further from the film's other main characters. George's musical taste is juxtaposed by the two songs on either side of it ('On Edge' and 'The Sound of Settling'). The other boys only really listen to what could broadly be termed 'alternative rock' throughout the film.

George is heavy-set, dresses in baggy clothes (in this scene he is wearing a bright orange shirt and camouflage cargo pants), wears a gold chain, and seems to come from a wealthier family than the others do. In addition to his camcorder, George's room contains a guitar, a snowboard, a skateboard, a computer, and a flat-screen television. The other characters all seem to come from a more working-class background – they live in smaller houses and in one case a trailer, and they dress in more basic jeans and t-shirts. George's awkward social interactions tend towards corny jokes, bizarre philosophy/fantasy, and downright offensive and aggressive behaviour. In this context, 'Fear Not of Man' helps construct George as an 'Other', albeit not racially. He may be wealthier than the rest of the main characters, but he is also an outcast. George's only true friend seems to be his camcorder. He may be using 'Fear Not of Man' in this scene to 'pump himself up' for the boat trip and to make himself feel cool, but the song takes on new meaning, particularly lyrically, when another part of his video is shown at the end of the film.

When the police are led to George's buried body, they also find his camcorder, which still contains the tape on which he filmed the bedroom scene. The video starts the same way as before, but this time George sets the camera down, sits on an inflatable plastic chair, and says "the inside of my mind has a zillion things about it...but...the people that don't see inside my mind don't know there are a zillion things." He goes on to say, "One day people will know, because that's my master plan." Documenting his life on film and burying the tape in a time capsule, he reveals, is his plan. This way, in the future, "some atlien[1] or highly evolved species will find it and understand." George's 'plan' straddles the line between creativity and delusion, but this hitherto unseen section of the tape gives more emphasis to the song's grand lyrics and is reinforced by them. He obviously feels that this song reflects the spirit he has inside him, as well as commenting on some life beyond his own. Statements George makes to the others about his dyslexia earlier in the film are followed by a similar self-comparison to superior extraterrestrial beings. It would seem that George feels some empathy – however misguided – with the past and present struggles faced by African Americans and identifies with the knowing intellect suggested by Mos Def's lyrics.

The filmmakers do not place as much weight on this song as George did, though. As he says the words "a zillion things about it" in the section of the tape shown at the end of the film, the music changes from 'Fear Not of Man' to original dramatic score. Strings take over and bridge the cut from George's tape to a police boat on the water during the search for his body, though George's words do carry on over the next scene of the police digging in the forest where he was buried earlier in the film. Finally, the film ends with a return to George on tape, still accompanied by the original score rather than the source music. The screen goes black when he turns off his camcorder and the soundtrack goes silent. The simple, minor key score of strings and piano replaces George's self-righteous fantasy with a tragic, sentimental tone that brings the perceiver back to the narrative, where George is very much dead. Thus, his monologue takes on a sad and somewhat pathetic quality where it was once optimistic and hopeful. This musical stripping of George's agency parallels the narrative theft of his life in the prime of his youth. Although the film does not engage with racial discourse in any way, George obviously finds value in the song, and likewise the song adds depth and dignity to the oddball, outcast bully that everyone else knows George to be.

In *Napoleon Dynamite*, Napoleon (Jon Heder) and his brother Kip (Aaron Ruell) use black music and culture in a seemingly uncritical manner, but the film does engage with racial discourse by other means. This story takes place in Idaho, where Napoleon and Kip live with their grandmother; the film is populated by exaggerated characters who embody stereotypes for comic effect. Sarcastic, deadpan performances clash with obnoxious, overzealous ones in a manner that nearly overshadows normal narrative concerns. The two bespectacled brothers are dry, difficult, and awkward. Napoleon is tall yet slouchy with curly hair, and Kip is short and stiff with a moustache. Neither is particularly adept at socialisation of any kind.

Napoleon's engagement with black music begins when he discovers a video cassette entitled *D-Qwon's Dance Grooves* in a thrift store. The cover of the video – which includes an invitation to "Get Your Groove On" – features a young African-American man with a flat-top haircut wearing a microphone headset and giving a 'thumbs up'. Later, Napoleon is shown inserting the tape into his VCR. With a cut to a sliver of Napoleon's slouched body visible behind his slightly open bedroom door, some very lo-fi, funky, electronic dance music begins to play from the videocassette. The music has a cheap keyboard aesthetic, similar to the original score throughout the rest of the film. Although the sound quality is the same, certain elements are changed to signify genre. A deep voice then announces, "Welcome to D-Qwon's Dance Grooves! Are you ready to get your groove on?" Napoleon replies with a deadpan "Yes." There is an obvious, intentionally comical juxtaposition in this scene, as well as other scenes I will discuss shortly, between Napoleon's nerdy whiteness and the Otherness of black music/culture. The comedy of this scene relies on ideas of 'coolness' present in discourse surrounding black music and dance, and their perceived opposition to the socially inept white nerd. In addition, the gender connotations of this contradiction are driven home by the unicorn poster on his bedroom wall and by a "Pegasus Crossing" sign (complete with a drawing of the mythical winged horse) on his bedroom door. Napoleon's whiteness is infused with nerdiness and femininity that contradict the black masculinity suggested by the music and the deep voice of 'D-Qwon'.

Later, Napoleon is given music by the film's only significant black character, Kip's girlfriend Lafawnda (Shondrella Avery), whom Kip met on the internet. Lafawnda meets a sweat-soaked Napoleon, who has been practicing dancing, in the kitchen of his house. Although she is a woman, Lafawnda's masculinity is accentuated by her clothing, close-ups of her large feet, and her towering size relative to Kip. This seems intentional to the point of making the perceiver question at times whether she may actually be a trans woman. Lafawnda is also cartoonishly sexual, especially in comparison to Napoleon and Kip. When Lafawnda and Napoleon meet, she asks him why he is so sweaty, and he tells her that he has been practicing. Her suggestive reply is "Mmmm...practicing what?" After Napoleon tells her that he was dancing, she asks in a sceptical tone, "You like dancing?", and then chuckles and gives a surprised and slightly impressed smile. Her disbelief that Napoleon could be interested in dancing follows the binary racial assumptions that the film exaggerates. Kip then enters the kitchen, dressed from head to toe in hip hop clothing. Up to this point in the film, Kip has been wearing polo shirts buttoned all the way to the top and glasses, which he no longer wears. Lafawnda then pulls an audio cassette from her purse and throws it to Napoleon, saying, "Here, you might like that. My cousin made it."

Once again, Napoleon is shown through a slightly open bedroom door, but this time he is dancing to funky, electronic dance music, presumably from the tape given to him by Lafawnda. At first her character seems to exist solely as a joke, but then again, every single character in the film is an exaggerated stereotype. In Lafawnda's case, her excessive sexuality and masculinity create an awkward tension with Kip and Napoleon's nerdish, feminine whiteness. Both Kip and Napoleon are somehow liberated by her presence, though. Kip finds true love and self-confidence, and Napoleon gains musical agency, mainly through dance. David Buchbinder (2008) claims that the film problematises normative masculinity in the following way:

> While Kip achieves a certain masculinity in this new-found relationship by adopting the clothes, gestures and attitude of a black man, his very whiteness undermines the machismo he affects. At the same time, however, that impersonation of the masculinity of the black other also demonstrates the performativity of gender itself. Napoleon, by contrast, in continuing to assert his awkwardness and lack of social grace, refuses the imperatives of the gender system that he conform to a particular model of masculinity if he is to succeed: his modest notion of success is measured by different indicators.
>
> (p. 237)

As Buchbinder also points out, there are several characters in the film who represent white masculinity (basically in the form of 'jocks'), but they, too, are exaggerated stereotypes. Kip finds love before he performs black masculinity, and Napoleon finds success in a final dance scene that, however unrealistically, undermines the importance of masculinity by winning over his entire high school through alliances with his

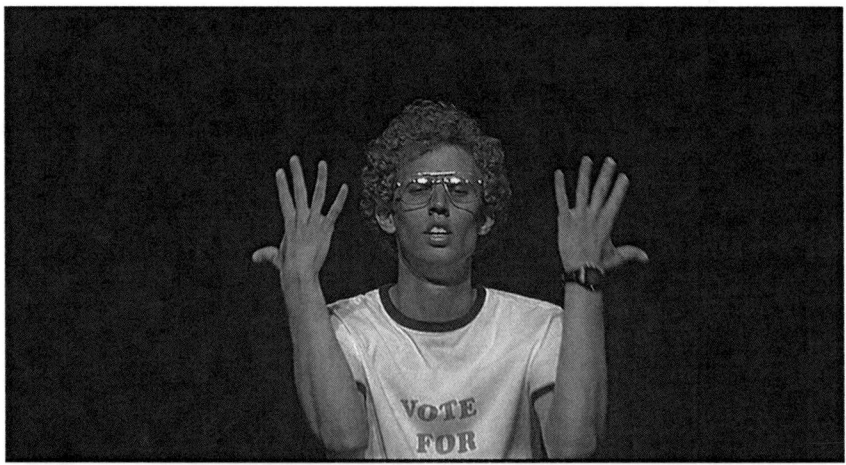

Figure 6.1 Napoleon shows off his moves in front of the students.

Mexican-American friend Pedro (Efren Ramirez) and Lafawnda, from whom he receives musical agency.

Napoleon's final triumph occurs after Pedro gives a disheartened speech to an auditorium full of students while campaigning to become class president. Unaware that he needed to prepare a skit to perform after his speech, Pedro has given up all hope of being elected. Sensing that he must act quickly, Napoleon delivers his audio cassette, still presumably the tape from Lafawnda, to the student controlling the auditorium's sound system, and takes to the stage. What follows is a dance Napoleon performs to the disco-funk of 'Canned Heat' by Jamiroquai. Although this dance is well choreographed and impressively executed, there is nothing hip about it. While Napoleon's moves are fluid, his performance is still, as Buchbinder states about Kip's display of black masculinity, undermined by his particular (and peculiar) whiteness. This makes the musical choice for the dance sequence all the more inspired. The singer and principal songwriter of Jamiroquai, Jason Kay (stage name: Jay Kay), is a white man born in Stretford, Lancashire, England. The two aspects of his performing style that stand out the most are his dancing ability and the fact that he sings just like Stevie Wonder. Thus, his use of black music parallels that of Napoleon in some ways.

When 'Canned Heat' cuts off abruptly, Napoleon slouches and walks off stage. His performance is followed, however, by a standing ovation from the student body. Regardless of its lack of authenticity, everyone loves his performance, and it serves to win the favour of his almost-girlfriend Deb (Tina Majorino) once and for all. Napoleon uses black music for agency, but he does so almost as an afterthought. His actions are presented as random, yet he commits fully to them. Napoleon achieves popularity without a modicum of enthusiasm. Even though he exists in an unrealistic world (not that any film portrayal of high school could be accurately described as realistic), Napoleon's musical agency is nevertheless brought about using a common strategy – borrowing coolness from black popular culture.

However, Stan Link (2008) claims that Napoleon's use of black culture is not as straightforward as that of non-nerd characters. Building on Mary Buchholtz's research into high school nerds, Link asserts that the nerd's appropriation of black culture is a critique of the ways that mainstream white characters use black culture to achieve coolness. This is because nerds normally "*eschew* the cultural assimilation of blackness into white culture as they decline their own social assimilation into their primarily white peer group" (no page). Link declares that Napoleon's skillful adoption of black dance moves only serves to highlight his whiteness even more. He goes on to say the following about the racial implications of the dance:

> The disparity between Napoleon's identity and that of his performance becomes a kind of choreographic blackface in which the whiteness of the mask's wearer is never totally hidden—peering out

around the edges to frame the mask itself. But Napoleon does not wear the mask as much as it wears him. On stage, Napoleon choreographs a theory of racial identity, which says that identity itself is at least partially a *performance*. The hyper-whiteness of Napoleon's dance lies in its use of blackness NOT to assimilate him into a mainstream whiteness, but rather to expose his own whiteness and hold it out for objective scrutiny.

(no page)

Thus, Link's argument is very similar to Buchbinder's – both emphasise the performativity of racially coded masculinity. But where Buchbinder sees a specifically white masculinity in some of the film's other high school students, Link suggests that white masculine coolness is based on the adoption of black mannerisms and culture. For both Link and Buchbinder, however, nerds actively resist normative masculinity, and the racial implications of this add a new layer of meaning to the appropriation of black culture that does not exist with non-nerd characters. Napoleon's dance is at once too accomplished to be ironic and yet too overshadowed by his particular nerdy whiteness to be perceived as an authentic performance of black culture. Overall, this film illuminates stereotypical elements of identity attached to race by presenting an excessive whiteness in Napoleon (emphasised by his use of black music and dance) and Kip, an excessive blackness in Lafawnda, and even an excessive Mexicanness in Pedro (who always appears to be sleepy and sometimes sweaty with no explanation). The film uses these crass stereotypes for humour, but in so doing, it forces the perceiver to think about their own assumptions and prejudices.

In *Black Magic*, Krin Gabbard (2004) uses the following paragraph to explain the book's underlying argument:

Because white culture has assigned black culture a central role in its own self-definition while simultaneously marginalizing or erasing black people, the films that perpetuate this project must often resort to what I have called magic. I use this term literally to describe a group of films in which African American actors play angels who improve the lives of whites; I use this term metaphorically to describe the enchanting effect that black music, black sexuality, and other aspects of African American culture have on movie characters, more often than not when the characters on screen are white.

(p. 6)

Throughout Part II, I have discussed examples that mostly relate to Gabbard's metaphorical meaning of magic, and yet many characters in these films could be thought of as angels. In some cases, these are characters in the traditional sense. Chenille and Derek both take Sara under their metaphorical wings in *Save the Last Dance*. While Chenille teaches Sara how not to dress 'country', Derek encourages her to start dancing again, teaches her to dance and behave with hip hop style, and encourages her to try again after she falls at the Juilliard audition. In *Napoleon Dynamite*, Lafawnda provides a sort of salvation for both Napoleon and Kip – through love and a makeover in Kip's case, and through provision of music and thus agency with Napoleon.

Some of the films considered in Part II contain songs by artists who are very much present as ethereal beings. In *Ghost World*, Skip James is brought into the narrative through Enid's repeated playing of 'Devil Got My Woman', and his name is mentioned when Enid and Seymour discuss the song. In fact, when she first hears the song, Enid is so enthralled that she looks as if she has seen a ghost. It is James who changes Enid's life dramatically, providing her with the closest thing she finds to an authentic musical experience, albeit one that ultimately rings hollow. Mos Def, although never actually mentioned in *Mean Creek*, is present through his words and music at two crucial points in the film. In the first instance, he merely provides George with strength and a sense of self-worth. However, at the end of the film his words speak for George from beyond the grave. Even though the song is cut off by original dramatic score this time, the part that is heard and the lyrics from the song's first occurrence lend a spiritual, eternal, and righteous dimension to George's dead body.

As I hope to have illustrated throughout Part II, black music is an important resource for white teenagers, both in film and in the real world. They use it to feel cool, to add 'spice' to their lives, as a vehicle for dance, and to gain some sort of spirituality, authenticity, or history – that is, to feel more real, more human, more whole. It is hard to think of examples where the binary opposite occurs, where African-American teens use white music for agency or to add meaning to their lives. How would this music be coded as white and what would the characters gain from this? One reason for the absence of such representations could be that the most popular of contemporary popular music, especially that which is made in the US, is more often than not based on some historically black form – such is the case with R&B, rap, soul, and rock 'n' roll. Some types of music that could be used to connote whiteness are Western 'classical' or 'art' music, indie rock, country music, punk, or even polka. But it is also true that genres largely considered white, such as indie rock or punk – though both come from African-American roots via blues music to some extent, are listened to by many black teens, yet few if any such characters are represented in US youth films.

Although their ultimate fates differ significantly, all of the characters in the films discussed in Part II benefit from black music in some way. In *Save the Last Dance*, Sara uses hip hop dancing to get into Juilliard, but her mixed-genre contemporary dance piece is far removed from the dancing that goes on in the club. Her experience with hip hop is beneficial only insofar as it gets her into Juilliard. It is unlikely that she will use many of the hip hop moves professionally. However, she does undergo a cultural transformation, at least for the duration of the film, and she learns a significant amount about the racial inequality that still exists today. Enid, on the other hand, finds something special in 'Devil Got My Woman', but ultimately uses it to move beyond her post-high school stasis, regardless of where she ends up. The Toros in *Bring It On* use black music dishonestly, if unknowingly, and only choose to do the right thing after they are humiliated by the Clovers. George gains a sense of self-worth from 'Fear Not of Man' in *Mean Creek*, and the song speaks for him after his death. Dying is not exactly a victory for George, but he is shown to have a deeper understanding of the music he listens to, and it does return the favour by expressing his feelings posthumously. Napoleon seems to benefit the most effortlessly from his use of black music and dance. As Link points out, he proudly asserts his nerdishness through his performance. Although Link reads Napoleon's appropriation of music and dance as a critique of both white masculinity and uncritical cultural borrowing, there is no evidence in the film to suggest that Napoleon reflects on this borrowing in a critical manner.

All of these characters use black music in different ways with different results. However, they each experience some increase in agency that would have been difficult to depict without the music. Those who use the music because of its cultural connotations of authenticity and masculinity only find temporary satisfaction in doing so – this is definitely the case with Enid, and possibly would have been with George had he survived. Sara seems to benefit more because she immerses herself in, or perhaps must become immersed in, hip hop culture. Similarly, Napoleon works hard to learn the dance moves, even if the racial implications are not made an issue beyond Kip's African-American girlfriend. All of the films I have discussed in Part II highlight the constructed nature of racial discourse by focusing on the connotations of black music for which many white people (and others) seek it out. Of course, this leads to the realisation that the terms 'black music' and 'white people' are equally loaded. But, to return to bell hooks' (1992) argument, which I discussed in the Introduction to Part II, the desire involved in the process of cultural borrowing, of 'listening to the Other' as well as 'hearing the Other', can be productive and progressive as long as what one searches for in this experience is not reduced to some essentialised form of blackness.

Note

1 The fact that George clearly says "atlien" may be a reference to the 1996 album *ATLiens* by Atlanta, Georgia rappers Outkast – further emphasising his interest in rap.

References

Buchbinder, David (2008) 'Enter the Schlemiel: The Emergence of Inadequate or Incompetent Masculinities in Recent Film and Television' in *Canadian Review of American Studies*, Vol. 38, No. 2, pp. 227–245.

Gabbard, Krin (2004) *Black Magic: White Hollywood and African American Culture*, New Brunswick, NJ: Rutgers University Press.

hooks, bell (1992) 'Eating the Other: Desire and Resistance' in *Black Looks: Race and Representation*, Boston, MA: South End Press.

Link, Stan (2008) 'Musical Misfits and Dancing Dorks: Nerds and the Musical Visibility of Whiteness', Keynote speech given at 17th Annual Screen Conference, Glasgow, Scotland, 4–6 July 2008.

Rose, Tricia (1994) *Black Noise: Rap Music and Black Culture in Contemporary America*, Middletown, CT: Wesleyan University Press.

Filmography

Bring It On (2000, USA) directed by Peyton Reed, music by Christophe Beck, music supervision by Billy Gottlieb, Universal Home Entertainment.

Ghost World (2001, USA) directed by Terry Zwigoff, music by David Kitay, music supervision by Melissa Axelrod and Christine Bergren, Icon Home Entertainment.

Mean Creek (2004, USA) directed by Jacob Aaron Estes, music by tomandandy, music supervision by Robin Urdang, Palisades Tartan.

Napoleon Dynamite (2004, USA) directed by Jared Hess, music by John Swihart, music consultancy by Tracy Lynch-Sanchez, Paramount Pictures.

Save the Last Dance (2001, USA) directed by Thomas Carter, music by Mark Isham, music supervision by Michael McQuarn, Paramount Home Video.

Part III

Unheard Ethnicities

Musical Construction of Ethnic Identity and Agency

Introduction

In Part III of this book I analyse the musical construction of ethnic identity with an intersectional approach, considering how music can suggest and reinforce difference within ethnic categories, as well as the influence it has on agency. The films I consider in Part III are *Real Women Have Curves* (Patricia Cardoso, 2002), *Quinceañera* (*Echo Park, LA* – alternate title, Richard Glatzer and Wash Westmoreland, 2006), and *Better Luck Tomorrow* (Justin Lin, 2002). All three films are set in southern California – the first two in Los Angeles and the third in Orange County. In my analyses of the first two films, I discuss the role of music in the construction of Latino/a ethnicity, with a particular focus on the relationships between ethnicity, gender, sexuality, and class. *Real Women Have Curves* and *Quinceañera* both feature working-class Latina protagonists, although *Quinceañera* also has an important gay teenage Latino character whose identity construction is central to the film's narrative. Finally, I will consider *Better Luck Tomorrow*, a film with East Asian-American[1] male protagonists and main characters. This film is interesting for the way it self-consciously manipulates audience ideas about Asian-American ethnicity and the teen film genre while using music without typical connotations of Other ethnicity to construct ethnic identity.

In *Unthinking Eurocentrism: Multiculturalism and the Media*, Ella Shohat and Robert Stam (1994) state that "Hollywood's geographical and historiographical constructs have a visceral impact" for US citizens due to their shared history of immigration (p. 221). They go on to say the following about Hollywood's inclusion and exclusion of countries in its re-construction of this history:

> [...] since immigration is at the core of this official master-narrative, the sympathetic portrayal of certain lands of origin and the caricaturing of others has indirectly legitimated links to Europe while undermining links to Asia, Africa, and Latin America. In this sense, Hollywood has imagined a monocultural history for a multicultural America (and for a multicultural world).
>
> (p. 221)

Immigrants from Latin America and East Asia are thus among those who have fallen into the category of cultures to be ridiculed in Hollywood cinema. Luckily, the influence of various parallel civil rights movements (e.g., the African-American, Mexican-American, and Asian-American Civil Rights Movements, particularly in the 1960s and 1970s) and the increasing presence of Latinos and Asian Americans in major roles in film production have resulted in the making of films portraying much more varied forms of ethnic identity.[2] To understand the historical context of these films, however, it is necessary first to consider the history of narrow ethnic representations in Hollywood cinema.

I begin with a discussion of literature on representation and stereotype of Latinos in Hollywood cinema. Asian-American representation is considered in Chapter 9. As with the treatment of any group other than straight, white, middle class, Anglo-Saxon men, Hollywood has historically been unkind to Latin Americans. Charles Ramírez Berg (2002) summarises the stereotypes of this diverse group in the following way:

> The history of Latino images in U.S. cinema is in large measure a pageant of six basic stereotypes: *el bandido*, the harlot, the male buffoon, the female clown, the Latin lover, and the dark lady. Sometimes the stereotypes were combined, sometimes they were altered superficially, but their core defining—and demeaning—characteristics have remained consistent for more than a century and are still evident today.
> (p. 66)

Though residues of these stereotypes remain, the films I will discuss largely avoid them, but do contain some reductive elements not related to character type. In this respect, the stereotypes described above tend to be avoided in contemporary cinema, yet more generalised images of Latino culture are still prevalent.

Edward Said's (1979) concept of 'Orientalism' has been modified by Ramírez Berg (2002) and Frances R. Aparicio and Susana Chávez-Silverman (1997) in an attempt to theorise the reduction of highly varied Latin-American cultures into a set of characteristics that disposes of differences between countries and cultures. Ramírez Berg uses the term "Latinism" to refer to "the construction of Latin America and its inhabitants and of Latinos in this country to justify the United States' imperialistic goals" (p. 4). He then goes on to explain the historical basis for this "discursive system":

> Operationalized externally as the Monroe Doctrine and internally as Manifest Destiny, U.S. imperialism was based on the notion that the nation should control the entire hemisphere and was willing to fight anyone who disagreed. For centuries, the precepts underpinning the Monroe Doctrine have been used as a rationale for U.S. interference in the internal politics of Latin America. On the whole, Hollywood

endorsed North American dominance of this hemisphere, and as often as it depicted that hegemony uncritically, movies helped to perpetuate it.

(p. 4)

For Ramírez Berg this is a historically-based unidirectional appropriation of another culture by various powerful institutions in the United States, including the Hollywood film industry. This representational strategy still affects the way films are made today. While the concept of "Latinism" is no doubt useful, especially for the study of older Hollywood cinema and some contemporary films, it is becoming somewhat more limited in a modern film industry and other areas of US culture where Latinos are actively involved in their own representations.

In the introduction of *Tropicalizations: Transcultural Representations of Latinidad*, Aparicio and Chávez-Silverman (1997) discuss a particular type of "Latinism" that involves a multi-directional representational process. They initially describe "tropicalism" in its unidirectional form more closely related to Orientalism:

> Clearly indebted to Said's "orientalism," the etymological correlative within the Latino context would be "tropicalism," the system of ideological fictions (Said 321) with which the dominant (Anglo and European) cultures trope Latin American and U.S. Latino/a identities and cultures. [...] Moreover, artists, journalists and poets have represented the countries and cultures "south of the border" in textualizations that have, in the main, reified the political, economic, and cultural hegemony of the "neighbor to the north." In order to account for the overarching discursive patterns inherent in these hegemonic *tropicalizations*, the notion of tropicality, overdetermined for the Caribbean, must be extended to embrace México, Latin America, and in more radical and innovative ways, the United States. In other words, our focus is perhaps better characterized as geocultural rather than narrowly geophysical.
>
> (p. 1)

Thus, "tropicalizations" often involve a reduction of Latin-American cultures, as well as Latino culture within the United States, to a discursive system of characteristics most closely associated with the Caribbean. But Aparicio and Chávez-Silverman move beyond this unidirectional process, as do the authors of the rest of the chapters in the collection, to a theory that allows for some Latin-American agency:

> In contrast to the unidirectional thrust implicit in Said's theory of orientalism, in which the Arab world is represented under the dominant western gaze, constructed by European discourses exclusively (and thus deprived of agency with regard to its own history

and collective cultural identity), the conceptual framework of *tropicalizations*—its plural form and multiple subject locations proposed in this volume—allows us to include, as Silvia Spitta observes about transculturation, "the dynamics of the colony from the space and the perspective of the colonized" (Spitta, in this volume). [...] we conceptualize *tropicalizations* precisely as a tool that foregrounds the transformative cultural agency of the subaltern subject.

(p. 2)

Their use of "tropicalizations" involves the "mythic idea of *latinidad* based on Anglo (or dominant) projections of fear" (p. 8), but they also wish "to inscribe Anglo, U.S. Latino/a and Latin-American subjects as self as well as other, margin and center, or as neither" (p. 15). Citing Henry Louis Gates, Jr., they argue against the oversimplified model of 'self' and 'Other'. I have at times found it useful in previous chapters to consider characters in terms of 'self' and 'Other' where Hollywood conventions ensure representations of binary racial identity. Where protagonists are Latina/o or East Asian American, however, conventions are not as set in stone. While stereotypical representations have existed throughout much of film history for these ranges of ethnicities, their presence as protagonists has been relatively limited, especially in youth films. Thus, films that place these ethnicities at the centre of the story have less history to impede the portrayal of varied subjectivities, although not all films take advantage of the opportunity to do so.

When considering these portrayals from within and without the Latin-American/Latino 'community', it is necessary to think about what 'Latino community' actually means. Juan Flores (1997), in a chapter in *Tropicalizations*, suggests that Latinos as a group are understood through three main approaches: demographic, analytical, and imaginary (p. 185). Demographic refers to numbers/population and the analytical approach adds some flesh to the bones of demographic data, including details of personal history such as country of origin, generation in the United States, sex, occupation, etc. (pp. 186–187). The imaginary approach, however, brings the self-conceptualisation of the people into the understanding of the group as a whole (or, rather, an imagined whole). Flores states the following about the imaginary community:

> The "Latino community" is an "imagined community"—to summon Benedict Anderson's well-worn though useful phrase—a quintessential present-day geopolitical landscape. The role of the social imagination and the imaginary in the self-conception of nationally, ethnically, and "racially" kindred groups is of course central, but must always be assessed with a view toward how they are *being* imagined, from the "outside," and to what ends and outcomes. Distinguishing between interior and exterior perspectives is thus a necessary step,

and given that in the case of Latinos the outside representation is the dominant one, any instance of cultural expression by Latinos themselves may serve as a healthy corrective to the ceaseless barrage of stereotypes that go to define what is "Latino" in the public mind.

(p. 185)

Of course, it has been argued that self-representation is important for any historically marginalised or stereotyped group, but "distinguishing between interior and exterior perspectives" is not always possible, and it could be argued that a clear separation is never possible. In the case of films, this is because every end product is the work of an ensemble. While writer and director have much to do with the final product, they do not control every aspect of the film, or how the film is understood by audiences. And regardless of who controls each aspect of a film's production, the individuals are always influenced by the history of representations. For this reason, I do not put too much consideration into the ethnicity of writers and directors. I am more interested in the audiovisual construction of identity and agency presented in the films themselves.

Every study of ethnic representation and identity in cinema should take music into account. Just as music is used to mark location in cinema, it is also used to mark the origin of bodies. Latin-American and Latino music are particularly varied and hybrid forms, and their origins are important to understanding this mix. A combination of traditional Latin-American styles, more contemporary fusions, and Anglo-American pop songs is used throughout the films with Latina/o characters that I examine in the first two chapters of Part III. I consider the music of East Asian-American musicians separately in the section on *Better Luck Tomorrow*, because in this film music does not signify ethnicity with the use of traditional or 'ethnic' musical styles.

In *The Latin Tinge*, John Storm Roberts (1999) examines Latin-American music's influence on music and culture in the United States. His discussion of this music illustrates the worldwide influences contained in a body of musical styles often imagined to be quite homogeneous:

The music of Latin America is fully as varied as one would expect of an area containing almost thirty countries and encompassing both tropical and temperate climes. It makes use of two European languages, embraces three cultures—European, African, and Amerindian—and within each of these subdivisions, there are further variations. Brazil's main European culture is Portuguese; the rest of Latin America's is Spanish.

(p. 3)

It seems strange that while arguing for great variation Roberts refers to European, African, and Amerindian as three cultures rather than three large regional groupings each encompassing a vast array of cultures. Yet, despite all of this diversity, Roberts still argues for an imagined musical community:

> The resulting unity-in-diversity is extraordinary. Even the smallest country has its own clearly identifiable musical culture, ranging from the simplest folk idioms to national conservatory styles. Yet from another perspective, all represent versions of one cultural mix, even though not all its elements are equal, or even present, in every country [...].
>
> (p. 3)

This cultural mix represented by the different countries of Latin America is just the beginning of the diversity. In the above passages, Roberts discusses some of the countries that have influenced Latin-American culture, but a closer examination of the music leads to a fascinating history of musical migration.

Roberts (1999) suggests that the main Latin-American countries to have a lasting effect on music of the United States are Cuba, Brazil, Argentina, and Mexico (p. 3). According to Alma M. Garcia (2002) one of the most popular styles of music to cross the border was music from the north of Mexico known as *música norteña* or *norteño*. This genre "originated in the northern states of Mexico such as Nuevo León, Tamualipas, and Chihuahua, and along the U.S.-Mexico border states, particularly Texas" and continued to evolve in the United States (p. 98). Roberts explains how *música norteña* originated in both Mexico and the US, and that the term applies to "an ensemble, consisting of an accordion lead, a guitar and/or *baja sexto* (a type of 12-string guitar), and sometimes a double bass". He goes on to say that this music "leans heavily on corridos and on dances like the polka, waltz, and schottische" (p. 21).

While the musical presence of these dances is obvious, it is something that I personally have, perhaps naively, always taken for granted. I never really questioned how these forms, and the accordion, made their way to Mexico. Roberts (1999) offers the following explanation of the music's origins:

> Contemporary norteño music [...] appears to be a fruit of U.S. cultural crossover. Chicano accordionists believe their instrument was introduced to the area by the German Bohemian and Czech engineers building the railroads between San Antonio and Monterrey, Laredo and Corpus Christi, as well as in the mines of Monterrey.
>
> (p. 21)

This theory adds German and Czech influences to the already well-known Spanish and Native American cultural mix. Garcia (2002) offers a similar, if perhaps too simplistic, account of the style's origins:

> Música norteña can be traced back to the latter part of the nineteenth century and the early part of the twentieth century. Mexican musicians

and songwriters built on the influence of German immigrants who brought their distinctive music styles with them from Germany in the nineteenth century to South Texas and Northern Mexico. Within their communities, Germans listened to and danced to German polkas and mazurkas. Immigrants from Germany introduced the accordion to their new homeland. As a result música norteña developed as a musical genre that blended elements of two cultures: German and Mexican.

(pp. 98–99)

In this account, the accordion and dance forms came solely from Germany, and Garcia refers to *música norteña* as a mix of two cultures. This statement takes for granted that Mexican music, which already mixes many different cultures, has become an individual and recognisable style over time. Garcia goes on to state that *música norteña* continues to evolve over time, on both sides of the border, as it absorbs elements of rock, pop, and techno (p. 99).

According to Roberts (1999), the arrival of the waltz and the continued popularity of 3/4 time in Mexican music are due to the great influence of French culture in the eighteenth and nineteenth centuries, and it is even possible that the polka made its way to Mexico from France (pp. 16–17). Roberts also states that Mexican music significantly incorporated Cuban (and therefore also African) elements from the middle of the nineteenth century onwards (p. 17). Thus, the history of Mexican music, as well as that of music from the rest of Latin America, is intimately linked to a history of immigration to and around the Americas.

I have discussed Latin-American music and particularly *música norteña* at length to illustrate the countless influences on this music from abroad and its evolution through its passage to and from the United States. The musical influences described by Roberts (1999) and Garcia (2002) from various parts of Europe and Africa, as well as those travelling around Latin America and the United States, resulted in an ever-changing set of hybrid musical forms that are at once separate and connected. This musical history not only accompanies those who have immigrated to the US, it also suggests a plurality of identity when music plays a role in constructing this identity. Although there are obviously some distinct musical forms that are linked to specific locations, Roberts asserts that much Latin-American music is hard to categorise:

Most Latin musical forms are remarkably resistant to being pinned down, since they usually involve a rhythm, a dance, a style or styles of playing, typical tempi and even subject matter. Moreover, their origins are often unclear and they frequently change greatly over a period.

(p. 5)

This hybridity of Latin-American music and its tendency to evolve while retaining its deep roots would seem to make the music very suitable for expressing identity and affecting agency in *Real Women Have Curves* and *Quinceañera* due to the tension between the traditional and the modern foregrounded in both films. This music, in its traditional and further hybridised modern forms, constructs identities that are as "resistant to being pinned down" as the Latin music that Roberts describes. The musical choices differ greatly in these films, however, and I consider the films in detail before examining a different type of musical representation of ethnic identity and agency in *Better Luck Tomorrow*. This film does not rely on traditional music, but rather suggests hybrid ethnic identities through musical forms that do not seem to be ethnically-coded in any superficial sense.

Notes

1 From this point onwards I shall use the typical US nomenclature, Asian American, to mean East Asian American.
2 Recent television (in its broadest definition) has been more inclusive than the period of cinema I discuss here.

References

Aparicio, Frances R. and Susana Chávez-Silverman (1997) 'Introduction' in Frances R. Aparicio and Susana Chávez-Silverman (eds), *Tropicalizations: Transcultural Representations of Latinidad*, Hanover, NH: University Press of New England, pp. 1–17.
Flores, Juan (1997) 'The Latino Imaginary: Dimensions of Community and Identity' in Frances R. Aparicio and Susana Chávez-Silverman (eds), *Tropicalizations: Transcultural Representations of Latinidad*, Hanover, NH: University Press of New England, pp. 183–193.
Garcia, Alma M. (2002) *The Mexican Americans*, Westport, CT: Greenwood Press.
Ramírez Berg, Charles (2002) *Latino Images in Film: Stereotypes, Subversion, & Resistance*, Austin, TX: University of Texas Press.
Roberts, John Storm (1999) *The Latin Tinge: The Impact of Latin American Music on the United States*, 2nd Ed., Oxford, UK: Oxford University Press.
Said, Edward W. (1979) *Orientalism*, New York: Vintage Books, Random House.
Shohat, Ella and Robert Stam (1994) *Unthinking Eurocentrism: Multiculturalism and the Media*, London: Routledge.

Filmography

Better Luck Tomorrow (2002, USA) directed by Justin Lin, music by Michael J. Gonzales and Semiautomatic, music supervision by Ernesto M. Foronda, Paramount.
Quinceañera (*Echo Park, LA* – alternate title, 2006, USA) directed by Richard Glatzer and Wash Westmoreland, music by Victor Bock and Micko Westmoreland, music supervision by Shaun Young, Metrodome Distribution.
Real Women Have Curves (2002, USA) directed by Patricia Cardoso, music by Heitor Pereira, music supervision by Margaret Guerra Rogers, Home Box Office Home Video.

Real Women Have Curves (Patricia Cardoso, 2002) tells the coming-of-age story of Ana García (America Ferrera), the daughter of Mexican immigrants who lives with her extended family in East Los Angeles. The narrative focuses on Ana's problematic relationship with her mother, her desire to seek further education, her developing sexuality, and the lessons she learns about pride, self-respect, and humility through working in her sister's dress factory, which Ana initially refers to as a "sweatshop". The film begins with Ana's mother Carmen (Lupe Ontiveros) summoning Ana to her bedroom where she lies in what appears to be a very ill state. It soon becomes clear that Carmen is a hypochondriac; when Ana tells her that she will not miss her final day of high school because her mother is feigning illness, Carmen immediately sits up in bed and reprimands her. After Ana walks out, Carmen asks Estela (Ingrid Oliu) what is wrong with her sister Ana. This scene sets up the often-antagonistic relationship between Ana and her mother that lasts throughout the film and becomes the source of both humour and heartbreak.

The rest of *Real Women* follows Ana's life as she is pulled by two opposing forces: the desire to go to college and the duty to fulfil the wishes of her family by working in her sister's dress factory. After Ana quits her fast food job on the last day of school, Carmen insists that Ana must work in Estela's factory to make money and help her sister meet tight production deadlines. Ana is initially resistant and complains about the heat in the factory and the fact that the women who work there are just cheap labour for upscale boutiques that sell the dresses at a handsome profit. But Ana's judgement is met with strong protest from the women who are proud of the work they do in the factory. They consider Ana's condescending attitude to be a sign of snobbery. However, Ana ultimately learns to take pride in her work at the factory as she begins to take pride in her own body and mind.

As convention dictates, *Real Women* has a romantic subplot. Unlike many youth films, however, this relationship is not the focus of the protagonist's efforts or the film's narrative. Jimmy (Brian Sites), the love interest, is a white fellow student at Beverly Hills High School who naively believes that Ana comes from a wealthy family like his and enjoys an equally privileged lifestyle. The reality is, however, that Ana was accepted into the school because of her intelligence, and that she must take two buses to get to school every day. The two must date without Carmen's knowledge, and they eventually have sex, resulting in Ana's increased confidence in her body and mind. With the help of her teacher Mr. Guzman (George Lopez), who has a convenient friendship with the dean of admissions at Columbia University, Ana applies to college and is accepted. Despite initial resistance from her parents, Ana decides that she will move to New York City to attend Columbia.

Real Women Have Curves is an independent film based on a stage play of the same name, written by Josefina Lopez, who also co-wrote the screenplay. According to Linda C. McClain, Lopez "drew on her experiences as an undocumented worker in her sister's East Los Angeles sewing factory, in which Lopez's mother and an older sister also worked" (2005, p. 733). In the film version, the focus was shifted from Estela and the factory to Ana and her experiences, and Carmen was turned into "a more antagonistic figure" (p. 733). In addition, the play featured a more in-depth examination of immigration and citizenship issues (Jillian M. Báez, 2007, p. 119). As a film, *Real Women* does not abandon its consideration of immigration and citizenship altogether, but rather moves these issues from the foreground to the background, instead using them to modify challenges typically faced by (often white) teenage girls in mainstream youth films.

Steven H. Cooper and Adrienne Harris (2002) summarise the film's themes and its representation of culture:

> It is a film about women and bodies, about mothers and daughters, and about the deformations class and work make upon body and psyche. The film brims with the complex mixes of speech patterns, accents, languages and cultures, the hybridity of modern and postmodern immigrant and urban life.
>
> (p. 1,481)

Unlike many of the films I discuss in Part II, *Real Women* does not present difference from the white middle class as Other. Or, at least, it does not make the representation of Otherness a central concern. Rather, Ana is simply presented as belonging to a mix of cultures. Ana is smart but is not a nerd. She has curves but is not undesirable. She is Latina but not Other. The fact that Ana is the film's protagonist goes some way in explaining her progressive characterisation, and yet some other films with non-white protagonists regularly fall back on stereotypes. Considering the Latina stereotypes historically presented in films (which have not disappeared altogether), Ana is a progressive character. She comes from a working-class immigrant family but is headed for higher education. Her class mobility shows not assimilation, but hybridity.

Hybridity is important to the portrayal of any Latina because, as my discussion of Flores (1997) in the Introduction to Part III indicates, it is a central element of the imagined Latino community. With regard to the protagonists of the films *Selena* (1997), *Girlfight* (2000), and *Real Women Have Curves*, Báez (2007) asserts the following:

> Each of these Latina protagonists embody a hybrid subjectivity—
> one in which identity is fluid and sometimes contradictory. Within
> these films, Selena, Diana, and Ana are all *new mestizas* in that
> all three are bilingual and multicultural—they occupy a third space
> in between Latin America and the U.S. These characters all chal-
> lenge notions of an "authentic" Latinidad in that they are not the
> foreign other—they are second- and third-generation Latinas that
> speak English without a Spanish accent and counter the notorious
> stereotype of the heavily accented Latina in Hollywood. Although
> working-class subjectivity is often subdued under the trope of
> Latinidad (Valdivia, 2000), here it breaks with conventional codes
> that often render Latinas as non-citizens or as Other.
>
> (p. 122)

Thus, Báez explains this hybrid subjectivity in terms of fluid identity – a variety particular to these "*new mestizas*". However, Ana does not really exist between places, even if the film tries to draw cultural lines. Rather, Ana is a US citizen, a Latina, a Mexican American, a young woman, a teenage girl, a high school student, a daughter, a sister, a lover, a future student of Columbia University, a former fast-food employee, a factory worker, and so on. It is also important to the story that Ana and her family are represented as working class and not just poor as a func- tion of being Mexican Americans, as Báez points out.

Real Women uses a mix of Latin-American musical styles to score Ana's experiences, and to a lesser extent, those of her family and acquain- tances. Ana's hybrid identity parallels the previously discussed hybridity of Latin-American music. The use of a variety of Latin styles in *Real Women* does not simply reinforce a generalised idea of Ana's ethnicity or the film's location in East Los Angeles. Rather, it foregrounds her exis- tence in a mix of cultures. The songs that appear during major events for Ana tend to combine more modern musical idioms that usually include some Latin form. However, the absence of songs with English lyrics, or even songs with Spanish lyrics in typically Anglo-American music genres, serves to steer her representation towards the Mexican side of her Chicana identity while ignoring the English-speaking environment where she at- tends high school, dates, and will be attending university. While the hy- brid musical forms highlight the film's central tension – Ana, the daughter of working-class Mexican immigrants, wants to go to college and there- fore separate from her family and class background – the exclusion of

Anglo-American popular music and Latin-American music with English lyrics serves to obscure a significant part of her identity.

'Chica Dificil' ('Difficult Girl'), by Colombian alternative Latin rock band Aterciopelados, is the first significant song associated with Ana in the film. It begins after she refuses to miss her last day of school because of her mother's apparently feigned illness. The song bridges a cut to Ana slamming open the front door of her house and walking out, and continues to score her trip to school. 'Chica Dificil' contains laid-back vocals, clean electric guitar, bass guitar, accordion, and light drums. The music has a shuffling, bluesy, lounge-jazz feel to it. The vocalist sings (in Spanish) about being a difficult girl who is worth the trouble, and explains how she is looking for a man who will do amazing things for her, but she insists she will not be easy to catch. For those who do not understand Spanish, the title and initial lyrics ("Soy una chica dificil") are fairly easy to comprehend (or at least to look up) and are arguably the most important words of the song with regard to Ana's character. Those who do understand will get the full meaning of the song's words included in the film. These lyrics give a general impression of Ana's character: she is in fact difficult, but she is also a worthwhile person to know with plenty of positive attributes. Rather than simply being stubborn, Ana is an intelligent, demanding girl with strong opinions. Thus 'Chica Dificil' sets up the exceptional agency that Ana has as the film's young, female protagonist, despite the somewhat comic quality the lyrics take on after the altercation between Ana and her mother.

The song follows Ana through her neighbourhood and onto two buses, ending after it bridges a cut to her classroom in Beverly Hills High School. As the song plays, visuals alternate between medium-to-long shots of Ana and scenes of her surroundings, possibly from her point

Figure 7.1 Ana watches as a woman serenades an invisible audience.

of view. As she walks to the first bus, Ana passes through her neighbourhood, which is colourful – literally and figuratively, visually and
aurally. After Ana is shown from behind passing bright flowers in her
front garden, the view switches to a long shot of her from a high angle,
with sneakers draped over a phone line taking up the lower left-hand
corner of the shot. Children play in the street and her father's landscap-
ing truck is visible in the driveway. Thus, the mise-en-scène signifies a
working-class neighbourhood. Ana waves to, but gets no reaction from,
an old woman who sings 'O Sole Mio' and slowly waves her arms as if
she is performing in front of an audience.

On her way to the bus Ana passes two Latino guitarists in cowboy
hats and matching shirts, as well as colourful murals on the fronts and
sides of buildings. She finally stands at the bus stop in front of brightly
painted ads for vegetables and a large painting of a farm on the front
of a market. Her neighbourhood is lively and cheerful, yet full of
working-class people with complicated lives. Downtown Los Angeles
looms in the background and a scruffy white man with a long beard and
bin bag full of possessions sits at the bus stop. 'Chica Dificil' may reflect
the ethnicity of Ana and her neighbours, but it also constructs a clever
yet difficult girl with a somewhat melancholic mood that is mirrored in
her vibrant yet hard-working neighbourhood. As Ana gets off the first
bus, an African-American man at the stop plays a flute. The flute blends
perfectly into the song – in its jazzy style, key, and volume – to the point
that one wonders if it is part of the recording. The flute is not in the
original song, but it enhances the melancholic, contemplative mood of
this instrumental passage. Thus, the boundaries between source music
and dramatic score become blurred. We share Ana's point of audition
through the source music (singing and flute) as well as identifying with
her subjectivity via the dramatic score. This underlines Ana's concerns
about her relationship with her mother, the fact that she has to take two
buses to school, and her desire to go to college despite serious doubts
that it will be possible. Ana is not alone in her musical world; many
people of different races, ethnicities, and religions appear on the same
streets. Thus, the music informs the perceiver about Ana's ethnicity and
personality, but it also connects her to the whole population of her city
via characters with whom she shares the scenes, additional source music from the old woman who sings and the man with the flute, and the
visible presence of downtown Los Angeles. This sequence foregrounds
hybridity of music and identity, developing Ana's character and suggesting the evolution of her agency in the remainder of the film.

'Chica Dificil' pauses after bridging a cut to Ana's classroom and
starts again after she quits her fast food restaurant job on the way home.
She picks up a final pay check from her bitter boss who says, "You know,
you can always just kiss my ass to get your job back." In response to
her boss's comment Ana flings her hand up in the air as she walks out
the door. The instrumental passage of 'Chica Dificil' starts with this

dismissive gesture as if Ana controls the music's entry. Mirroring the way she quits the job on her own terms, the reappearance of the song reinforces her agency in this matter and cements her determination for the rest of the film. The song later ends as Ana walks into her house and closes the door behind her. The fact that 'Chica Dificil' begins as Ana leaves her house and ends as she returns suggests that her agency lies outside of this domestic space. Her life in this house is controlled by her mother, and the music locates her power in the outside world, foreshadowing her need to leave home.

Musically, Ana's need to leave home is suggested by the more international (that is, less traditionally[1] Mexican) sound of songs associated with key moments in her coming-of-age. While 'Chica Dificil' suggests something about Ana's personality, it is also heard at a time when she is making important decisions and contemplating her future. Another featured song with an even more international feel is 'Minha Galera' ('My Gang' or 'My People') by Manu Chao, a French singer born to Spanish parents. The song's lyrics are in Portuguese, and Chao uses some Brazilian Portuguese to reference Brazilian culture. A guitar and a keyboard playing a gentle reggae rhythm accompany the vocals.

'Minha Galera' plays during Ana and Jimmy's first date and continues through several other events. Before they meet, Ana walks her grandfather to a bar on the corner, from which lively tejano music pours out into the street. John Koegel (2002, p. 107) describes tejano as "the general term for contemporary Texas-Mexican popular music, [encompassing] many earlier and present-day musical styles to create a hybrid mix: polka, *ranchera*, blues, rock, jazz, *cumbia*, and so forth". This music contrasts with that heard in the scene immediately following it. The tejano ends and 'Minha Galera' begins with a cut to the restaurant where the date takes place. The outside seating area of this restaurant is ornately decorated with cactuses, flowers, and a large statue of the Virgin Mary, adorned with several strings of Christmas lights and surrounded by mosaic tiling. The hip, young, seemingly affluent crowd, albeit multiracial, contrasts with the more working-class Latino neighbourhood from which Ana has just come. This adds to the impression that the stylised decoration, with its exaggerated display of religious icons, fetishises Mexican culture.

The combination of the restaurant with the light reggae feel and Portuguese vocals of 'Minha Galera' places Ana and Jimmy in a space somewhere between both of their usual worlds. This appears to be a more upscale Mexican restaurant, and to Jimmy, who comes from a wealthy, white family and has a narrow and sometimes vulgar knowledge of Mexican and Chicano/Latino culture, this may represent an 'authentic' experience. Likewise, the fact that the song is sung in Portuguese with a Brazilian slant by a French singer with Spanish ancestry further complicates any notion of a fixed national/cultural identity.

For Ana, the restaurant has familiar if stylised iconography and presumably serves Mexican food. However, it may not have the kind of food she would eat at home and is probably not the type of restaurant where her family would eat, if they can even afford to eat out.

The guitar and vocals are delivered in a poppy, quirky style, with Chao humming at one point, seemingly mimicking a kazoo or perhaps a trumpet. This quirky, innocent feel of the song highlights the awkward interactions between Ana and Jimmy: Jimmy is caught staring at Ana's breasts, and Ana declares, "I made this list of topics to talk about so that we wouldn't run out of things to talk about." The volume of the song also changes at key moments during the date. When Jimmy tries to make light of the shared awkwardness by asking if big breasts are on Ana's list, the volume of the song jumps to echo the laughter and rise in emotion of the two characters. The song then bridges a cut to Ana and Jimmy walking through various parts of Ana's neighbourhood until they reach the corner where Ana dropped off her grandfather. The song again jumps in volume, although more subtly, when Jimmy kisses Ana goodnight. Again, the humming enters as the song bridges a final cut to Ana waking up in her bed and smiling in a dream-like state as she recalls the events of the night before.

Unlike 'Chica Difícil', 'Minha Galera' does not end when Ana walks through the door of her house. The song accompanies her memory of the date and the kiss, and it returns when she takes decisive steps to improve her life and the lives of her family. But first, Ana's blissful slumber is interrupted by the sound of traffic, then a cut to an exterior shot of the factory, followed by what sounds like the metal gate of the factory being opened and then the sounds of steam and sewing machines – sonic simulacra of factory toil. These sounds accentuate the jarring change of scenery and mood from Ana's plush bed to the sweaty workplace. What follows is a scene of hardship. Pancha (Soledad St. Hilaire), one of the workers in the factory, observes the anniversary of her father's death, and recalls how she had to sneak him out of the hospital when he died because she could not pay the bill. Next, a man comes to ask Estela when she will pay rent and threatens, in a faux-polite manner, to kick her out of the factory if she does not pay soon.

In the following scene, Ana visits her father at work to ask if he will lend Estela the money to pay rent so she can keep the factory open. He eventually agrees, and after she hugs him, 'Minha Galera' returns as he smiles at her. The song bridges a cut to Ana writing her personal essay for college applications – she has obviously decided at this point that she needs to attend college to avoid ending up in a financial situation similar to that of Pancha and Estela. 'Minha Galera' then bridges another cut to Mr. Guzman seated at his desk and Ana enters with her essay. After she hands him the essay he smiles, and the song bridges one further cut to Estela, sketching a dress design on a body that obviously belongs to Anna (the face is expertly drawn), and the music ends. When Pancha asks about and compliments the design, Estela replies that she is working on her own line, and asks if Pancha would buy a dress like the one she has drawn. Pancha replies that she would if it would be large enough to fit her. Thus, 'Minha Galera' carries Ana's good feelings and positive action through to Estela and perhaps inspires her to follow her own dreams. The design of the dress on Ana's body and the fact that Pancha assumes a dress like that would never come in her size both fore-shadow later events: Ana laments that she will never get to enjoy one of the beautiful dresses laboured over in the factory, Estela presents Ana with a dress made just for her, and the women in the factory (except for Carmen) declare their acceptance of, and even love for, their own bod-ies. All of this is indirectly made possible by Ana's maturation, and her music carries this newly found agency from scene to scene.

The second Aterciopelados song enters the film when Ana and Jimmy decide to have sex for the first time. After they climb into bed and start to get undressed, Jimmy turns off the lights, but Ana asks him to turn them back on so he can see what her body looks like. When the lights come on she is standing naked (only shown from the shoulders up) in front of a mirror, and Jimmy walks over, puts his arm around her, and says *"qué bonita"* ("how beautiful"). At this point, the song begins with a strummed acoustic guitar, soon adding a shuffling rhythm and melan-cholic vocals, and eventually incorporating squelching electronic flour-ishes. The low-key song, 'Luto' ('Mourning'), then bridges a cut to Ana tying back her hair, fully clothed. When Jimmy says that he will write to and email her after he goes to college, Ana says "no". She tells him not to worry about her anymore, that they will not have anything to talk about once he is in college, and that he will probably meet a skinny girl.

In this scene, Ana seems self-conscious about the fact that her parents will not let her go to Columbia University even though she has been ac-cepted, and that Jimmy will be moving on with his life while she stays to work in the factory. Although it appears that she will miss Jimmy, and he says that he will miss her, the 'mourning' of the song's title seems to refer more to Ana's loss of an opportunity than to her loss of Jimmy, or the loss of her virginity. The nonchalance with which Ana treats this first sexual encounter and loss of a boyfriend is unusual for a teenage girl in cinema.

For Cooper and Harris, "Jimmy, [...] is a transitional figure between Ana's disavowal of wishes to learn more and become more assimilated and her wishes to be loyal to her family, even if her family is driving her nuts" (2005, p. 1,485). While Ana no doubt cares about Jimmy, she does not harbour some ridiculous fantasy of marrying him. But nor does she show any desire to "assimilate". The idea to have sex is Ana's, and she makes a point of buying condoms beforehand. The desire to have sex before Jimmy leaves is empowering for her character, and once again, it is a more modern sounding song with contemporary international influences that accompanies her agency. The music bridges one final cut to the couple walking out of Jimmy's house, hand-in-hand and smiling. As they get into his car and drive away, the mood is level, perhaps even somewhat triumphant, even though the music is sorrowful. The song ends as the car is driving away but bleeds somewhat over the next cut to Ana admiring herself in the mirror. Her empowerment continues in this scene. After Ana's mother guesses that she has lost her virginity, she calls Ana a "*puta*" (whore) and slaps her. Following this, Ana tells her mother off and slams the door in her face.

More traditional-sounding Mexican and Latin-American songs are generally heard when Ana is with her family or working in the factory. However, this is not simply a conservative music strategy to represent ethnicity. 'No le Hace' ('It Doesn't Matter') and 'Tenemos la Culpa' ('It's Our Fault'), both by Banda Llaneros, are heard when Ana is being driven to the factory in her father's truck. It is not clear if these are source songs playing on the radio, but this seems more likely in the case of 'Tenemos la Culpa'. It is difficult to tell the difference between brass instruments and their electronic counterparts in this type of music, but the songs of Banda Llaneros sound like more traditional banda music, rather than technobanda, an electronic version of banda music that became popular with young Latinos in the 1990s "as a space for cultural affirmation" and a way of making a political statement (Helena Simonett, 2001 p. 80). Either way, the music has its own history and takes on some of the political meaning of technobanda in its present context, representing the solidarity of a migrant 'community'.

In other cases, as previously mentioned, tejano music flows from a local bar, and mariachis approach Jimmy to ask if he wants them to perform while he stands against his car waiting for Ana. The musical fabric of East Los Angeles is both audible and visible in the streets. This mix of sounds blends traditional Mexican and other Latin genres with cross-border music and, in the case of 'Aquí No Será' ('It Will Not Be Here') by Ozomatli, a hybrid of more traditional forms with modern political lyrics. 'Aquí No Será', a song that could be broadly described as a slow tango, appears three times in the film. The first two instances occur in one scene in the factory and no vocals are heard at these times. The song first enters when Ana takes a bite of flan in defiance of her mother and bridges a cut to the steamy factory where all of the women are miserably hot and sweaty. After Ana removes her shirt to cool off, her mother tells Ana that she looks terrible and asks if she is not ashamed of herself. Once again Ana is defiant, asserting that there is more to her than her body, and telling her mother that no one should criticise her for the way she looks. 'Aquí No Será' returns when Ana and the other women start to remove more of their clothes to compare cellulite and stretch marks. Again, the music is cued by Ana's actions – this time it starts when she unzips her jeans. Carmen eventually walks out in disgust, but the rest of the women are pleased with themselves, sharing in Ana's agency that is highlighted by the song. In this instance, the music that accompanies Ana's agency sounds more traditional, but this makes sense in a scene where she finally and completely bonds with the other women in the factory – thus finding pride in her own working class Chicano family history. I will discuss the last appearance of 'Aquí No Será', as well as the cultural significance of Ozomatli, when I consider the film's ending.

After this, the women return to work in their underwear, and Ana enthusiastically exclaims that they should finish the dress order that night. She then turns on the radio, from which the snappy 'Qué Rico el Mambo' ('How Rich/Nice the Mambo') by Pérez Prado blares. The women dance happily to the mambo while they work, feeling revitalised and comfortable in their own skin. At the end of the scene there is a fade to black, accompanied by a rise in volume, and the song ends with a cut to a lawnmower. As before, Ana's musical agency carries over into further action as she once again visits her father at work. This time she wants to tell him that she has decided to go to Columbia University despite her parents' previous refusal of the idea. Before she can conjure the words, however, her father anticipates with "you have my blessing".

Ana's major actions and important experiences throughout the film are coupled with music. With 'Chica Dificil', 'Minha Galera', and 'Luto', more modern, hybrid styles reflect Ana's youth and desire to move away from her family, her neighbourhood, and the factory, and go to college. But just as importantly, by the end of the film Ana has come to accept her own body – both in terms of size and in terms of her ethnic/socioeconomic background. She still wants to go to Columbia, but she also learns to appreciate the work that she and her colleagues do at the factory. Perhaps this understanding is reflected in the more traditional sounding 'Aquí No Será' and 'Qué Rico el Mambo'. When these songs play, or when she plays them, she is happy and in control, unlike the earlier appearances of the Banda Llaneros songs in her father's truck.

Although Ana leaves at the end of the film with her father's blessing, her mother does not even come out of her bedroom to say goodbye. It is only as Ana, her father, and her grandfather, drive off on their way to the airport that she finally looks out the window. After Ana says goodbye to her father and grandfather at the airport and walks away there is a cut to Ana ascending from the New York subway near Times Square. She has adopted a more fashion-conscious style and 'feminine' walk (as encouraged by her mother earlier in the film) for her new life. As she surfaces, 'Strawberry Tango Parts 1 & 2' (written by Marty Stuart, originally from the *All The Pretty Horses* [Billy Bob Thornton, 2000] soundtrack) starts to play. The instrumentation is a mix of acoustic guitars, percussion, and syncopated low brass. The traditional genre of this song connects Ana to her home and family, even as she struts through New York City.

As in the rest of the film, the fact that the music is 'Latin' is more important than whether or not it is Mexican or Mexican-American. The exceptions to this are generally with the more specifically Mexican or Mexican-American source music in Ana's father's truck and the bar on the corner – music that serves to connect Ana's parents and grandfather to their country of birth and thus signify their lives as immigrants, as well as reflect the predominant ethnicity of the neighbourhood.

The genre of 'Strawberry Tango' is not the only thing that conjures Ana's old neighbourhood. After Ana has been walking confidently and excitedly surveying her surroundings, the music slows with some sustained minor chords strummed on the guitar. When the song picks back up, the camera pulls away from Ana. At this point strings enter the song and add a layer of sadness and anxiety to the music. It is at this exact moment that the perceiver separates from Ana's subjectivity visually, but not aurally. Up to this point, the top half of Ana's body is shown in a medium close-up tracking shot as she walks down the street, her face expressing a mix of excitement and apprehension. But once the camera pulls away the perceiver gets farther and farther from Ana; other pedestrians pass between Ana and the camera, and she becomes part of the crowd and the unfamiliar city. As Ana approaches a corner, the camera crosses the street but she does not. Instead, she looks around as if she is unsure of where to go, and as the pedestrian signal facing the camera flashes "DON'T WALK" in red, Ana turns the corner and walks off screen. The ambivalence of this shot is emphasised by the music, which slows to a few sustained, melancholic notes that seem to mirror Ana's sense of being alone in an unfamiliar and slightly menacing metropolis. A few final sustained electric guitar notes with a heavy tremolo effect add to a sense of unease as the scene fades to black.

This ambivalent ending suggests that Ana may have been better off in Los Angeles – an impression that is strengthened by the end credit sequence. The split subjectivity at the end of the New York scene creates uncertainty as to whether Ana regrets leaving home or whether the film is judging her for doing so. After the fade to black, there is a cut to a close-up of a radio. When a hand reaches into the frame and turns the radio on, the familiar 'Aquí No Será' returns. The song continues over a montage of scenes that resemble those shown in concert with 'Chica Difícil' when Ana is walking through her neighbourhood early in the film (although she does not appear in the end credit sequence). Brightly coloured spools of thread, a running sewing machine, scenes of the neighbourhood, religious icons, walking musicians, the family's parakeets, and the charismatic old woman who sings 'O Sole Mio' at the start of the film, are all shown. While these scenes are colourful, both literally and metaphorically, they are interspersed with shots of dirty bus windows and a tangled mess of phone lines, among other ugly aspects of life in Ana's old neighbourhood. Mostly, however, the scenes tend to suggest nostalgia for a comfortable, vibrant community with whose long roots Ana has become disconnected.

This ambivalence recalls "the assimilation narrative" and conflicted endings of "Chicano social problem films" that flourished from the 1930s to the 1960s as discussed by Charles Ramírez Berg (2002, p. 114). According to Ramírez Berg, the troubled protagonists of these films had to navigate a path between the values of their root culture, material success, and assimilation. In these narratives, the ethnic culture of protagonists was always rose-tinted:

> The best course of action is for ethnic/immigrant/class/gender Others to go home to their old ethnic neighbourhood, the locus of all that is good and true. Abandoning their aspirations of mainstream integration and success, these characters can remain content in the knowledge that they have gained morality, a prize far greater than fame or fortune.
>
> (p. 114)

For Ramírez Berg, the nostalgic tendencies of these ethnic representations did not serve to celebrate diversity, but rather to suggest that the best place for Latino characters to stay was on the economic margins. Despite the audiovisual return to the old neighbourhood and its nostalgic suggestion of ethnic wholesomeness at the end of *Real Women Have Curves*, Ana does not end up back where she started. Nor does she 'assimilate'. Rather, she goes to Columbia University and carries her old neighbourhood and ethnic pride with her, and the inclusion of 'Aquí No Será' in the end credit sequence problematises the accompanying nostalgic images.

The lyrics of 'Aquí No Será', which seem to criticise the US government's support of El Salvador's violent military regime during the Salvadoran Civil War, only serve to amplify the dour mood of the song and credit sequence. This song, especially to those who understand Spanish, adds to the feeling that Ana's old neighbourhood is a somewhat tragic place, or perhaps it is a critique of white, hegemonic US culture and the fact that Ana is an exception to the lack of agency possessed by many others from her background. But at the same time, there is a definite air of nostalgia in these scenes, amplified by the inclusion of the song that previously accompanied Ana's ultimate bonding with the other women in her sister's factory.

A brief discussion of Ozomatli will help to understand the context of their music and the role that 'Aquí No Será' plays in the film. Victor Hugo Viesca (2004) states the following about the local music scene that Ozomatli is a part of: "East Los Angeles is the center of a flourishing musical cultural scene with a renewed 'Chicana/o' sensibility. This scene is being led by a collective of socially conscious and politically active Latin-fusion bands that emerged in the 1990s" (p. 719). For those familiar with the band, the inclusion of Ozomatli's music reinforces the location of the film and thus the location of the film's end credit sequence, as well as adding a sense of social and political awareness. According to Viesca, Ozomatli is an overtly political band that has played at many charity gigs and connects with older Chicano identity politics and indigenous Mexican identity. But Ozomatli is not a musically traditional band; their music combines traditional Latin-American genres with rap, rock, and other types of music into a trans-generational hybrid style. It is therefore appropriate that the band's music should enhance the idea of Ana (re)connecting with her own working-class Chicana identity – an event that, paradoxically, seems to enable her to move away from it, both socially and economically. However, Ana's newly strengthened ties to this identity probably make it harder for her to leave, as suggested by the musical ambivalence in the final scene in New York.

Báez (2007) asserts that, due to the film's tropicalised representation of Boyle Heights (Ana's neighbourhood) it comes to signify the "Third World", while Beverly Hills High School represents the "First World" (pp. 121–122). The tropicalism referred to by Báez with regard to Latina bodies can be seen and heard in the previously discussed factory scene where the undressed women dance to 'Qué Rico el Mambo'. In addition, when Ana is walking through New York, the very prominent syncopated low brass in 'Strawberry Tango' can be heard to represent the movement of her body in a crude way. But this same element of the song could also represent Ana's personality since it is very strong and sometimes confrontational.

So Ana's character is conflicted, pulled between two worlds, and yet she is strong enough to act decisively to ensure the future opportunities she desires. Both Báez (2007) and Chris Holmlund (2005) discuss the

Figure 7.2 A 'Chica Difícil' waits for the bus to school.

feminist elements of Ana's character and the film overall. For Báez, "Ana experiences an internal contradiction between solidarity with her fellow Latina workers and the upward mobility promised by the American dream", and this "marks a new kind of *Latinidad feminista* – one that demonstrates the social hierarchy and tensions between different generations within Latina/o communities" (p. 120). Ana does seem to understand her family and the factory from a position other than the one she was raised to occupy. She eventually comes to empathise with and nearly occupy the position of her co-workers. Yet this position, like Jimmy's presence in her life, is transitional. Ana will never return to factory work after attending Columbia University. Báez goes on to observe that since "Ana's mother reinforces patriarchy, traditions of the 'Old World' are gendered feminine, while her father's, grandfather's, and teacher's support of her pursuit of higher education genders the progress of the 'New World' as masculine" (p. 121). This coding contradicts feminist elements that exist in the film. However, Estela and the other women in the factory occupy an intermediate position. While they do work under the same conditions as Ana's mother and mock Ana for the arrogance she displays when she starts working in the factory, these women do not discourage Ana's ambitions and they eventually bond with her over a shared progressive view towards their bodies. Furthermore, Estela has ambitions of designing her own line of clothing, even though it may never happen. The position of these characters between "Old World" and "New World" complicates the male/female division that Báez describes. Holmlund (2005) recognises the temporary nature of Ana's appreciation of working in the dress factory, and the contradiction between feminist and postfeminist elements of the film, but she concludes that *Real Women* ultimately conveys a feminist message. Ana does criticise the factory at first, but she later comes to appreciate the meaning of the work done by the women there. She is the only one with the agency to change her situation, though, due to her education at Beverly Hills High School. Her only real interest in the factory stems from a desire to help her sister. The rest of the women will continue working at the factory, with the possible exception of Estela, should her new clothing line ever come to fruition. Although they may be proud of the work they do there, they seem to have no other choice. Thus while Ana shows concern for, and ultimately identifies with, the other women in the factory, her achievement is hers alone.

Throughout *Real Women*, songs serve to reinforce Ana's ethnicity and that of her community. But the music does not do this in a simplistic manner. The songs that accompany important moments in Ana's story tend to be more modern fusions containing elements of rock, reggae, and electronic music, and those that represent her parents and community are often more traditional in style. However, when considering the film's central tension, whether it be described as 'Old World' versus 'New World', 'First World' versus 'Third World', or solidarity versus upward mobility (Báez), a tension created by class conflict and class movement (Cooper and Harris), or the tension between postfeminism or liberal feminism and feminism that accounts for historically-based socioeconomic conditions (Holmlund and Báez), it is odd that songs with English lyrics do not appear in connection with Ana. As my discussion has suggested and discussions of other scholars have supported, Ana is a hybrid character. Her ethnic background is an important part of her life and more varied musical styles represent her, but the side of her that identifies with mainstream US culture is not highlighted musically. Aside from 'Minha Galera' by Manu Chao, which is sung in Portuguese, all of the songs associated with Ana have Spanish lyrics. Thus, the omission of songs with English lyrics excludes some aspects of Ana's personality and her cultural context, both present and aspirational, but the film's soundtrack nevertheless plays a key role in the representation of a hybrid character.

Note

1 While I acknowledge that 'traditional' is a relative and somewhat problematic term, I will be using it throughout this chapter to refer to identifiable musical styles that, despite being present in modern forms, were already established by the early-to-mid-twentieth century.

References

Báez, Jillian M. (2007) 'Towards a *Latinidad Feminista*: The Multiplicities of Latinidad and Feminism in Contemporary Cinema' in *Popular Communication*, Vol. 5, No. 2, pp. 109–128.

Cooper, Steven H. and Adrienne Harris (2005) '*Real Women have Curves* (2002)' in *International Journal of Psychoanalysis*, Vol. 86, No. 5, pp. 1,481–1,487.

Flores, Juan (1997) 'The Latino Imaginary: Dimensions of Community and Identity' in Frances R. Aparicio and Susana Chávez-Silverman (eds), *Tropicalizations: Transcultural Representations of Latinidad*, Hanover, NH: University Press of New England, pp. 183–193.

Holmlund, Chris (2005) 'Postfeminism from A to G' in *Cinema Journal*, Vol. 44, No. 2, pp. 116–121.

Koegel, John (2002) 'Crossing Borders: Mexicana, Tejana, and Chicana Musicians in the United States and Mexico' in Walter Aaron Clark (ed.), *From Tejano to Tango: Latin American Popular Music*, London: Routledge, pp. 97–125.

McClain, Linda C (2005) 'Bend it Like Beckham' and 'Real Women Have Curves': Constructing Identity in Coming-of-Age Stories' in *Depaul Law Review*, Vol. 54, No. 3, pp. 701–754.

Ramírez Berg, Charles (2002) *Latino Images in Film: Stereotypes, Subversion, & Resistance*, Austin, TX: University of Texas Press.

Simonett, Helena (2001) *Banda: Mexican Musical Life Across Borders*, Middletown, CT: Wesleyan University Press.

Viesca, Victor Hugo (2004) 'The Battle of Los Angeles: The Cultural Politics of Chicana/o Music in the Greater Eastside' in *American Quarterly*, Vol. 56, No. 3, pp. 719–739.

Filmography

All The Pretty Horses (2000, USA) directed by Billy Bob Thornton, music by Larry Paxton, Marty Stuart, and Kristin Wilkinson, music supervision by Barry Cole and Christopher Covert, Miramax Films.

Real Women Have Curves (2002, USA) directed by Patricia Cardoso, music by Heitor Pereira, music supervision by Margaret Guerra Rogers, Home Box Office Home Video.

8 "Neighbourhood is sure changing, isn't it?"
Evolving Traditions and Complex Identities in *Quinceañera*

Quinceañera (Richard Glatzer and Wash Westmoreland, 2006) tells the story of three outcasts who find solace and agency in each other's company: Magdalena (Emily Rios), a 14-year-old girl who is kicked out of her house after accidentally becoming pregnant, Carlos (Jesse García), Magdalena's cousin who was thrown out of his parents' house after they discovered he was gay, and Tio Tomás (Chalo González), the great great uncle of Magdalena and Carlos who takes them both in, has never married, does not have any children, and practices Marian devotion (i.e. a worship of the Virgin Mary that does not necessarily involve any Christian denominational tie – in this case, specifically The Virgin of Guadalupe [Aurelio Espinosa, 2009]) as opposed to the evangelical faith of the families of Magdalena and Carlos. The film is bookended by two *quinceañera* ceremonies, the first for Magdalena's cousin Eileen (Alicia Sixtos), and the second for Magdalena herself.

The *quinceañera* is a wedding-like celebration in honour of a girl's fifteenth birthday. This celebration has religious meaning and involves a mass, whether Catholic, evangelical, or otherwise, as well as a party. Alma M. García (2002) explains that the *quinceañera* is a religious milestone, a coming-of-age within the celebrant's religion. It also has cultural significance in connecting Mexican immigrants and Mexican Americans to their ancestral homeland. García explains how this public display of a girl's commitment to her religion "brings honor to herself and to her entire family, particularly her parents whom the community recognizes for raising a traditional Mexican daughter" (p. 73). Honour plays an extremely important role in this film, since it is the perceived assault on the family's honour, for both Magdalena and Carlos, which results in their expulsion from their families' homes.

Carlos lives with Tio Tomás from the start of *Quinceañera*, but Magdalena only moves in after her father Ernesto (Jesus Castaños-Chima), an evangelical pastor, discovers that she is pregnant and tells her to go away. Magdalena's pregnancy is a shock to everyone, including herself, because she never actually had penetrative sex. Her pregnancy, as she later discovers, was the unfortunate result of sexual activity with her almost-boyfriend Herman (J.R. Cruz). Initially Herman promises to be a supportive father but the disapproval of his mother is enough of a deterrent (or an excuse) for him to abandon Magdalena. Thus, she moves in with Carlos and Tio Tomás, a kind old man who is known to everyone in the neighbourhood as the old man who sells *champurrado* (a traditional Mexican warm chocolate drink) from a shopping trolley. Tio Tomás has lived in his rented house for many years, and he has made it his own with religious icons throughout the house and an altar in the garden.

Tensions in *Quinceañera* emerge from three parallel yet intertwined subplots aligned with the three main characters. First there is the pregnancy of Magdalena, her father's temporary abandonment of her, Herman's eventual abandonment of her, and the fact that she is approaching her fifteenth birthday and is due to have her own *quinceañera*, with the ceremony to take place in her father's church. Secondly, there is Carlos' homosexuality. When he shows up at his sister Eileen's *quinceañera* party near the beginning of the film, he is yelled at and punched in the face by his father and then punched again by another attendee. The film initially implies that Carlos is a troublemaker and possibly a gang member (his sexuality is not made clear until later on). This is a red herring – the audience will later discover his kindness and sense of family loyalty, as well as the real reason for his father's abuse. In addition, tension results from a relationship that develops between Carlos and Gary (David Ross) and James (Jason L. Wood), the gay white couple who buy the house in which Tio Tomás lives and move into the upstairs apartment. At first the two men, who together with their other affluent friends fetishise Latino boys, both have occasional casual sex with Carlos. But eventually Carlos starts to see Gary, the younger of the two men, without James' knowledge. James eventually finds out about the affair and this leads to the third major tension – Tio Tomás is served with an eviction notice. He is 85 years old and is being forced to vacate a house that he has been renting for many years in Echo Park, a neighbourhood that was mostly Latino and affordable but is now experiencing rapid gentrification and the accompanying rise in property values. Carlos loses his job after vandalising Gary and James' car post-eviction notice, and Magdalena has no income, so finding a new home like the one Tio Tomás has been living in will be almost impossible with the elevated prices of newly renovated apartments in the area.

Music in *Quinceañera* serves several different functions and can basically be split into three categories: songs, character themes, and other dramatic score. I will mainly focus on the first two categories, since they are the most important with regard to the construction of identity and agency. The songs mostly follow the central themes of the film that are paralleled in the *quinceañera* celebration itself. They construct binaries of traditional/old/religious and modern/young/commercial. The character themes are pieces of original score that are named after the three main characters – Magdalena, Carlos, and Tio Tomás – on the soundtrack album. Each theme signifies information about the character and her or his subjectivity at that particular point in the narrative. I will discuss music from the film's opening first, and follow on with a consideration of songs and themes connected to the three main characters.

The primary genre of modern popular music associated with the film's teenagers, especially Carlos, is reggaetón. Since this music has a complex yet short history and a reputation for sexual explicitness, an extended discussion of the genre and its connotations is warranted. According to Philip Samponaro (2009), "since 2000, reggaetón has emerged as the defining music of Latino youth culture, displacing salsa, which previously held the distinction for thirty years" (p. 489). Samponaro goes on to describe the genre's characteristics and its origins:

> Named for Jamaican reggae, which influences its dance beat, reggaetón has gained increasing popularity over the last decade and a half in Puerto Rico, from where it has spread to the United States and where a common misconception has it originating in the *caseríos*, or projects, of Santurce and Bayamón. Reggaetón's fame may have originated in Puerto Rico, but its first creators were Panamanian artists (*raperos Panameños*) performing raps in Spanish styled after Jamaican dancehall rap.
>
> (p. 489)

Further emphasising the music's broad and powerful influence, Kim Kattari argues that "reggaeton, like salsa before it, became extremely popular among a pan-Latino audience in the United States specifically because of its musical hybridity" (2009, p. 117). She goes on to suggest that, due to "musical influences from an array of Latin-American cultures, different Latino groups will each find something in the music to enjoy and appreciate" (p. 117). While members of different Latino groups are probably attracted to the music as much for its particularity as a genre as they are for its traditional influences, it nevertheless has become a widespread phenomenon. The use of reggaetón songs in *Quinceañera* employs the music's hybridity to construct the social and private worlds of Carlos and, to a lesser extent, Magdalena and her friends.

Reggaetón also carries negative connotations – this is partially due to controversial lyrical content, but also due in large part to racist judgements surrounding the origins of the music. Samponaro (2009) explains the following about the music's racial history and connotations:

> In Puerto Rico (and elsewhere in the Caribbean), reggaetón reflects regional variation, which has heightened the ethno-racial or national appeal of the genre outside Panamá through the incorporation of the respective local music styles, which are considered "black," or poor people's music. As George Reid Andrews's work on Afro-Latin America suggests, race defines class in Latin America. An Afrocentric music, reggaetón thrives on the styles of the popular classes.
>
> (p. 493)

Thus, reggaetón's appeal and its perceived threat both stem from the mix of racially coded musical styles that are considered "poor people's music". But Samponaro asserts that the music was created by young people and appeals to young people because in this demographic "racial boundaries have not yet formally jelled" (p. 495). Unfortunately, not unlike rap artists, many reggaetón performers have incorporated sexism and homophobia into their lyrics, and these themes have been used to improve record sales through generation of controversy (p. 498).

This mix of racist judgments of the music and explicit lyrical content – sometimes sexist and homophobic, other times just sexual – has led to damning government intervention, which nevertheless helped to propel the music commercially:

> Because of its association with the dark-skinned *caseríos* of Santurce, reggaetón was immediately considered too "racy" for airplay. The Puerto Rican Senate even banned its beats, considering its lyrics, full of sexual innuendo, a negative influence on the island's youth. These circumstances earned the genre an early designation on the island as "underground" culture, where both the music and dances were to be performed clandestinely. The scenario also spoke of the fundamental battle over race and the corresponding association between people of color and debauchery, as symbolized in the action taken by the traditionally white Senate.
>
> (Samponaro, 2009, p. 499)

Yet this controversy also defined the music's intrinsic racial struggle, and the music's origins make it a tool of empowerment for all Latinos. According to Samponaro, reggaetón artists come from a mix of racial backgrounds and promote "a sense of cross-racial tolerance that in fact mirrors the reality of the Latino heritage". He goes on to state that "artists have even played off race to address the colonialism that has made skin color so divisive among Latinos in general" (p. 495). Despite some misogyny among male performers, both male and female performers have used the music to promote political causes, religion, and feminism (pp. 501–502). Samponaro and Kittari each discuss how the music has fostered a shared sense of pride, uniting people from across all ethnic/racial Latin-American and Latino backgrounds.

With this cultural context of reggaetón in mind, I will now discuss the music from the first part of the film in greater detail. The film actually begins with silence; a scenic landscape of lush pine forest and water becomes the background for Ernesto's opening remarks at Magdalena's cousin Eileen's *quinceañera*. A cut to the outside of the evangelical "Church of God" shows the boys and girls of the *quinceañera* party (dressed like bridesmaids and groomsmen in a wedding) hurriedly preparing for the ceremony. 'Marcha Triunfal De Aida', composed by

Giuseppe Verdi (for the opera *Aida*) and performed by The Multimusic Stars, starts with a cut back to the inside of the church and continues as the boys and girls walk slowly down the aisle in pairs, stop in two lines, and hold up roses to form an arch. Eileen and her escort then walk down the aisle, in a white dress and black suit respectively, and stop, with a close-up of the bouquet of flowers in Eileen's hand, in front of which the film's title appears. Eileen then sits in a large, white chair trimmed with roses and looks up at Ernesto, waiting patiently to be declared a woman by the preacher. The triumphant march then bridges a cut to a large fountain, in front of which the boys and girls have their pictures taken in various configurations as the opening credits continue.

With a cut to the inside of the Hummer limousine that Eileen's parents have rented for the occasion, there is an immediate and powerful contrast, both musically and in action, with the preceding scenes. The music changes to 'Don't Stop', a reggaetón/R&B hybrid performed by Moses McClean, featuring Malika. The behaviour of the boys and girls also changes from quiet, composed walking and posing for pictures to shouting and dancing. With the adults and the ceremony out of the way, the teenagers are now letting their hair down, yelling, laughing, and daring each other to dance on the illuminated pole in the middle of the limo (which a couple of girls and a boy do). 'Don't Stop' has a mix of male rapping and female singing, and the lyrics, which are all in English, are about dancing or sex depending on how one wishes to interpret them.

In reggaetón, according to Samponaro (2009), a "common musical strategy among male artists to express dominance is to incorporate female voices as the chorus in a call-and-response pattern with lyrics that reinforce female submission" (p. 498). In the example that Samponaro gives, the female responds to the male's call with submissive sexual suggestions. In contrast, the male and female positions are reversed in 'Don't Stop' with the woman singing the call part and the man rapping the response. Although the man's response to the woman's "don't stop, don't stop, keep it right there" is more sexually suggestive and clearly about a woman's body, there is a reversal of positions that gives the woman control. During the verse, the woman sings about a man watching her, but she is in control of the vocals and the scenario. Likewise, both girls and boys dance on the pole in the limo, and all seem to be having fun rather than doing it for the visual pleasure of the others. Lest this veer towards a postfeminist reading of the scene, it should be acknowledged that the act of a girl dancing on a pole is obviously more sexualised due to the broader context of exotic dancing, whereas the boy dancing on the pole is presented in a more humorous light. It bears mentioning that neither Magdalena nor Herman dance on the pole, but they do exchange awkward glances at the end of the scene, suggesting a complicated romantic situation.

Figure 8.1 Serious dancing at the *quinceañera*.

'Don't Stop' drops in volume and fades out after a cut to the outside of the limo. With a cut to the inside of the reception hall, 'Vals Fascinación' (Fascination Waltz), performed by Mariachi Los Palmeros, begins. The scene starts with a close-up of an elaborate cake-top statue of a woman in a white dress, flanked by two pink balloons with white text that reads "Mis Quince Años" ("My Fifteen Years"). Next, there is a cut to Eileen and her escort swaying back and forth awkwardly in front of an elaborate display of cakes and balloons. The rest of this sequence shows all of the teenagers and some children performing a traditional dance that they have obviously practiced for the occasion, while the rest of the guests patiently watch in silence. As the mariachi band that is positioned on a stage beneath an arch of pink balloons plays the song, the young people dance mechanically with little enthusiasm, frequently switching partners as convention dictates. Herman and Magdalena uncomfortably discuss another girl who is interested in Herman as they dance, and he denies having any feelings for her.

While watching the dance, Magdalena's father Ernesto and Eileen's father Walter (Johnny Chavez) discuss Magdalena's rapidly approaching *quinceañera*. When Walter tells Ernesto to "get ready to pay through the nose", Ernesto replies that Magdalena's *quinceañera* will not be like Eileen's because Magdalena is a more traditional girl. To this Walter dryly replies "alright Ernesto, if you say so", suggesting that he is aware of Ernesto's naïve view of Magdalena as traditional and unconcerned with material things and status symbols. In Ernesto's mind Magdalena is still a little girl, as his reaction to her pregnancy makes clear later in the film. The three songs that have appeared so far in the film have little to do with the development of the main characters. Rather, they begin to juxtapose and construct the tension between the traditional and the modern that lies at the heart of the film, which the protagonists must ultimately transcend, just as Ana did in *Real Women Have Curves*. The traditional conventions of the *quinceañera* seem important to the teenagers, yet all of them go through the motions in a manner that suggests a fun yet obligatory ritual rather than a tradition for which religious devotion breeds great enthusiasm. This celebration is more of a party, an important social event, and a backdrop to their normal activities; the guests at the reception look somewhat bored as they watch the dance, and Magdalena and Herman converse insecurely about their feelings and teenage dramas while they dance.

The song drops in volume as it bridges a cut to the kitchen where a series of close-ups show traditional Mexican food being prepared by the women of the family. After Eileen's mother Silvia (Carmen Aguirre) offers to alter Eileen's *quinceañera* dress for Magdalena, one of the women asks where her son Carlos is and why he is not coming to his own sister's *quinceañera*. Silvia angrily replies, "don't talk to me about that boy" and walks out of the room. Just after she says this, the 'Carlos' theme (dramatic score) begins with a jarring electronic pulse and bridges a cut to a shaky, hand-held tracking shot of Carlos from behind. The close-up of the back of Carlos' head and neck shows that he has "213"[1] tattooed on his neck. The theme has a reggaetón beat with pizzicato strings and a trembling synth melody that has a sound quality similar to that of early video game music. This high-pitched melody could, to some, recall synth parts from the early-1990s gangster rap subgenre G-Funk, popularised by the songs of Dr Dre and Snoop Dog.

With a cut to a frontal medium shot Carlos approaches a roadside flower market. He nonchalantly reaches down, picks up a rose from the flower stand, and begins to walk away. After the shopkeeper spots him and starts to yell, Carlos runs off and is chased by the yelling flower attendant. The Carlos theme then ends with a cut back to the party. This introduction of Carlos, starting with the shaky, hand-held tracking shot from behind that emphasises the tattoo and moving on to the rose theft, is obviously meant to give the perceiver the idea that Carlos is of dubious character and is possibly a gang member. The music plays a crucial role in this depiction, with its elements of reggaetón that draw on the genre's previously discussed negative connotations. At this point, all that has been divulged is that Carlos is not expected to attend his sister's *quinceañera*, and that his mother does not want to talk about him. The theft of the rose, while a minor crime, also suggests dishonesty. This short scene sets Carlos up as a criminal, although it later becomes clear that he is one of the film's most honest characters.

With a cut back to the party, everyone dances to 'Pica Pica' ('Hot Hot'), an up-tempo merengue performed by Mangana. After this song ends, 'Pa Toda Las Mamitas' ('For All the Little Mamas'), a reggaetón song performed by Noel, begins. Many young people are shown dancing suggestively to this song. One young man takes his shirt off

Figure 8.2 Queering *el perreo*.

while he dances. In addition, a boy and girl who took part in Eileen's *quinceañera* ceremony dance *el perreo*, a dance particular to reggaetón[2] that Samponaro (2009) describes in greater detail:

> [...] women participants have practiced submission through the performance of the defining dance that accompanies the production of reggaetón music, "*el perreo*." Translatable as "the doggie dance," *el perreo* simulates the sex act between dogs with the female dancing in a submissive position beneath the male, who dominates her from behind. This dance is everywhere present: in clubs, house parties, and on videos like The Score, which features female dancers in almost-pornographic postures.
>
> (pp. 498–499)

Indeed, in this scene the boy dances behind the girl, who is bent over, and he pushes down slightly on her back with his forearms. A cut to an older, seated couple shows expressions of surprise and slight disgust on their faces as they watch. Two younger men also look on with amusement. The dominance in this dance is soon complicated, however, by the addition of a third dancer. A second young woman joins the dance behind the boy. This could be considered a further addition to the boy's pleasure, except for the fact that the new dancer has a rather butch appearance – she is wearing jeans, a black button-up shirt, and a tie, and has slicked back hair that is clipped short at the sides and underneath. In addition, she dwarfs the rather diminutive boy in size and dances fully upright, arms swinging and pelvis thrusting, with a 'raunchy' facial expression. She takes over as the dominant partner and queers the otherwise aggressive heteronormativity of the dance.

As 'Pa Toda Las Mamitas' continues, Magdalena walks outside to check her phone and read a romantic text from Herman, who is then shown inside, dancing innocently with one of Magdalena's aunts (they are not doing *el perreo*). In this way both Magdalena and Herman are removed from the racial and sexual connotations that come with reggaetón music. This distancing of Herman and Magdalena from reggaetón serves to present the characters as somewhat 'wholesome', perhaps to position the perceiver in opposition to Ernesto's disgust later in the film when he discovers that Magdalena is pregnant. However, this sexual/innocent binary problematically reinforces Ernesto's patriarchal policing and judgement of his daughter's sexuality.

While Magdalena is standing outside, Carlos arrives at the party. With a cut to inside the reception hall, Carlos sneaks up behind Eileen as 'Pa Toda Las Mamitas' continues to play. Eileen turns around in shock and asks what Carlos is doing there after he presents her with the stolen rose and wishes her a happy birthday. With fear in her voice, Eileen tells Carlos that he had better leave. But within seconds Carlos is spotted by his father, Walter, who rushes towards him and asks why he is there. During the argument that follows, the music stops and Walter tells Carlos that he disgusts him. As a response, Carlos shoves his father, who then punches him in the face, knocking Carlos to the floor. Two large young men then escort Carlos outside. When he tries to go back inside, one of the men who dragged him out punches Carlos yet again. He finally decides to leave after Tio Tomás tells him to go home. Once again, Carlos is presented as a questionable character. Several people accuse him of ruining his sister's "big day", but it is still not clear why his father is so disgusted with him. It is significant, however, that Carlos arrives when reggaetón is playing, instead of a more traditional genre that would lack reggaetón's negative connotations.

A few minutes later, after the *quinceañera* party is over, a variation on the 'Carlos' theme enters with a cut to the inside of a house with a few close-ups of religious statues. The theme begins with a vaguely Latin-sounding acoustic guitar. The camera then cuts to a coffin-shaped case that is opened to reveal several joints and some rolling papers. Carlos takes a joint from the case and, as he lights up, the music mimics the sound of the flame as a hip-hop beat fades in and continues to propel the song. This version of 'Carlos' is more relaxed, with the same melody as before, but this time with a hip hop beat rather than a reggaetón rhythm. Although different, this variation draws on hip hop for similar connotations of criminal behaviour as Carlos, bruised and wearing a blood-stained, white tank top undershirt, smokes marijuana in Tio Tomás' house. The theme fades out and Carlos hides his marijuana as Tio Tomás and Carlos' aunt and uncle enter the house, discussing the fact that Carlos was kicked out of his house and that his parents will not divulge their motivation for doing so. The secrecy surrounding Carlos' expulsion from the family home, in combination with his audiovisual characterisation, continues to encourage audience assumptions of criminal behaviour that will eventually be proven unsubstantiated, forcing audiences to confront the implications of their own presumptions.

Figure 8.3 A misleading introduction to Carlos.

The connection between Carlos and reggaetón music is strengthened by his association with another song and different versions of his theme. 'No la Mola Tu Tombao', which is also performed by Noel, plays on one occasion when Carlos is working at, and walking home from, a car wash. The song also returns during the end credits, which emphasises the position of Carlos as the film's central character, even if the film's title and significant plot concerning Magdalena's pregnancy would suggest otherwise. (The only other song during the end credits is '*Quinceañera*' by The Multimusic Allstars, a saccharine song that plays earlier on the videotape of Eileen's *quinceañera*.)

The 'Carlos' theme returns two more times in its original form and on one other occasion as a variation, 'Carlos II'. In one scene, the original 'Carlos' theme plays from Carlos' mobile as his ring tone. Later, after James discovers that Gary is cheating on him with Carlos, Carlos overhears the couple arguing and Gary saying that Carlos is just some kid about whom he does not care. 'Carlos II' begins as Carlos listens in and bridges a cut to him walking around at night and smoking marijuana. The instrumentation and rhythm of 'Carlos II' differ from the original theme. This version has strings, a piano, and swirling keyboards, and has neither the reggaetón rhythm nor the hip hop beat. The overall effect is a more ominous feel, and the processed swirling keyboard sounds reflect Carlos' confused and depressed mental state, as well as the influence of the marijuana.

James' discovery of the affair results in the eviction of Tío Tomás, Carlos, and Magdalena. The original 'Carlos' theme returns once more when Carlos is working at the car wash and his boss tells him to wash a Mustang, which belongs to James and Gary. As his theme plays, Carlos carves an obscenity in the car's paint with James' keys. His boss soon notices what he is doing, however, and Carlos is chased and beaten up (although the fight is not shown). Carlos is associated with reggaetón throughout the film – not only through his theme but also with 'Pa Toda Las Mamitas', which is playing at Eileen's *quinceañera* party when he shows up and 'starts trouble' (although it is really his father who causes the trouble), and 'No la Mola Tu Tombao'. This music suggests criminality through its history and popular connotations derived from racism, but it also carries ideas of aggressive heterosexuality and male dominance, as previously discussed.

Carlos gains strength from his theme and the other reggaetón songs, however. The agency he shows when vandalising the Mustang results in the loss of his job, but it is also a turning point in his life. Just after this event, he decides to look for a better career and offers to take care of Magdalena and her baby, since Herman has completely disappeared from her life by this point. Crucially, his statement of these intentions causes Tio Tomás, who is listening from another room, to smile proudly. Tomás is aware that he may die soon, and he finds comfort in the knowledge that Carlos will become a responsible adult. Much like the reggaetón that was banned in Puerto Rico, Carlos does not deserve the damning judgement from his father, so he refocuses the negativity and his anger on improving the circumstances of Magdalena and himself. It is appropriate that Carlos is aligned with a musical culture that, at least in Puerto Rico, had to go underground due to being banned. Carlos has had to take his sexuality 'underground' in a similar manner, but he still manages to thrive under these circumstances.

It is also interesting that Carlos, like the butch young woman at Eileen's *quinceañera* party, turns the sexual connotations of reggaetón on their head. The fact that he is gay problematises the heteronormativity and domination associated with reggaetón and gives the music fresh meaning. For Carlos, reggaetón is a source of strength and pride in a life full of struggle, just as Samponaro (2009) and Kattari (2009) suggest it is a source of Latino pride and unification. When Tio Tomás dies, Carlos gives a very moving, heartfelt speech at his funeral. At this point, it becomes clear to all of the attendees that they had misjudged Carlos, just as reggaetón music plays a significant role in coercing the audience into initially misjudging him.

Unlike Carlos, Magdalena does not have musical ties that highlight certain aspects of her personality or draw on complex genre connotations. She is often associated with original score that comments on her emotional state. However, her theme, much like Carlos' theme, does co-incide with a turning point in her confidence and an increase in agency. The 'Magdalena' theme enters after Carlos tells Magdalena that he will get a better job and take care of her and the baby. Earlier in the film, Magdalena was worried about her pregnancy, the reaction of her father, and the increasing distance of Herman. From this point on, however, she takes control of her future. 'Magdalena' is an optimistic sounding theme containing guitar, harmonica, and drums, with a generic light folk-rock feel. Rather than telling the audience about Magdalena's identity, the music gives a positive feel to the scene and suggests an increase in confidence. This theme continues as Magdalena picks up a house rental magazine and starts to look for a prospective home for herself, Carlos, and Tio Tomás. Although she has no initial success, Magdalena does connect with one woman who eventually drops the rental price in return for an offer of free cleaning and gardening. The fact that Magdalena and Carlos still move into the apartment after Tio Tomás dies is suggested by the owner's presence at Magdalena's *quinceañera* at the end of the film.

Magdalena's theme is generally associated with growing up, due not only to her increase in agency, but also because of the song's presence when she finds Tio Tomás dead. Unlike Carlos and Tio Tomás, Magdalena's ethnicity is not really made an issue in the film. Her interest in her *quinceañera* is more like the interest of a girl in her prom in a typical youth film. But Magdalena does fit the stereotype of the pregnant minority teenage girl, and the ultimate treatment of her pregnancy is somewhat regressive. After Magdalena's mother tells her father that a doctor verified she never had penetrative sex he finally believes her. Furthermore, he instantly forgives Magdalena and calls the pregnancy a "miracle". Even after Magdalena insists that there is a scientific explanation, Ernesto says, "God works in mysterious ways." Earlier in the film, Magdalena refuses to tell her father about this proof of her virginity because she feels that she should not have to just so he can regain his pride. However, at this point she accepts his forgiveness with no resistance, and his offer to make it up to her results in the renting of a Hummer limo for her *quinceañera*. By the end of the film, everything has been forgiven and her father performs the ceremony. The lack of musical complexity in relation to Magdalena's character fits this simplistic, conservative ending.

The film musically represents Tio Tomás' ethnicity in a somewhat obvious manner, yet his music highlights the issues of gentrification and ethnic displacement brought up throughout the film. On two separate occasions, Tio Tomás is associated with 'Vagabundo' ('Vagabond'), performed by the Puerto Rican group Los Tres Reyes. This is a mid-tempo folk song with an Afro-Latin sound. In both of the sequences where 'Vagabundo' plays, Tio Tomás is walking around the neighbourhood selling *champurrado* from his cart. The first sequence contains scenes of Tio Tomás preparing the drink with large quantities of raw ingredients, as well as colourful shots of the neighbourhood, similar to those previously discussed in *Real Women Have Curves*. These scenes show a man scooping up large chunks of tropical fruit that he is selling from a cart, Latino musicians in cowboy hats, a woman with dark curly hair and a short black dress walking by a man selling colourful balloons, and a barbershop where Latino men are getting their hair trimmed. As Tomás leaves his house (also wearing a cowboy hat) he passes by his new neighbours/landlords, Gary and James, who have just pulled into their driveway in a red Mustang convertible with new chairs stacked in the back. Later in the scene, Tio Tomás jokes with the obviously familiar customers to whom he sells *champurrado*. During the second occurrence of 'Vagabundo', Tio Tomás sells *champurrado* and discusses the rising house prices in the neighbourhood with some local women. He also comments on how much the neighbourhood has changed.

The Puerto Rican sound of 'Vagabundo' combines with the colourful scenes to tropicalise the neighbourhood somewhat, but the traditional feel of the song connects with Tio Tomás, an old man who was born in Mexico and sells *champurrado*, the making of which suggests artisanship rather than cooking. The 'old world' character of Tio Tomás suggested by his Marian devotion, his occupation, his cowboy hat, and 'Vagabundo' are juxtaposed in these two sequences with his new landlords (wealthy, gay, white, young) and the rising house prices that are the result of similar young professionals moving into the newly hip neighbourhood. Tomás' familiarity with his customers shows a connection to the neighbourhood and a traditional closeness of community that is also suggested by the shot of the barbershop. Both of the sequences containing 'Vagabundo' construct Tio Tomás as a traditional character in a changing world – here represented by a working-class Latino neighbourhood experiencing gentrification. In addition, these scenes foreshadow the disappearance of Tio Tomás' way of life, and the ultimate disappearance of Tio Tomás. Lyrically, the song is about a vagabond who cannot find love and wanders alone. These words also suggest the loneliness of the old man and the fact that he is without a permanent home, especially since he will soon be kicked out of the rental in which he has lived for so long.

Like Carlos and Magdalena, Tio Tomás has a theme bearing his name. This theme is first heard after Tio Tomás tries to convince Ernesto to talk to Magdalena about the pregnancy and bridges a cut to Tomás placing a picture of Magdalena on the altar in his garden and doing the Christian 'sign of the cross'. 'Tio Tomás' is a simple, contemplative, melancholic, generically 'Latin' theme played by two guitars. As with Carlos and Magdalena, Tomás' theme is present at times of agency. In this scene, he prays for Mary to intervene in the problems of Magdalena and Ernesto. 'Tio Tomás' is also heard before and after Tomás' funeral. Although he is dead at this point, the music carries his good will, tolerance, and sense of forgiveness. While Tio Tomás is traditional in many ways, it is suggested that he knows about Carlos' sexuality, even though he tells some relatives that he does not know why Carlos was kicked out of his parents' house. At one point, he tells Carlos that he is glad he has a "special friend". While Carlos is never shown mentioning his sexuality or the fact that his friend is a man to Tio Tomás, this scene implies that Tomás understands the situation. 'Tio Tomás' plays just before the funeral, at which Carlos gives a moving speech about his great great uncle's warmth and generosity. After the funeral, the 'Tio Tomás' theme starts just before Ernesto asks for Magdalena's forgiveness. The presence of 'Tio Tomás' musically suggests that the man's tolerance, forgiveness, and kindness live on through those he has been close to.

The music in *Quinceañera* creates and re-enforces ethnically coded ideas of tradition and change. It also serves to broaden representations of Latina/o characters through the construction of complex identities, especially in the case of Carlos. Original themes use elements of popular styles to suggest certain traits that draw on the cultural history of genres such as reggaetón. One major difference between the music, characters, and narrative of *Quinceañera* and those of *Real Women Have Curves* is that in *Quinceañera* there is not such an emphasis on the traditional/modern (old world/new world) divide as an either/or choice that must be made. Rather, in *Quinceañera*, Magdalena, Carlos, and Tio Tomás continue to live in a changing world that bridges the old and the new in a specifically Latino context. None of these characters are planning to move away from their neighbourhood or families. The incorporation of more specifically modern music genres in *Quinceañera* helps to create a present in which the young characters can live and grow without having to decide between leaving and being held back.

In her discussion of *quinceañera* ceremonies and how women navigate ideas of tradition and change, Karen May Davalos (1996) says the following about how women regard the role of *quinceañera* ceremonies in the modern world:

> The *quinceañera* is an anchor between two cultures. It is a space in which *mexicanas* position themselves outside of and within dominant narratives about Mexican woman and the United States. [...] Nonetheless, as Gloria Anzaldúa points out, *mexicanas* move through the uncomfortable territory, "this place of contradictions" between their Mexico and their United States, between patriarchy and equality in order to make sense of their lives. It is a territory that permits two or more cultures, multiple meanings, and complicated constructions of a *mexicana*. It is a site of negotiation in which people and cultural practices are not coherent, whole, or distinct. The discourse and practice of the *quinceañera* encourage us to examine the paradoxical and ambiguous nature of "tradition." The discourse and practice suggest that what we intend as "cultural" is fluid, slippery, contradictory, spontaneous, and chaotic.
>
> (p. 123)

This discussion perfectly reflects many of the themes present in the film. The negotiation of tradition and identity by Magdalena, Carlos, and Tio Tomás is at the heart of the film. Much like the women Davalos describes, these characters have many sides to them that do not reflect simplistic conceptions of Mexico and the United States. The film's music plays a key role in conveying elements of fluid identity to the audience. This is done especially effectively in the use of reggaetón by drawing on simplistic genre connotations only to later subvert them with complex character identities.

Both *Real Women Have Curves* and *Quinceañera* use a mix of modern and traditional musical styles to construct the ethnic identity of their characters. These films mostly correlate modern styles of music with young characters' moments of agency. In the next chapter I discuss *Better Luck Tomorrow*, a film in which music does not reflect ethnic identity in such a straightforward manner. In this film, Asian-American characters are associated with songs that have English lyrics and do not directly connote any ethnicity within the US. However, a closer examination of music in this film reveals character identities constructed in more complex ways through associations with feminist music and the manipulation of teen film genre conventions.

Notes

1 213 is the telephone area code of downtown Los Angeles. It was also a rap group consisting of Snoop Dog, Warren G, and Nate Dogg before the three artists found fame through other projects.
2 For an ethnographic study that problematises *el perreo* and the gender connotations of reggaetón in Cuba, see Jan Fairley (2006).

References

Davalos, Karen May (1996) '"La Quinceañera": Making Gender and Ethnic Identities' in *Frontiers: A Journal of Women Studies*, Vol. 16, No. 2/3, pp. 101–127.
Espinosa, Aurelio (2009) 'Home Altars and the Virgin of Guadalupe in *Quinceañera*: Historical and Critical Perspectives' in *Journal of Religion and Popular Culture* [Internet], Vol. 21, No. 1, Available from: http://www.usask.ca/relst/jrpc/articles21(1).html [Accessed 15 July 2010].
Fairley, Jan (2006) 'Dancing Back to Front: *Regeton*, Sexuality, Gender and Transnationalism in Cuba' in *Popular Music*, Vol. 25, No. 3, pp. 471–488.
García, Alma M. (2002) *The Mexican Americans*, Westport, CT: Greenwood Press.
Kattari, Kim (2009) 'Building Pan-Latino Unity in the United States through Music: An Exploration of Commonalities between Salsa and Reggaeton' in *Musicological Explorations* [Internet], Vol. 10, September, pp. 105–136, Available from: http://journals.uvic.ca/index.php/me/article/view/149/181 [Accessed: 16 July 2010].
Samponaro, Philip (2009) '"Oye mi canto" ("Listen to My Song"): The History and Politics of Reggaetón' in *Popular Music and Society*, Vol. 32, No. 4, pp. 489–506.

Filmography

Quinceañera (*Echo Park, LA* – alternate title, 2006, USA) directed by Richard Glatzer and Wash Westmoreland, music by Victor Bock and Micko Westmoreland, music supervision by Shaun Young, Metrodome Distribution.
Real Women Have Curves (2002, USA) directed by Patricia Cardoso, music by Heitor Pereira, music supervision by Margaret Guerra Rogers, Home Box Office Home Video.

9 Reimagining the All-American Teenager

Inaudible Ethnicity and Agency from the Margins in *Better Luck Tomorrow*

Better Luck Tomorrow (Justin Lin, 2002) is one of the few mainstream US youth films in which all of the major characters are Asian Americans.[1] The plot of this film revolves around the academic and criminal activities of four Orange County high school students – Ben (Parry Shen), Virgil (Jason Tobin), Han (Sung Kang), and Daric (Roger Fan). The story begins on a sunny day with the discovery of a body buried in a backyard. Ben and Virgil sit discussing plans for their future when a phone rings. After checking their own phones, the pair crawl along the ground and dig, finding a body just beneath the surface, where they also discover the ringing phone. With a tornado of swirling sounds and sped-up images, the title of the film appears on screen, followed by a flashback to "Four Months Prior". From this point, the story is narrated by Ben and focuses on his academic and extra-curricular activities. Every action in the lives of Ben and the others seems to exist solely for creating the perfect college application. Eventually, however, Ben, Virgil, Daric, and Han get involved in criminal pursuits, seemingly motivated by nothing more than boredom.

Starting small with the sale of cheat sheets, the unlikely gang eventually moves on to drug pushing and complicated schemes involving the theft of computer equipment. Throughout this development, Ben deals with a crush on his lab partner, Stephanie (Karin Anna Cheung), while transforming into a cocaine-vacuuming robot, all consumed by academic study and petty crime. Eventually Ben decides to clean up his act, focusing on his studies and a growing friendship with Stephanie, complicated only by the fact that she has a boyfriend. But like most protagonists who attempt to turn away from a life of crime, Ben is eventually pulled back in. The gang decide to take on one last job when Stephanie's boyfriend Steve (John Cho) asks them to rob his parents' house to "teach them a lesson". After some initial apprehension, the gang choose to take the offer, but rather than loot the house they decide to teach Steve a lesson by ambushing and assaulting him. Everything goes terribly wrong, however, when Steve gets a hold of one of the gang's guns. After hearing a gunshot, Ben rushes into the garage where the rest are assaulting Steve. Even though the gun is wrestled away from Steve, something inside Ben snaps and he ends up beating Steve to death with a baseball bat. The boys then bury the body in the back yard and try to forget about the whole thing. The film comes full circle with a repeat of the body discovery from the beginning and continues to show the deleterious effects of the murder on the four friends.

Better Luck Tomorrow is an important film because of the inclusion it insists on for Asian Americans in youth films in general and in the teen film genre in particular. Unlike the music in *Real Women Have Curves* (Patricia Cardoso, 2002) and *Quinceañera* (Richard Glatzer and Wash Westmoreland, 2006), the soundtrack of *Better Luck Tomorrow* does not use traditional styles to re-enforce ethnicity in any way. In her exploration of representation, masculinity, and parody in *Better Luck Tomorrow*, Margaret Hillenbrand (2008) argues that the racial makeup of teen film protagonists is usually limited to the white middle class, with African Americans present mostly in explorations of more complex social issues (p. 63). Asian-American characters are often only involved in the capacity of racist stereotypes. Hillenbrand goes on to discuss more specific examples of roles traditionally given to Asian Americans:

> For women, the representation possibilities continue to be defined, and delimited, in erotic terms. Thus dragon ladies, China dolls, Miss Saigon/Madame Butterfly, and single Asian females seeking their white knights are still the major blueprint – all highly fevered but barely differentiated creations of the white male mind as it pursues fantasies of sexual otherness that are as old as empire itself. For the Asian American males who are displaced by this interracial erotic configuration, the constraints are stricter still. Seldom granted a cinematic space outside the laundry, the triad, the kung-fu club, or the academic decathlon, Asian American men are so far from landing roles where they might "get the girl" that access to fully fledged, three-dimensional masculinity (even if it is defined in heterosexist, homosocial terms) is denied them – and in the blithest, most unreflecting of ways – across the popular culture terrain.
>
> (p. 50)

To Hillenbrand, this film is especially important when considered in relation to the history of feminised representations of Asian-American males in popular culture. Taking into account this feminisation and the restrictive stereotypical roles usually on offer, the making of a teen film with an Asian-American lead cast is a tricky undertaking. Mainstream teen films have evolved a standardised vocabulary; the set of conventions by which these films operate dictates that working with any type of difference might necessarily mean breaking with convention, thus moving the film outside the teen genre to a more niche setting.

Figure 9.1 All-American boys.

Better Luck Tomorrow works hard to get beyond the oversimplified label of 'Asian-American Teen Film' while staying within teen film genre boundaries (with perhaps the exception of the murder). As Tasha G. Oren (2005) asserts:

> the power and appeal of *Better Luck Tomorrow* and *Secret Asian Man* to mainstream audiences is neither in the transcendence of their particularities (the secret handshake of racial experience) nor the humanist "universal" of "race blind" (or "practically white") narratives. Instead, their cultural work is in reconfiguring Asian American experience into the common vocabulary of mainstream entertainment fiction and its history.
>
> (p. 356)

This navigation between outright representational politics and performing in 'white face' involves a tightrope walk that may be elusive on first exposure to the film. For Hillenbrand, *Better Luck*'s success in accomplishing this move to the mainstream involves a more complicated strategy than simply adapting to genre conventions. She argues that the film successfully makes the jump while avoiding simple assimilation due to its parody of other genres:

> [...] the film articulates Asian American masculinity via the long-established codes, cues, and conventions of Hollywood, moving away from the self-referentiality of the Asian American cinematic tradition toward the open waters of the mainstream. Unlike its movie predecessors – which often express their protest through the

content-based devices of plot and character – *Better Luck Tomor-row* articulates itself through narratology, borrowing magpie-like from the mainstream and using allusion to create a metacinematic parody. [...] parody both legitimizes and undermines the object of its attentions: insofar as it is imitative, the parodic impulse flatters its original in the sincerest of ways. Yet its citations are also ironic and as such operate subversively.

(pp. 56–57)

Hillenbrand goes on to say that *Better Luck* mainly parodies two genres: "the American teen movie, particularly in its 1980s and 1990s incarnations" and "the 'ethnic' gangster movie in its various guises. Most obvious is the debt to Martin Scorsese's *Goodfellas* (1990)" (pp. 61–62).

Although Hillenbrand's parody argument is satisfying with regard to the subversive power it affords the film and its cast and is perhaps appropriate when considering the "'ethnic' gangster movie", it is somewhat problematic when the generic traits of teen films are taken into account. While it is true that some youth films are concerned with more serious social issues (racism, pregnancy, LGBTQ identity, poverty, violence resulting from marginalisation, etc.), mainstream teen films often concern less serious subject matter. In fact, one defining characteristic of mainstream teen films is that they are meant to be funny and light in tone. Films such as *Porky's* (Bob Clark, 1981) and *Revenge of the Nerds* (Jeff Kanew, 1984) set the standards for future teen comedies like *American Pie* (Paul Weitz, 1999), while clever films like *Heathers* (Michael Lehmann, 1988) and *Clueless* (Amy Heckerling, 1995) brought sharp wit, irony, and satire to the genre. And the string of John Hughes hits in the mid-1980s including *Sixteen Candles* (John Hughes, 1984), *The Breakfast Club* (John Hughes, 1985), *Weird Science* (John Hughes, 1985), *Pretty in Pink* (Howard Deutch, 1986 written by John Hughes), and *Ferris Bueller's Day Off* (John Hughes, 1986) contained such exaggerated characters and absurd situations that recklessly breaking the bounds of verisimilitude was fair game for any teen films that followed. Those that did follow often parodied Hughes' sappy romantic scenarios, as well as his incorporation of pop songs into grandiose emotional climaxes. Contemporary teen films possess a tongue-in-cheek self-awareness of their ridiculous plots and characters and regularly parody the very genre to which they belong. How then can *Better Luck Tomorrow* be a parody of teen films? While it is true that a few films such as *Not Another Teen Movie* (Joel Gallen, 2001) are intended to parody the genre, the line between parody and genre film is practically non-existent in these films. In taking absurdities already existing in the genre to their limit, it really is *just another teen movie*.

Better Luck Tomorrow's level of parody is far too subtle to break away from the absurdities of the typical teen film. Yet Hillenbrand's argument becomes more convincing when she insists that it is the awkwardness of the presence of Asian-American bodies in these stereotypically white, masculine, teen film stock roles and situations that makes the film subversive. In this sense it is not only the parody of generic traits (from both teen and gangster films) but the self-consciously faithful reproduction of them. The film's soundtrack seems to support this part of her argument by sitting uncomfortably in the teen film genre.

In a party scene that Hillenbrand considers, the boys end up getting into a fight with stereotypical 'jocks'. This scuffle results in Daric pulling his gun, which causes the jocks to back down. The techno music at the party ends abruptly when Daric draws the gun, suggesting that the protagonists dominate the space sonically, as well as through violence. After a cut, the boys are shown celebrating their new gangster personae by playing rap music as they drive around. However, when a car full of 'real gangsters' (so implied because they have darker skin[2] and are brandishing larger guns) pulls up beside the boys, the bass of the rap music from the gangsters' car overpowers the boys' music in the same way that their 'authentic' gangster personae displaces the boys' role-playing. At this point Daric turns the music off, as if to diffuse any perceived challenge to the real gangsters. These gangsters put an end to the protagonists' musical transformation, drawing attention to the protagonists' awkward fit in any mainstream cinema character type.

Hillenbrand asserts that the boys are out of place, both as typical students at the party (Daric is taunted by one of the jocks for wearing a letterman jacket awarded for tennis; Ben is referred to as the "Chinese [Michael] Jordan") and as ethnic gangsters (pp. 66–67). While she does mention the overpowering nature of the music from the 'real' gangsters' car, she states it drowns out the protagonists' music, neglecting important details regarding when music stops, both at the party and in the car, and who controls this

Figure 9.2 Confrontation at the party.

music. The fact that the boys willingly back down with regard to music (by reducing the volume) suggests an emasculating subservience fitting with Asian-American male stereotypes. As evidenced by the party scene, the boys are not allowed to be jocks or gangsters, and throughout the film, other typical teen roles prove equally problematic for them.

While the use of rap music in the driving sequence contains fairly obvious connotations of gang violence and dominance, music throughout the rest of the film has a more complicated relationship with the characters. The majority of songs on the soundtrack could be placed into one of three broad categories: (1) distorted alternative rock, (2) electronic music, and (3) lighter acoustic rock. While not strict genres, these categories are distinct enough to influence the way one perceives characters and plot action accompanied by the songs. Particularly interesting are the meanings the songs from the first two groups bring to characters and narrative.

To begin with, I will consider the distorted alternative rock songs. There is only one song in the film by a well-known band with connections to riot grrrl music: 'Let's Run' by Le Tigre. Nevertheless, the placement of this song sets the feeling and semantic relations for the rest of the film. Kathleen Hanna, singer of Le Tigre, was also in well-known riot grrrl band Bikini Kill, although Le Tigre is a popular feminist band in its own right. 'Let's Run', with its distorted, simple, driving guitar line and slightly angry, disinterested sounding female vocals, appears early in the film. The song starts with a cut to school buses parked outside and continues over a montage of cheerleaders dancing, male students watching the cheerleaders, various students and teachers walking around the high school, and Ben entering the school in slow motion. In combination with the previously described musical elements of the song, the montage uses choppy editing and speed-altered shots of still objects and students walking, goofing around, etc. Several elements of this montage, particularly Ben's slow-motion entrance and a jock's insistence on Ben sliding his exam over so he can cheat, do play on conventions and stereotypes. But nothing in this clip stretches the boundaries of the teen film genre enough to justify completely Hillenbrand's argument for parody. Two elements that do stand out in the teen film context, however, are the centrality of Asian-American characters and the use of a Le Tigre song. These are particularly important with regard to the film's comment on Asian-American representation.

Several of the tracks in the distorted alternative rock category are performed by bands signed to Kill Rock Stars – the label that signed Bikini Kill, as well as other riot grrrl and feminist bands such as Huggy Bear, Bratmobile, Sleater-Kinney, and Kathleen Hanna's solo project Julie Ruin. The following description of the label appears on the Kill Rock Stars website:

> KRS's mission is to continue putting out exceptional records by important artists, and our tradition of being queer-positive, feminist, and artist-friendly continues as well. We are now distinguished by

being one of the few female-run indie labels in the US, which we are proud of, but all that really means is get out there and start your record labels, ladies!

This mission statement outlines political views that are important to the label and to its artists. In addition to Kathleen Hanna's connection to Kill Rock Stars, the following artists featured on the *Better Luck Tomorrow* soundtrack are currently or were previously signed to the label (with the number of songs contributed to the soundtrack): Bonfire Madigan (2), Emily's Sassy Lime (2), Mocket (1), and Semiautomatic (7). Thus, at least these 12 songs have a connection to a feminist label, even without consideration of the lyrics or each artist's politics. And, as previously mentioned, many of the songs by these bands (with Semiautomatic being an exception that I shall return to later) and others featured on the soundtrack are musically similar to 'Let's Run' by Le Tigre.

This inclusion of feminist bands and bands signed to a label with a well-known feminist stance is interesting considering that all four protagonists are male. The lone female character of note is Stephanie, Ben's cheerleader love interest, and she is only associated with the lighter alternative songs in scenes portraying the tender feelings and developing relationship between the two characters. Thus, the four male protagonists are propelled through their journey by these unlikely musical selections. I would like to suggest, however, that this music has a stronger connection to Ben, Virgil, Han, and Daric than may be immediately apparent. The alignment of these four Asian-American teens with feminist music makes more sense when one considers the marginalisation and oppression that has been experienced by both women and Asian Americans.

In addition, popular cultural representations have tended to feminise both Asian-American males and women. (This is most true with white women, however, since representations of women of colour tend to be more complex with respect to gender – see Halberstam below.) Such feminising tendencies have led to book-length gender studies such as David Eng's *Racial Castration: Managing Masculinity in Asian America* (2001) and Judith Halberstam's *Female Masculinity* (1998). Halberstam argues the following regarding masculinity:

> Masculinity [...] becomes legible as masculinity where and when it leaves the white male middle-class body. Arguments about excessive masculinity tend to focus on black bodies (male and female), latino/a bodies, or working class bodies, and insufficient masculinity is all too often figured by Asian bodies or upper-class bodies; these stereotypical constructions of variable masculinity mark the process by which masculinity becomes dominant in the sphere of white middle-class maleness.

(p. 2)

Filmic representations of Asian Americans and women do not simply ignore difference, they construct a false reality – one in which Asian-American men are never truly masculine and white women are always feminine, unless they are clearly identified as 'abnormal' – tomboys to be corrected or lesbians to be contained. Both groups are refused masculine privilege in dominant representations. This shared history of real oppression and representational constraint makes the pairing of music and characters in *Better Luck Tomorrow* entirely appropriate; the politics and energy of the music empower the protagonists throughout the film.

Semiautomatic, the band listed above with the most songs on the soundtrack, fits into the electronic music category. Their songs differ in texture and style from the other Kill Rock Stars bands featured in this film, and they play a somewhat different role in the narrative. Electronic music by Semiautomatic and other musically similar bands regularly functions as dramatic score and often appears during scenes depicting the gang's criminal activity and Ben's drug use. Bass and beat heavy music plays during scenes of petty crime, drug use, and more serious criminal offences. Semiautomatic's music plays during two scenes where the protagonists buy computer equipment from a store and return it with different stickers to make a profit. Similar music appears when they steal computers from the school, when Ben uses cocaine with Stephanie's boyfriend Steve and later wakes up with a bloody nose, when the gang drink shots of tequila during academic decathlon practice at Daric's house, and when Ben explains that stealing feels good because it is the one thing that does not go on his college applications.

Electronic dance music has a history of association with drugs and crime, whether perpetrated through moral panic in print media, through its affiliation with deviance in film and television, or simply because real drug use in club cultures is well documented.[3] Therefore, it is not surprising that this type of music is used during scenes depicting crime and drug use in the film. But this music also reflects the duality of the four protagonists that Hillenbrand refers to in her discussion of Robert G. Lee's concept of the "'model minority as gook': the honor student who turns triad in Chinatown, and thus embodies 'the popular Vietnam War trope of the female Viet Cong fighter emerging from a crowd of friendly villagers to kill … the American savior'" (pp. 58–59). Hillenbrand then expands on what she sees as the parodic duality of the protagonists:

> Alternating metrically between "geek" and "gook," their split subjectivity reaffirms hoary white fears about the inscrutability of the "Oriental" [...] But the stereotype is not played straight, of course, and the gook/geek gang seems instead to point to an Asian American masculinity that defies such absolutes. [...] the gang fuses the two

disjoined halves of the model minority stereotype into a single subject position. Needless to say, any such fusion makes most sense as
satire: the boys cannot be geeks because they are gooks, nor gooks
because they are geeks, and the Jekyll and Hyde *leitmotif* is exposed
as racist melodrama. Through this anti-syllogism, which enables
Ben and his friends to be both "good" and "bad" Asians, often in a
single scene, the absurdity of the stereotype is revealed at the same
time as its "truth" is parodically affirmed.

(p. 59)

Hillenbrand's argument for parody is stronger in this passage, and the
use of electronic dance music in the film enforces this fusion of the good
and bad Asian stereotypes "into a single subject position". The music
works in this way for a couple of reasons. I have already discussed the association of electronic dance music and drugs/deviance, but the making
of such music also necessitates a 'geeky' relationship with technology –
proficiency with computers and/or synthesisers requires more diligence
than it takes to play three chords on a guitar. Thus, the presence of this
music in scenes of criminal enterprise reflects the duality of the characters, while at the same time helping to construct this duality.

   In addition to the previously discussed relevance of riot grrrl and electronic music to the musical agency of Ben, Virgil, Han, and Daric, the
use of songs by Asian-American artists adds an extra layer of meaning
to the soundtrack, and in fact relates directly to the central dilemma of
the film as discussed by Hillenbrand: *Better Luck Tomorrow* is at once a
niche film and a mainstream teen film. Alternatively, it is at least a niche
film trying to be a mainstream teen film. Or, it is a niche film that parodies mainstream teen films so carefully that it becomes one. The film's
position between niche and mainstream mirrors current Asian-American
involvement in the music industry as discussed by Oliver Wang (2001).
Wang argues that, unlike Asian-American musicians of the 1970s, those
of the 1990s were not solely concerned with identity politics. Although
some were still primarily political, others looked to reach a wider audience with less overtly principled music:

   [...] a wave of young Asian Americans are now entering into the
   popular music industry as singers, rappers, rockers, and musicians.
   While they have yet to crack the glass ceiling in the recording industry (merely a handful are signed to major labels), they have become
   a viable and, in some cases, seminal force in popular music. They
   are spearheading a major push into the popular media by working
   independently and thriving in smaller niches of the music market.
   In contrast to the previous generation, who made music "for, by
   and about" Asian Americans, many of the new artists seek to make
   music for an audience beyond their ethnic constituency. This doesn't

equate to a rejection of an ethnic audience, but they're not seeking dialogue solely with that community. Their music is, as the cliché goes, "for everyone."

(pp. 456–457)

This niche-yet-mainstream musical activity mirrors the uncomfortable status of *Better Luck Tomorrow* as a teen film and the awkward representation of the film's protagonists as All-American teens. At least five of the bands on the soundtrack (Ee, Semiautomatic, Emily's Sassy Lime, Versus, and IQU) have one or more Asian-American members. The independent label affiliations and music of these artists reflect the trend discussed by Wang. Ethnicity is inaudible in the soundtrack, but the marginality of the music still sides with and lends further musical agency to the film's protagonists.

Musically, culturally, and biographically, the songs in this film and their recording artists represent marginality and struggle that has been present throughout the history of Asian-American representations in film. An unlikely alliance of the main characters with feminist music draws on a shared history of feminisation and oppression to enhance character agency. Furthermore, music throughout this film constructs identities beyond the mono-ethnic. Rather than using obviously ethnically-coded songs, or even hybrid songs with some ethnic connotations, the film's soundtrack draws on subversive elements of riot grrrl and electronic music genres to construct ethnic identities that challenge reductive preconceptions about Asian Americans and their place in mainstream US film.

While *Real Women Have Curves*, *Quinceañera*, and *Better Luck Tomorrow* all deal with ethnic identity differently, they all have interesting ways of moving beyond simplistic musical representations of ethnicity. The music I have discussed from these films performs many of the functions of what Anahid Kassabian (2001) refers to as "identifying music", that is, music that "can convey or evoke all of the things mentioned in the definition of leitmotiv – 'a character, a place or an object, a certain situation, or a recurrent idea of the plot' – as well as period, time, depth of field, and certain sociological factors" (pp. 56–57). Kassabian goes on to discuss how music in the film *I Like It Like That* (Darnell Martin, 1994) "marks out both community and class for perceivers unfamiliar with contemporary Latin music in North America" (pp. 57–58). Kassabian also states that identifying music addresses perceivers as "members of the dominant musical culture" and that the cultural background of audience members will affect their understanding of the music's meaning (p 58). With regard to the music in *I Like It Like That*, Kassabian suggests that for the community portrayed in the film, "it makes clear generational distinctions between salsa and merengue and rap" (p. 58).

Much of the music in *Real Women Have Curves* and *Quinceañera* signifies ethnicity more obviously in this way, providing information on multiple levels based on the cultural experience of the perceiver. Genre differences and context within the film make this pretty apparent in both films, although some songs do bridge the generation gap and speak for characters of all ages. In *Real Women*, music tends to outline Ana's choice that is central to the film's narrative – home, family, and factory work or New York City, individuality, and Columbia University. Particular ethnic connotations of the music locate Ana's choice with regard to family, tradition, class, and gender. As I have suggested, though, more modern sounding songs that have a vaguely Latin sound, as well as songs like 'Minha Galera' with its reggae feel, serve to distance Ana somewhat from tradition and family. However, these songs still reflect her Latina identity – that is, an identity formed in Spanish and English, with influences of a culture that is at once Mexican and US American, but at the same time is something else entirely. Class is also more visible and audible in *Real Women* than in *Quinceañera*. Factory noise is very prominent in the sound mix and some of the dramatic score that I did not have the space to consider in Chapter 7 reflects the pain and alienation of a lifetime of hard work for Carmen. In *Quinceañera*, the working class status of Magdalena's family is only really highlighted when her family's financial situation is compared with the wealth of her Uncle Walter and Aunt Silvia. However, class connotations do transfer to Carlos via the historical context of reggaetón music, and Tio Tomás' poverty takes centre stage later in the film when he is evicted.

Music in *Better Luck Tomorrow* comments on characters' ethnicity without referring to it specifically. The difference in class context between *Better Luck Tomorrow* and the other two films considered in Part III could account for the differences in musical representations of ethnic identity. All of the characters in *Better Luck Tomorrow* live in Orange County as opposed to East Los Angeles, and they all seem to be from more affluent or at least middle class families. In fact, these characters are completely removed from their families. Parents play no role in this film whatsoever, aside from Steve's desire to rob his obviously wealthy parents, who are also never shown. In a way, this distance from parents liberates the characters and allows them to have more varied identities beyond ethnicity. This is important to the film's drive to at once be a teen film and also critique the genre's overwhelming whiteness. However, this distancing of the protagonists from their families also distances them from their ethnic backgrounds, and from the strength gained through community, solidarity and history.

True agency in all three of these films, however, comes from music that reaches across cultures and political agendas. In her critique on the concept of 'diaspora', Floya Anthias (1998) outlines what she considers the main theoretical shortcomings of the term:

> My argument is primarily that the concept of diaspora, whilst focusing on transnational processes and commonalities, does so by deploying

a notion of ethnicity which privileges the point of 'origin' in constructing identity and solidarity. In the process it also fails to examine trans-ethnic commonalities and relations and does not adequately pay attention to differences of gender and class.

(p. 558)

While I do not intend to make a major intervention into the debate surrounding the term 'diaspora' or its theoretical relatives at this point in time, I do find Anthias' argument compelling and useful when it comes to the musical moulding of identity and agency in these three films.

The music associated with agency in these films is not the music that enforces a character's ethnicity most forcefully. Instead, moments of agency occur with hybrid styles that connect across ethnic, racial, and national boundaries. In Ana's case, this includes the Latin-alternative rock of Aterciopelados and the Latin reggae of Manu Chao's 'Minha Galera'. For Carlos, it is reggaetón, a Latin take on Jamaican dancehall. Magdalena is an exception in this case, since her theme is not particularly Latin sounding and does not draw meaning from any specific popular genre, but acts more as typical dramatic score with a light rock feel. For Ben, Virgil, Daric, and Han, musical agency comes not from ties to their own ethnic backgrounds (aside from the invisible Asian-American members of some bands as previously discussed), but rather from their alliance with feminist music. Anthias (1998) asserts that 'diaspora' has trouble sustaining the "capacity to be trans-ethnic in terms of forging solidary bonds with crosscutting groups, both from within the dominant category or with other groups also on the margins" (p. 574). Musical trans-ethnic solidarity is precisely what provides most of the protagonists in these three films with agency, and it allows for representations of ethnic identity to move beyond stereotype and the ethnic margins. While visible representations of ethnicity have been widely studied, audible representations have been largely ignored. A close examination of musical identity construction, however, can bring a new level of understanding to the ways that ethnic identities are restricted or opened up in films, as well as provide clues to how certain ethnicities are allowed or denied access to mainstream US culture.

Notes

1 According to Margaret Hillenbrand (2008), "the casting and delineation of the protagonists themselves, which suggest a definition of what constitutes Asian America, and Asian Americans, [...] is disappointingly circumscribed. By and large, 'Asian American' means 'Chinese American' or 'Korean American' in *Better Luck Tomorrow*" (p. 69).
2 Hillenbrand states that "for some audiences, the gangbangers are Filipino-American, while for others they are Latino" and gives references for examples of each (p. 75, note 50).

3 See, for example, Steve Redhead (1993) and Sarah Thornton (1995). For a study of Asian-American ethnic identity and drug use in dance scenes, see Geoffrey Hunt, Molly Moloney, and Kristin Evans (2011).

References

About *Kill Rock Stars* [Internet], Available from: http://www.killrockstars. com/about/ [Accessed 28 October 2016].

Anthias, Floya (1998) 'Evaluating 'Diaspora': Beyond Ethnicity?' in *Sociology*, Vol. 32, No. 3, pp. 557–580.

Eng, David (2001) *Racial Castration: Managing Masculinity in Asian America*, Durham, NC: Duke University Press.

Halberstam, Judith (1998) *Female Masculinity*, Durham, NC: Duke University Press.

Hillenbrand, Margaret (2008) 'Of Myths and Men: *Better Luck Tomorrow* and the Mainstreaming of Asian American Cinema' in *Cinema Journal*, Vol. 47, No. 4, pp. 50–75.

Hunt, Geoffrey, Molly Moloney, and Kristin Evans (2011) '"How Asian Am I": Asian American Youth Cultures, Drug Use, and Ethnic Identity Construction' in *Youth and Society*, Vol. 43, No. 1, pp. 274–304.

Kassabian, Anahid (2001) *Hearing Film: Tracking Identifications in Contemporary Hollywood Film Music*, New York: Routledge.

Oren, Tasha G (2005) 'Secret Asian Man: Angry Asians and the Politics of Cultural Visibility' in Shilpa Davé LeiLani Nishime, and Tasha G. Oren (eds), *East Main Street: Asian American Popular Culture*, New York: New York University Press, pp. 337–360.

Redhead, Steve (ed.) (1993) *Rave Off: Politics and Deviance in Contemporary Youth Culture*, Aldershot: Avebury.

Thornton, Sarah (1995) *Club Cultures: Music, Media and Subcultural Capital*, Cambridge, UK: Polity.

Wang, Oliver (2001) 'Between the Notes: Finding Asian America in Popular Music' in *American Music*, Vol. 19, No. 4, pp. 439–465.

Filmography

American Pie (1999, USA) directed by Paul Weitz, music by David Lawrence, music supervision by Gary Jones, Universal Home Entertainment.

Better Luck Tomorrow (2002, USA) directed by Justin Lin, music by Michael J. Gonzales and Semiautomatic, music supervision by Ernesto M. Foronda, Paramount.

The Breakfast Club (1985, USA) directed by John Hughes, music by Keith Forsey, music supervision by Keith Forsey, Universal Pictures.

Clueless (1995, USA) directed by Amy Heckerling, music by David Kitay, music supervision by Karyn Rachtman, Paramount Home Video.

Ferris Bueller's Day Off (1986, USA) directed by John Hughes, music by Arthur Baker, Ira Newborn, and John Robie, music supervision by Taquin Gotch, Paramount Home Video.

Heathers (1988, USA) directed by Michael Lehmann, music by David Newman, Anchor Bay Entertainment.

Not Another Teen Movie (2001, USA) directed by Joel Gallen, music by Theodore Shapiro, music supervision by Pilar McClurry, Columbia TriStar Home Video.

Porky's (1981, USA) directed by Bob Clark, music by Paul Zaza and Carl Zittrer, music consultancy by Gerry Young, 20th Century Fox Home Entertainment.

Pretty in Pink (1986, USA) directed by Howard Deutch, music by Michael Gore, music supervision by David Anderle, Paramount Home Video.

Quinceañera (*Echo Park, LA* – alternate title, 2006, USA) directed by Richard Glatzer and Wash Westmoreland, music by Victor Bock and Micko Westmoreland, music supervision by Shaun Young, Metrodome Distribution.

Real Women Have Curves (2002, USA) directed by Patricia Cardoso, music by Heitor Pereira, music supervision by Margaret Guerra Rogers, Home Box Office Home Video.

Revenge of the Nerds (1984, USA) directed by Jeff Kanew, music by Thomas Newman, music supervision by Martin Schwartz, 20th Century Fox Home Entertainment.

Sixteen Candles (1984, USA) directed by John Hughes, music by Ira Newborn, music supervision by Jimmy Iovine, Universal Home Video.

Weird Science (1985, USA) directed by John Hughes, music by Danny Elfman, Jimmy Iovine, and Ira Newborn, music supervised by Kathy Nelson, Universal Pictures.

Conclusion
The Continuing Relevance of Film Music to Identity and Agency

> Music is a device or resource to which people turn in order to regulate themselves as aesthetic agents, as feeling, thinking and acting beings in their day-to-day lives. Achieving this regulation requires a high degree of reflexivity [...]
>
> (Tia DeNora, 2000, p. 62)

The use of music to construct self-identity and regulate agency, and the reflexivity central to this process, both play a vital role in determining how perceivers understand film characters. When people reflect on why they have chosen a particular song to perform a specific function in their daily lives, they are engaging in a process that draws meaning from the mediation of that particular song and related music in popular culture, as well as from their own experience of the song in their personal history. Decisions can be based on instrumentation, mood, tempo, lyrics, and other elements of the song text. But choices also rely on connotations resulting from discourse about the genre or artist, or from a song's previous use in various audiovisual forms (films, computer games, television programmes, advertising, and various forms of new media). While musical meaning is partially understood through shared cultural knowledge, its comprehension is also largely personal.

All of this bears a direct relation to how identity and agency are presented in films and how perceivers understand them. Filmmakers use music to draw on the same types of connotations that perceivers use for their own identity construction. However, the vast array of sources of meaning for musical choices described above ensures that filmmaker intention and audience perception do not always match up. This makes music a powerful tool for constructing identity in film, but it also ensures that identity can never remain fixed. Characters change with each new song and with each new narrative engagement with instruments and recorded music. Identity can only be understood as produced through music, sound, visuals, and narrative events, and it is constantly changing, forever realigning itself with the present audiovisual context. While the categories generally used to discuss identity (gender, ethnicity, race, sexuality, class, etc.) are considered to be stable to varying degrees (e.g., race is more 'fixed' than gender), musical connotations used to construct character identity in films show that all of these categories contain a plethora of variations within them. In the end, perceivers draw meaning from some of the available connotations and not others, and it is by this process that character identity is constructed and modified through time. This process suggests that none of the common identity categories should be considered stable or fixed.

Of course, music does not work alone to construct identity in films. Other narrative elements interact with musical meaning to foreground certain connotations available in the music. Filmmakers use this strategy to steer character identity and the narrative in certain desired directions. Closer attention to the use of specific musical genres, for instance, can illuminate the contradictions between musical connotations and other narrative elements. It is through these contradictions that the guiding hand(s) of the filmmaker(s) becomes most audible. It is also through these contradictions that a film's politics, as well as the politics of the society within which the film was made, can be understood.

This is where the study of musical agency becomes particularly important. Different characters are allowed different levels of agency, and this agency is intimately connected to identity. Characters tend to have the greatest amount of musical agency in films with the fewest internal contradictions – i.e., areas of tension between music, identity, and storyline. In such films, characters tend to use music to their benefit, or at least benefit from music that is used to characterise them. Another consideration of arguments from earlier chapters with a revised focus on this aspect of musical agency will help to develop the concept further.

In Part I: 'She's a Rebel? Girls, Guitars, and Agency', the focus on guitar playing made internal contradictions easy to identify and examine. Using the gender connotations of guitar playing as a starting point, I went on to consider the meaning behind the type of guitar played and different characters' access to public performance. Strong gender connotations of the electric guitar and restrictions to performance make guitar playing an important site of struggle for young women.

In *10 Things I Hate About You* (Gil Junger, 1999), Kat is characterised in the storyline as a feminist, but by the end of the film, her shrew is tamed. Kat's initial resistance to patriarchy is contained by a narrative that uses connotations of feminism from riot grrrl music and the 'angry women in rock' discourse of the time to suggest a political stance that proves to be disingenuous by the end of the film. The fact that Kat has to wait for Verona to buy her a guitar further emphasises her lack of musical agency. The tension in this film between the musical connotations of riot grrrl feminism and the less political alternative pop of Kat's preferred music, as well as that between Kat's initial posturing and eventual acquiescence, aligns with her overall lack of musical agency. *Love Don't Cost a Thing* (Troy Beyer, 2003) contains an ongoing tension between Paris the cheerleader and Paris the aspiring musician. While resolution of this contradiction is important to the narrative, Paris' musical identity and agency never really come to fruition. In the end, she does choose Alvin over her professional athlete ex-boyfriend, but she never gets to become the person she dreams of being. As I discuss in Chapter 1, the alternate ending in which Paris gets on stage with her guitar and her new look would have resolved the film's internal contradictions much more completely. However, without this scene Paris remains Alvin's cheerleader prize, since the film short-changes her agency and foregrounds her physical appearance.

In *Juno* (Jason Reitman, 2007), there is a tension between Juno's sarcastic attitude/professed love of punk rock and the twee folk soundtrack that serves to infantilise her character. Although she does play the acoustic guitar on a couple of occasions, she can only worship Mark's electric guitar. Both a public performance where Juno plays the electric guitar and sings and a montage that uses more aggressive music set to highly active scenes were cut out of the released film. The inclusion of these scenes would have aligned Juno's musical representation more with her professed taste in music and greatly enhanced her musical agency. However, these scenes would have disrupted the consistency of the folk soundtrack and changed Juno's identity significantly; their inclusion would have made the film's internal musical tensions all too evident to audiences. But when one listens closely enough, the contradictions are not too difficult to hear.

All Over Me (Alex Sichel, 1997) contains the tightest fit between music, identity, and narrative. From the start of the film, distorted, angsty, female-fronted bands populate the soundtrack. Furthermore, just after the opening scene it becomes clear that Claude plays the electric guitar. She eventually meets Lucy through a local music scene that seems much more in the legitimate riot grrrl mode than the club in *10 Things I Hate About You*. She eventually plays her own electric guitar with Lucy, amplified for the first time in the film, and the connection is made between Claude's sexuality and musical agency. Importantly, Claude's musical agency is never made an issue in the film – her musical taste and guitar playing are consistently asserted throughout the film, never suggesting the unspoken question of whether or not a girl should be playing the guitar or listening to aggressive or angry music. This alignment of Claude's musical taste, identity, and agency show a clear strategy by the filmmakers to construct her as a strong character who engages with music without tripping over the traditional gender hurdles. There is no narrative excuse to present Claude as traditionally feminine, and thus she is allowed a high level of musical agency, especially with regard to guitar playing.

The films I examined in Part II: 'Listening to the Other: Cultural Borrowing and Critical Reflection' tend to afford their characters a higher level of musical agency than those considered in Part I. This has much to do with the fact that these are white characters using black music to their own ends; the focus of the chapter necessitates that, in the chosen films, the characters control their engagements with music. Due to the foregrounding of racial difference used to construct the films' narratives, there are necessary contradictions between character identity and music in the films. What is important in these films, then, is the level of critical engagement involved in the borrowing of the Other's culture. I have chosen to study these films for the cultural borrowing involved, and thus some level of musical agency is already a given for their protagonists. But at what price is this agency acquired, how do the characters benefit from it, and how are the political implications of their actions dealt with in the narrative?

In *Ghost World* (Terry Zwigoff, 2001), Enid tries out multiple musical identities before she becomes fixated on an old blues song. She does not engage directly with the implications of borrowing black music, but this is dealt with in other parts of the film's narrative. At one point, Enid and Seymour have a conversation about the history of racist representations in the marketing of the company for which Seymour works. In this scene, Seymour expresses his ambivalence about the history of race relations, acknowledging that things are probably better in the present even though he obsesses over archaic black culture in a way that suggests the existence of a more authentic past. Enid's uncritical engagement with black music ultimately leaves her unfulfilled, however, as does Seymour's barely critical consideration of his listening practices. Thus, regardless of the musical agency both characters possess, neither finds happiness through the misguided search for an authentic experience they expect to find in black music.

Save the Last Dance (Thomas Carter, 2001), however, presents cultural borrowing with greater critical engagement. Sara's adoption of hip hop culture is situated in a narrative that questions her right to do so. In the end, Sara uses hip hop dance to achieve her ultimate goal of attending Juilliard, but she also makes African-American friends and has an African-American lover, changes her clothing style, and becomes a regular at a local dance club. However, her trans-cultural engagement may turn out to be nothing more than a phase she is going through. Regardless of whether or not this is true, Sara has greater musical agency than Enid does. This is the result of Sara's deeper relationship with black culture and African-American people – a connection that lessens the contradictions of her musical practices by lessening the distance between Sara and the culture from which she borrows.

In the other three films, *Bring It On* (Peyton Reed, 2000), *Mean Creek* (Jacob Aaron Estes, 2004), and *Napoleon Dynamite* (Jared Hess, 2004), whiteness becomes more visible as more exaggerated forms of whiteness are juxtaposed with black music. Again, since the internal contradictions are emphasised in these films, the question shifts from the existence of musical agency to the implications of musical agency. Much like Sara in *Save the Last Dance*, the cheerleaders in *Bring It On* (the Toros) are forced to contemplate their cultural borrowing (or in this case, theft). Even after they are made aware of the theft, they decide to continue using the stolen routines for their own benefit. It is only after the cheerleaders from the other school (the Clovers) embarrass them that the Toros stop using the stolen routines. Ultimately, the Toros come in second to the Clovers in the championships; thus the film passes judgement on the earlier cultural theft that denies the Toros musical agency.

George's use of black music is limited in *Mean Creek*, and not explicitly critical. While he does not really benefit from this music, he does use it in the construction of his self-identity. Through this process, George attempts to shift his identity from bully/awkward outsider to something more respectable and intelligent while he waits for the others to pick him up for an ultimately fatal boating trip. This uncritical cultural borrowing cannot magically reinvent George, however, when he has been so antagonistic towards his fellow students. Thus, he has little musical agency. The contradictions between his internal and external identities are too great to overcome. However, George's use of 'Fear Not of Man' by Mos Def (1999) implies an identification with some aspect of the song; he imagines himself to have a deeper understanding of life than his peers, which is reflected in the song's lyrics.

Finally, in *Napoleon Dynamite*, Napoleon uses black music and dance to impress the rest of the students at his school at the end of the film. Napoleon's particular geeky whiteness, as well as the whiteness of almost the entire student body, is juxtaposed against black music and dance for comic effect. While Napoleon is not critical in his cultural borrowing, the film shows its critical treatment of difference through its presentation of exaggerated racial and ethnic stereotypes in Napoleon, Pedro, Lafawnda, and Kip. Thus, Napoleon's musical agency is possible through the negation of tensions by the film's excessive treatment of musical and racial contradictions.

Unlike the characters in Parts I and II, those in Part III: 'Unheard Ethnicities: Musical Construction of Ethnic Identity and Agency' do not consciously engage with music. In Part III, I considered how music is used to construct ethnic identity, and what the relationship is between the resulting identities and musical agency. Ethnic markers within the music interact with other elements of characters' identities to produce a wide range of ways one can understand characters. For these films, it is not so much the contradictions between the music and the characters that are important, but rather the ways that characters' identities resist simple ethnic coding. This resistance seems to stem from either the use of less traditional ethnically-coded music or the ways that characters' hybrid identities refuse to be labelled by music. Musical agency in these films results from the narrative resolution of tensions in some cases and from narrative exploitation of contradictions in others.

In *Real Women Have Curves* (Patricia Cardoso, 2002), a mix of more traditional music from Mexico and other parts of Latin America, as well as more modern, hybrid Latin-American styles, parallels the central tension between 'Old World' and 'New World' that Ana must navigate. It is from this tension that Ana gains confidence and develops her self-identity. Ana's greatest moments of musical agency come when the modern hybrid styles play on the film's soundtrack. These songs conflict less with Ana's modern Latina identity than do the more traditional songs, and they seem to lend her character agency by allowing her to forge a life and identity different from that of her parents and sister. Ultimately, the film is ambivalent with regard to Ana's leaving of Los Angeles, but the music constructs her identity as more complex than simple conceptions of ethnicity can explain.

Quinceañera (Richard Glatzer and Wash Westmoreland, 2006) contains a similar 'Old World'/'New World' tension, but it is treated less as a narrative hurdle than in *Real Women Have Curves*. Rather, this tension is something that all three of the main characters have to live with. None of them has immediate plans of moving away from their present cultural context. Rather, they must learn to live with forces beyond their control – for Magdalena they are teenage pregnancy and abandonment, for Carlos, homophobia and lack of opportunities in his working class context, and for Tio Tomás, gentrification and old age. The characters all gain strength through the elements of their identities that are acted upon by these challenging forces, however. Their musical agency is greatest when they come to terms with these challenges and find ways of living with them. In this film, Carlos has the greatest musical agency, because the musical construction of his identity takes full advantage of certain connotations that come with reggaetón music. The narrative and soundtrack then flaunt the contradictions that exist between the real Carlos and the musical connotations of violence and misogyny. The film also takes advantage of the positive ideas about struggle and solidarity that come with reggaetón, however. The contradictions that exist within the music and between Carlos and the music are, in this case, central to his musical agency.

Finally, in *Better Luck Tomorrow* (Justin Lin, 2002), ethnically-coded music is avoided altogether. Tensions between 'Old World' and 'New World' for these characters only remain as a residue evoked by the absence of ethnically-coded music on the soundtrack. This could be due to distance from the country of ancestry, or time passed since the migration of ancestors. However, it seems likely that the absence of ethnically-coded music has something to do with the implied middle to upper-middle class context of the characters, as well as the film's self-conscious staging as a 'teen film'. While the ethnicity of these characters is emphasised by the previously discussed presence of their Asian-American bodies in a typically white teen film context, their ethnicity is conversely de-emphasised by this same context, due to their taken-for-granted status as the film's protagonists. In combination with the characters' middle-class background, this seems to construct their identities as somehow 'less ethnic'. Nevertheless, these characters gain musical agency through their alignment with female-fronted and feminist bands, as well as electronic music, due to the previously discussed connotations of marginality and geek/criminal duality, respectively. Again, as with the other films from Part III, the musical agency of these characters seems to result from the foregrounding and manipulation of the film's contradictions.

As I hope to have shown throughout this book, a close examination of identity construction through music and its interaction with other narrative elements can provide a wealth of information about cultural connotations present in music, as well as how these ideas are used to modify characters' race, gender, ethnicity, sexuality, and other aspects of identity. Because music brings so much information to films, identities that draw on musical meaning must always be fluid, changing from scene to scene, song to song. Likewise, perceivers must always consider identity as a process due to the constant presentation of new musical information. While this process may differ for every perceiver based on one's knowledge and experience of musical discourse and song history, I have presented musical information available within the films themselves and the surrounding discourse rather than making assumptions about how different perceivers would understand films, although some shared cultural competency for audiences of US youth films can probably be assumed. Furthermore, a focus on musical agency highlights the access to power that certain types of identities have within the narrative, and this reflects back on connotations in the music in a way that reveals much about stereotypes and common conceptions of culture.

The films examined in this book span a period in which technological developments, particularly mobile phones and the internet, not only dramatically changed how teenagers engaged with and shared music, but also changed how they constructed their self-identities in relation to their peers via social media. In a sense, the films I have chosen reflect older types of relationships with music, with most compiled soundtracks displaying a stylistic or generic coherence. While it is beyond the scope of this book to examine how songs have been used in more recent youth films, soundtracks have undoubtedly reflected changes in how young people access, listen to, and make music. From mp3s and iPods to Spotify and mobile phones, the ability to listen to almost any song at almost any time has meant that albums no longer dominate and young people are not limited by radio programming and musical tastes of friends and relatives when it comes to the exploration and discovery of new sounds. The ways in which these new technologies have influenced the listening habits of young people, and how these changes have been reflected in recent youth films, will be fruitful avenues for future scholarship. However, this does not mean that current listening practices mark a complete break from the past. One significant development in the age of streaming is the renewed popularity of records, both for their physical presence and their fidelity, or at least the perception of a more authentic sound.

What is more important for this book, though, is that the relationship between music and identity remains a relevant concern for scholarship on youth films. Technological advances and increased access to a range of music do not negate differences within teenagers. One obvious example of this is that class continues to be relevant in relation to technology. If one cannot afford a mobile phone, or high fidelity headphones, or a laptop on which to create songs, then one's relationship with music will undoubtedly be different to that of someone who has access to all of the latest technology. In addition, the intersectional nature of identity means that class is not separate from race and gender, for example. Regardless of different levels of access, new technology has not completely wiped away all traces of older power relations. In a feminist study of the listening practices of university students in Stockholm and Moscow, Ann Werner and Sofia Johansson (2016) discover that, despite the so-called democratisation of the internet and increased availability of music and knowledge about it, the discourse around listening practices remains gendered. They also argue that there is no such thing as a neutral user of new music technologies. Werner and Johansson find that, despite some cultural differences reflected in responses, students continue to use a gendered discourse in discussions of music and related technology, and there is a patriarchal element in their discussions of taste, where the father is an important figure for the passing on of what is understood as more authentic musical taste and knowledge. With regard to the discursive masculinisation of technology, Werner and Johansson state, "the participants who talked about themselves as active were often young men [...] Activity in music use connoted control over and knowledge of the music and the technological devices" (p. 183). This mastery of knowledge and technological dissemination threatens to maintain old gatekeeping strategies and limit access to young women, even if the discourse does not accurately reflect gendered divisions in listening practices. Student responses also reflect other classically gendered divisions, such as the pop/rock and art/commerce binaries. Werner and Johansson warn against taking an overly simplistic view of the gendered discourse, however, pointing out that exceptions such as young women mastering new technology over their fathers (teaching them how to use Spotify, for example) provide a more nuanced understanding of the relationship between gender and listening practices. Nevertheless, they argue that "the increased need for advanced technology in order to listen to the latest music has rendered the user even more affected by gendered ideas about technological expertise and musical experts", and despite the increased access facilitated by new technology, "uses of technology continue to be firmly situated in discourse and social contexts" (p. 189).

As the above study suggests, identity remains central to young people's engagement with music in the real world, so the relationship between identity and music must not be ignored in future youth film scholarship. Questions of identity and agency are still very relevant in the twenty-first century, particularly considering that while society becomes more tolerant with regard to difference there are still many social and legal forms of discrimination against those whose identities defy simplistic binaries, traditional ways of life, and misplaced moral judgements. The challenge is to develop new and interesting approaches to studying identity and agency that address gaps in existing scholarship, taking into account the ways that cultural and technological shifts are affecting conceptions of identities and their representations on screen.

References

DeNora, Tia (2000) *Music in Everyday Life*, Cambridge, UK: Cambridge University Press.

Werner, Ann and Sofia Johansson (2016) 'Experts, Dads, and Technology: Gendered Talk about Online Music' in *International Journal of Cultural Studies*, Vol. 19, No. 2, pp. 177–192.

Filmography

10 Things I Hate About You (1999, USA) directed by Gil Junger, music by Richard Gibbs, music supervision by Alfonso E. Chavez, Buena Vista Home Entertainment.

All Over Me (1997, USA) directed by Alex Sichel, music by Miki Navazio, music supervision by Bill Coleman, Alliance.

Better Luck Tomorrow (2002, USA) directed by Justin Lin, music by Michael J. Gonzales and Semiautomatic, music supervision by Ernesto M. Foronda, Paramount.

Bring It On (2000, USA) directed by Peyton Reed, music by Christophe Beck, music supervision by Billy Gottlieb, Universal Home Entertainment.

Ghost World (2001, USA) directed by Terry Zwigoff, music by David Kitay, music supervision by Melissa Axelrod and Christine Bergren, Icon Home Entertainment.

Juno (2007, USA) directed by Jason Reitman, music by Mateo Messina, music supervision by Peter Afterman, 20th Century Fox.

Love Don't Cost a Thing (2003, USA) directed by Troy Beyer, music by Richard Gibbs, music supervision by Michael McQuarn, Warner Home Video.

Mean Creek (2004, USA) directed by Jacob Aaron Estes, music by tomandandy, music supervision by Robin Urdang, Palisades Tartan.

Napoleon Dynamite (2004, USA) directed by Jared Hess, music by John Swihart, music consultancy by Tracy Lynch-Sanchez, Paramount Pictures.

Quinceañera (*Echo Park, LA* – alternate title, 2006, USA) directed by Richard Glatzer and Wash Westmoreland, music by Victor Bock and Micko Westmoreland, music supervision by Shaun Young, Metrodome Distribution.

Real Women Have Curves (2002, USA) directed by Patricia Cardoso, music by Heitor Pereira, music supervision by Margaret Guerra Rogers, Home Box Office Home Video.

Save the Last Dance (2001, USA) directed by Thomas Carter, music by Mark Isham, music supervision by Michael McQuarn, Paramount Home Video.

Index